Creating Innovative Products and Services

Creating Innovative Products and Services

The FORTH Innovation Method

Gijs van Wulfen

Routledge
Taylor & Francis Group

LONDON AND NEW YORK

First published 2011 by Gower Publishing

2 Park Square, Milton Park, Abingdon, Oxon OX14 4RN
711 Third Avenue, New York, NY 10017, USA

Routledge is an imprint of the Taylor & Francis Group, an informa business

First issued in paperback 2016

British Library Cataloguing in Publication Data
Wulfen, Gijs van.
  Creating innovative products and services : the FORTH
  innovation method.
  1. New products. 2. Brainstorming. 3. Creative ability in
  business. 4. Group decision making.
  I. Title
  658.5'75-dc22

  ISBN 978-1-4094-1754-5 (hbk)
  ISBN 978-1-138-26964-4 (pbk)

Library of Congress Cataloging-in-Publication Data
Wulfen, Gijs van.
  Creating innovative products and services : the FORTH innovation method / Gijs van
  Wulfen.
    p. cm.
  Includes bibliographical references and index.
  ISBN 978-1-4094-1754-5 (hardback)
  1. New products. 2. Product management. 3. Production planning. I. Title.
  HF5415.153.W85 2011
  658.5'75--dc22

                                                                        2010044357

Contents

List of Figures

List of Tables

Foreword

Innovation is crucial to all organisations, whether large or small, new or established. It is of the utmost importance that you keep your product and service portfolio up to date and appropriate, as this will have a stimulating effect on your employees. By challenging them to consider new products or market combinations, you stimulate their creativity and extend their responsibility. Innovation is not an option. If you do not innovate, it leads to stagnation whereby good employees may leave the company and before you realise it, it is the beginning of the end.

Sanoma Publishers has a good track record in the marketing of magazines in the Netherlands. Well-known brand names such as *Libelle*, *Margriet*, *Viva*, *VTWonen*, *Donald Duck* and *Story* belong to the cultural heritage of the Netherlands. However, the world is changing rapidly and with it the behaviour of not only consumers but also advertisers. Anticipation of these changes can only occur if you innovate or purchase. At Sanoma we have chosen to do both. With regards to the Digital Media we have strengthened our position on the market through take-overs and purchasing. Good examples of this are Startpagina, Nu, Kieskeurig and SchoolBANK. Being in the top position, both on and offline, is great, but to stay in this position we must continue to be creative and innovative. The management is therefore obliged not only to keep this position but also to extend and develop it.

Innovation is often associated with 'totally new', because doing something new seems more exciting and should you succeed you can write history, even if only within your own company. However, the chance of this happening is small. Which company has created innovation through the selling of books online? Amazon. com? Wrong. Amazon.com is a good example of the current misconception that you have to be a *fast mover* in order to be profitable. However, if you are quick enough to consolidate your innovations and then to upgrade them, you can earn much more. Markides and Gerski describe it as *being fast second*.

Innovation of an existing brand and its position on the market is equally important. For this reason Sandra Dol, publisher of women's magazines at Sanoma, discussed the position of the magazines *Libelle* and *Margriet* after 2015 with me. Both brands will then be more than 75 years old and will undeniably still hold their strong position on the market. But we wanted more. During the past ten years both brands were strengthened by the so-called 'line and brand extension', which included not only books, agendas and thematic specials, but also duvet covers and bicycles. Great, but nothing new or pioneering apart from the *Libelle* Summer Week and the *Margriet* Winterfair, two very successful and profitable events.

Sandra and I consider ourselves stewards of these brand names and it is our task to initiate ideas from which our successors will be able to profit. This is how we came into contact with Gijs van Wulfen (whom we already knew) and his FORTH innovation method. We have implemented this technique and I must admit that it was an exciting and very successful course. At this very moment there are three detailed Mini Business Cases completed, which together are worth an income of €7.3 million within three years after their introduction. All three of the new concepts are innovative, suitable to the brands and have earned credibility with our clients. The next step is to decide which concept(s) we are going to develop in greater detail before launching it.

Some aspects have caught my attention during the FORTH journey:

- Firstly, the fantastic enthusiasm and drive this process creates within the participants.
- Secondly, the thoroughness of the process. In general people are creative and can produce 12 new concepts per hour, flawlessly. Yet the postponing of both the brainstorming session as well as the giving of your opinion, together with the will not only to understand the resistance of the customer but also to gain a deeper insight into new markets, were extremely useful. I am convinced that it led to improved and achievable concepts without affecting the ambition or the drive of the team.
- Thirdly, the necessity of a strong project management team, as during the process you experience every emotion from euphoria to the deepest depression and then back again.
- Finally, the necessity of an extended team, which includes the board of directors, even if only for support during the journey.

I highly recommend the FORTH innovation method. When you apply it well, it becomes a beautiful voyage with incredible discoveries and great advantages. I wish you a successful journey.

Henk Scheenstra
COO Print Sanoma Publishing Ltd

Preface

Imagination is the beginning of creation:
You imagine what you desire,
You will what you imagine,
And at last you create what you will.

(George Bernard Shaw)

My son came to visit me at my office in the Netherlands once. While sitting on the swing in the room where I usually hold my brainstorming sessions, he asked me the question all boys ask their fathers at one time: 'Dad, what do you do for a living?' I answered that I help people to invent new products and services for the businesses they work for. 'Cool', he said (which means something similar to 'great' if I remember correctly). 'So, you help people and then they do the work themselves. And you even get paid for it?' At that moment I realised, yet again, how strange my job is.

So, what is my job? I call myself an innovation facilitator, and with this book, whether you are a director, manager, marketer, product developer, innovation specialist, innovation consultant or brainstorming mentor, I would like to provide you with a practical and effective method to generate a flying start to innovation.

I wrestled with the idea of innovation for a long time, firstly, as a marketer in the food sector, where I tried to be innovative with brand names such as Honig (soup), Red Band (sweets) and King (peppermint). This was usually associated with blood, sweat and (sometimes) tears. However, my inspiration did not falter and with the occasional much-needed success of the Red Band Treasure Boxes, it kept my imagination and hopes alive. Following this, I worked as a management consultant at Ernst & Young Consulting and later at Boer & Croon, striving to help large organisations. At these organisations I took on the classic role of advisor: the expert standing on the sideline, analysing, interpreting and determining the direction. And even though, in most cases, the board of directors and the management were convinced a chosen direction was the right direction, in practice, nothing ever materialised in terms of the development of real new markets and products. This was due to what I call 'a false start in innovation'. Looking back, I realise that there were four reasons for this: it was not the right time for innovation as there was no urgency within the company; the people who had to realise the innovation were not totally convinced of the direction chosen; there was no suitable method for implementing the invention and developing the new product concepts; and there was no basis for new products, especially if people were not directly involved.

As a direct result of the experience gained, I opened my own innovation consultancy in 2003. The main aim was to give tangible help to organisations for rapid innovation; this led to the development of a practical method for the front end of innovation. This method, which enables the development of innovative products and services, is named the FORTH innovation method and is based on five stages: Full Steam Ahead, Observe and Learn, Raise Ideas, Test Ideas and Homecoming. It is an innovation method which works in practice. Many businesses and organisations of all sizes, in various sectors, have successfully implemented it to generate innovative services as well as products.

The first edition of the book appeared in Dutch in 2006. What is so distinctive about the book, given the number of titles on innovation already published?

Most of these books focused solely on the required success factors and the constraints. I realised that not only do you need the support of the top management, but that an innovative enterprising culture is also essential and a good innovation method is indispensable. Few books have been published about *how* one can successfully put innovation into practice. My experience lies in this field, and it is this practical knowledge I would like to share with you in the book, but also at www.forth-innovation.com where you will find the FORTH innovation method explained and where you can download the 15 innovation checklists mentioned in this book.

Why, after two Dutch editions, do I find it necessary to publish this book in English? Innovation is a worldwide phenomenon. During the past five years, the FORTH innovation method has been successfully implemented by many organisations; for example one of the largest insurance companies in the Netherlands, Univé VGZ IZA Trias, has been consistently using the FORTH innovation method. Despite the struggle many organisations seem to have with innovation, there has been little progress in developing an international method for innovation. The FORTH innovation method has proved itself a method which can be applied to the development of new services and this is where the greatest need exists. Whereas in manufacturing companies the research and development department is often at the forefront of promoting innovation via new patents and new applications, 75 per cent of people in developed economies work in the service sector, such as health and government, where no natural booster for innovation exists. The struggle to innovate rapidly is most urgent in these organisations and the FORTH innovation method is not only appropriate but can and will provide a structured way to get them off to a flying start.

The knowledge and experience which I have gained over the past five years stems from my involvement in the workplace and through innovation workshops with my clients. Consequently, I would like to take this opportunity to thank the following businesses for giving me the chance to continue to develop the FORTH innovation method: Univé VGZ IZA Trias, AB Oost, NEA International, EuroForum, Sanoma Publishers, ProRail, BoBike, VAK Delft, FNV Formaat en InteraktContour. There are also other companies who have applied the FORTH innovation method independently and I would like to thank them for putting their trust in the method, for their feedback and for their suggestions on how the FORTH innovation method can be improved.

Although I have learned much from all my clients, I would especially like to thank Univé VGZ IZA Trias for the intensive cooperation in implementing FORTH as their ideation method. I have trained the innovation facilitators and project leaders and had the privilege of guiding them as FORTH coach. I am very appreciative of all the project leaders, facilitators and participants of Univé VGZ IZA Trias and would like to extend a special thanks to Jan Dijkstra and Jaap van 't Kaar for the many great moments, exciting workshops and memorable times we have shared. I am also grateful to Bart Schouten, the Business Innovation Director who, with little fear of the risk to his reputation, initiated the FORTH innovation method within Univé VGZ IZA Trias. I am also extremely grateful for the cooperation and permission to publish the case study FORTH New Mobility Services.

Furthermore, I would like to thank the following people who, in one way or another, have contributed to this book:

- Johan Buigholt, Karel Bolckmans, Marc Heleven, Anita Mooiweer, John Resink, Jaap Vessies and Jeroen Verbrugge.
- Henk Scheenstra who, I am honoured to say, was willing to write the Foreword and to share his experiences with innovation as COO of Sanoma Publishers and as someone who has witnessed the FORTH innovation method first hand.
- Lex Dirkse, a great cartoonist, who is always present at every two-day FORTH brainstorming session and whom I would like to thank particularly both for his unparalleled humorous cartoons of which many are still on display in the boardrooms of numerous clients, but also for the inspiring cartoons in this book.
- Jonathan Norman of Gower Publishing for helping develop the idea for the English edition.
- Dalene Kettmann for her excellent translation of the original document.
- Peter Boterman (strategist and innovator at Heinz) and Richard Stomp (Chief WOW officer at WOW Ideas), for their feedback and inspiration at the start of the book in 2006.

Since then, 15 FORTH innovation facilitators have been trained and certified by me. I wish Ina Mohrmann, Benjo van den Boogaard, Rogier Braak, Isabel Verhoeven, Alexandra Luyk, Arjan Evers, Marien Gramser, Pieter van Haren, Ewoud Liberg, Cock Meerhof, Enno Meines, Carolien Nauta, Mathijs Niehaus and René Salemink much success with their own FORTH innovation projects and I hope that we will be able to continue working together.

I have always found it an awful cliché when an author ends the preface with a word of thanks to his wife and children. That is, until I wrote this book. With this, the English edition, there was a constant tug-of-war for my attention at home. I was asked 'Daddy, what are you thinking about?' more than once when I sat staring during dinner time. Natasja, Wisse, Brechtje: Thank you. Love is … when you allow your father and husband to write a book!

Utrecht, June 2010

Gijs van Wulfen
FORTH Innovation Group
Ondiep-zuidzijde 6
3551 BW Utrecht
the Netherlands

gijs@forth-innovation.com
+31–302456320
+31–651483575
www.forth-innovation.com

THE FUZZY FRONT END

Introduction

Long ago explorers did not only go on journeys to gather information and to observe new things but they were also eager to conquer and hoped to find new trade routes or fantastic cities filled with treasures. At times, people left their own country because of the hardship they had to endure as the country could not produce enough to support so many people.

(Atlas of the Voyage of Discoveries)

Innovation is an important managerial instrument and has become extremely popular. Even though the economy finds itself in a recession, everybody is talking about it and much is written about it in the *Financial Times*. Due to new technology and the changing needs of customers, acting upon new products, services and business models in time keeps your product portfolio up to date and different. Therefore for organisations which, in an already saturated market, have high market shares, innovation is the way to penetrate new markets, target groups and distribution channels. It is the way to growth.

WRESTLING WITH INNOVATION

When walking through a forest you notice that almost nothing grows under huge trees where it is dark, dry and mouldy. There, in the shadows, you only find moss and fungus. Small plants need much water and light, otherwise they wither and die. This image can be applied to organisations as well. While working as a marketer in a food company, I have often experienced the process of innovation as a struggle. Now, at my innovation consultancy, when I explain the metaphor of the huge trees to managers, an awkward smile appears on their faces, after which they try to defend themselves by saying that this is the way it has always been, and they are still the head of marketing. Or they try to justify their lack of innovative power by referring to the competition where things are not much better. Many managers feel they are not able to change things. In my opinion, however, no organisation should accept or conclude that the apparent inability to innovate effectively is a permanent situation. Something can be done about it.

THE DIFFICULT START

During the past 10 years many organisations have introduced modern methods to better structure and manage their innovation process. However, much has gone wrong before the process has even started. The process usually starts with the generating of new products or services, which are scarce, and should there be any new ideas, the question always remains whether they relate to the needs of the market. This, the first step in innovation – generating and selecting good and new ideas – is called the fuzzy front end of innovation. In other words it is a vague beginning to the innovation process. Vague, because how you generate new product ideas is not yet clear. In reality, everybody does what they believe is right. The following reasons are given as to why the innovation process has a vague and slow start:

1. There is not enough urgency within the organisation.
2. New ideas for products or services do not happen automatically, so where do you start?
3. People have no idea in which direction they can find chances for innovation.
4. There is a lack of insight into what the customer wants and needs.
5. There is no brainstorming, or not enough professional brainstorming.
6. There is a lack of internal support for the development of new products or services.

In short, there is no good ideation phase – the technical term for the phase which includes the creation of the idea until a decision is reached whereby the concept (or the product) will be developed.

In a new and young market which grows sporadically and where technology plays a large role, it is often discoveries or new technological applications which form the starting point for new products. Technology is often seen as the booster of the innovation process. The research and development department has developed something new: what can we do with it? Are we going to use it to improve current products or develop new products? Furthermore, the invention of new product ideas is more complicated for companies in an existing, stable, non-technological market, such as the service sector. Where does one start? Technology is not obvious, and if the company is large or well established, the problem becomes even more complex. Are there other departments or branches within the organisation which are also busy with innovation? And what have they come up with? Is it better to do it together or not? In this situation the additional value of a well structured, effective process to invent new products or services becomes even greater.

THE CONTENT OF THIS BOOK

This book is about the creation of new products and services. It is not only about physical products such as an Apple iPhone or Campbell Soup, but also about services such as digital training concepts and new health-care services. It offers a practical approach in five stages with which managers, innovation specialists and co-workers can develop attractive new product ideas themselves. It is about attractive ideas – for the market and the company – for which there is internal support and with which the innovation process can be filled in order to bring it to successful introduction onto the market as soon as possible. In this way organisations can grow in terms of their sales, profit, market shares, customer-satisfaction and especially pride, because they have introduced something new to the market successfully.

Really new products and services are scarce, yet the need for them in large organisations is huge. In Chapter 1, the struggle with the difficult start of innovation is discussed extensively. Usually, large companies follow the approach whereby a yes/no decision is taken after every step. This is called the Stage-Gate model. However, in this approach, the ideation phase has not been structured properly, and when the innovation pipeline is not filled with potential product ideas, nothing sensible comes from it.

There are five success factors for the creation of new products and services. These factors are described in Chapter 2. Thorough attention is given to the urgency, focus, real customer understanding, 'inside out' thinking and an effective creative process with good internal support.

The way in which new products and services are created is compared to a journey, and Chapter 3 gives the outline of this innovation journey. It is not an individual journey but a group travel, whereby everyone has the same goal: getting back home with momentous innovative souvenirs. The methodology is called FORTH, an acronym of the five stages which have to be completed: 1. Full Steam Ahead, 2. Observe and Learn, 3. Raise Ideas, 4. Test Ideas and 5. Homecoming. Each stage is described in a separate chapter.

Full Steam Ahead is the topic of Chapter 4. Before you go on a journey, you have to define where you are going and with whom. Before the ideation team can get going, the innovation focus workshop, the innovation assignment and the choosing and recruiting of an ideation team are crucial activities in preparing for the innovation journey.

Chapter 5 is all about discovery: Observe and Learn. This stage of discovery serves to get the managers, business developers, marketers, product developers and other co-workers from behind their desks so that they can obtain relevant customer insights by visiting customers and sources of inspiration, explore trends, new technology and explore their own opportunity for innovation.

Chapter 6 describes the development stage: Raise Ideas. This stage forms the creative *pièce de résistance* of the FORTH innovation method. A two-day brainstorming session for new products or services is on the main menu and for dessert, a concept development workshop. In a structured and creative process more than 500 product ideas are generated, 25 idea directions formulated and finally 12 attractive, achievable, new concepts developed.

Chapter 7 is about reflection: Test Ideas. Customers have the opportunity to reflect, in a qualitative research test, on the most attractive new concepts developed by the ideation team. In consultation with the internal client, the ideation team then chooses three to five concepts for further development in the last stage.

Finally, Chapter 8 deals with the stage: Homecoming. The three to five new product concepts are now developed into mini new business cases. Even though a single concept might perish in this final stage, the remaining concepts are then presented to the management and carefully passed on to the multidisciplinary development teams. They then start with the actual physical product development (in manufacturing companies) or with the development of the concept into a fully fledged business case (in the service sector). The journey for the ideation team has now ended because in the development process the development team gets going.

This book contains a real and concrete FORTH case study of one of the largest insurance companies in the Netherlands: Univé VGZ IZA Trias. They have been using the FORTH method consistently as their regular innovation method. The stages in the FORTH innovation method are described using the ways in which they have implemented it in practice regarding their innovation project FORTH New Mobility Services. At the end of Chapters 4 to 8 you will find practical checklists (totalling 15) which will guide you through the stages of the FORTH innovation method accurately.

The book contains two appendices. Appendix I lists 15 facilitators who have been trained and certified to supervise the process of the FORTH innovation method. Appendix II is a description of the 30 brainstorming techniques for the new product brainstorming session, with a practical manual regarding the application method of each technique. A short film about the FORTH innovation method, the FORTH facilitators, the users of the FORTH innovation method and the 15 checklists can also be found online at www.forth-innovation.com.

TO DIRECTORS, MANAGERS, ADVISORS AND INNOVATION SPECIALISTS

This book has been written for directors, managers, advisors and innovation specialists in organisations who are responsible for, or involved in, product innovation. The FORTH innovation method has additional value for the four groups in an organisation which are involved in the development of new products and services:

1. Managers and directors, whose responsibility includes the strategic positioning of their organisation on the market of the future, such as general directors, business unit managers and commercial directors.
2. Marketers, such as marketing directors, marketing managers, product and sectional managers.
3. R&D specialists, such as R&D managers and product developers.
4. Innovation and new business development specialists, such as innovation managers, specialists, facilitators, NBD managers and NBD project leaders.

A PRACTICAL TOUR GUIDE

The creation of new product or service ideas is contradictory. On the one hand it requires a 'soft approach', such as creativity to search for the 'insane' and to invent something which does not exist. On the other hand it requires a 'hard approach', such as building a business case to convince the management in order to break through the old product concept pattern. These two worlds are allergic to each other: the creative, vague futurists versus the practical line managers who want results today. They clash and do not work well together, which brings about frustration whereby they try to avoid each other as much as possible.

The greatest value of the FORTH innovation method which has been presented in this book is the solid bridge which is built between, on the one hand, creative brainstorming and, on the other hand, the support obtained by line managers who think in terms of new business cases. It does not end in a tasteless compromise but creates a successful marriage.

This book will help you bring the thought process regarding new products or services in your organisation to a professional level. It offers a practical tour guide and a chest full of usable tools with which the ideation team can apply the five stages of the FORTH innovation method at a comfortable pace. This method has proved itself over the past few years, both within the service sector as well as with manufacturing companies. By using this method correctly you will be able to add good mini new business cases to your innovation pipeline in order to get a flying start to your innovation process as 'the sticky back end' which follows, is often difficult enough.

STRUGGLING WITH INNOVATION

1   The Difficult Start of Innovation

Not because it is so difficult, don't we dare, but because we don't dare, it is so difficult.

(Seneca, Spanish-Roman philosopher)

If you always do what you always did, you will always get what you always got.

(A. Einstein, scientist and inventor)

Gradual growth is the worst enemy of innovation.
(N. Negroponte, Head MIT Media Lab)

1.1 INTRODUCTION

Innovation is not only advisable, it is essential. Organisations who want to grow have to adapt to the rapidly changing environment; to adjust their current products or services to the shifting needs of the customer; to develop a variety of products to reach out to new customer groups or distribution channels; and to invent new products and new business models to conquer new markets. Innovation is a popular theme amongst managers. According to the innovation monitor of the consultant agency The Bridge, 'the increase in revenue through innovation has risen to the most important strategic priority, bypassing independent growth and growth through purchasing'.[1]

Even though innovation is the main topic of interest, managers are human and consequently not much is happening. The rose-tinted perspective portrayed by many is over-optimistic in the extreme and this in times when things are not going so well economically.

It seems as if we treat innovation the same way as we treat the environment: everyone is concerned about it but we only do something when it is really necessary. This applies to young as well as experienced managers. Innovation means taking risks, but many are inhibited by the world around them where they are discouraged from making (any) mistakes. In many organisations, innovation is postponed until they really cannot wait any longer. It is not unusual to hear, *'we will have to innovate'* in the corridors of a company.

And once you start the innovation process there is no certainty that the result will bring about the long-awaited success. Research done in countries such as the United States of America, the United Kingdom and Australia shows that only 45 to 67 per cent of the products launched are successful (in other words performed in

---

1   Innovatiemonitor 2007/2008, Scherper Kiezen Beter Innoveren, p. 7. The Bridge business innovators.

accordance with management expectations).[2] And I have seen some much lower success rates quoted than this.

Organisations, whether a multi-national company such as Shell, or a large insurance company such as AIG, an enterprise involving public transport such as Deutsche Bahn or an association such as the Red Cross, are organised in order to control their current operational processes and to give account of the results produced by these processes. Should the size and complexity of the organisation increase, innovation becomes more difficult and less effective. The process of innovation seems counter cultural, particularly amongst larger organisations, although I have noticed this phenomenon with smaller organisations as well.

1.2 REALLY NEW SERVICES AND PRODUCTS ARE SCARCE

This book describes the creation process for new product ideas. It is all about the creation of new products or services. But what does that mean? The answer is as simple as the question: new products or services are products or services which did not exist before. A more complex definition is:

A new physical or virtual offer in a specific packaging with a specific brand name that is delivered to a specific group of customers with a certain business model through a specific distribution channel.

This definition has been chosen to include both physical products as well as services in the consumer and business-to-business markets. When relevant for the creation of new products, the method will be adapted to distinguish between both types.

A HUNDRED NEW PRODUCTS AND SERVICES – JUST LIKE THAT

A capsule camera for the inspection of the small intestine, Virgin Galactic space flights, bread which rises when cold, feeding bottle for adults, a sound box made of a carton, the iPad, apartments for pigs, the Fiat 500 Nuova, a Levi jacket with built-in electronics, Ramadan text messages, a T-shirt with protection against GSM rays, Linkedin, the Centre for Fathers, NutriDelight (Procter and Gamble's enriched orange drinks for developing countries), long-lasting flowers, a burial codicil, Pepsi Raw (100 per cent natural), a smoke-free ashtray, Realitybid.com – an internet site for auctioning houses, push-up snack, the very cheap EasyCruise, an energetic mouse pad, an open fire without a chimney, a self-heating tin (Canned Heat), Siemens HomeDeliverybox, nPower Personal Energy Generator, an indestructible sandwich, Mars snack vendor for dogs, Bolletje rusks with grooves, a ladies' urinal, Dyson's washing machine, a whispering trailer, a hybrid bus, a disposable duster, a footrest for skates in the winter, Freeze ice cream, a delivery bicycle for postmen, road surfaces with silencers, The Door (a door without a handle), Bertolli-lunchroom, Smoke

---

2   S. Cierpicki, M. Wright and B. Sharp (2000). Managers' Knowledge of Marketing Principles: The Case of New Product Development. *Journal of Empirical Generalisations in Marketing Science*, vol. 5, 777.

Shop 451F, Nintendo Wii Fit, Qool (a low-alcohol wine), TravelJohn (a disposable plastic bag), Philips Wake-up Light, ringing dustbins, Aldi-PC, a web supermarket, a patented reed for synthetic reed roofs, aeroplane pizza, braces which prevent snoring, a plasma scalpel, LG Steam dishwashers, Miss Molly cosmetics for children, salmon pâté for cats during menopause, Green Heinz Ketchup, an inflatable bath for the home, Tupperware shops, a sensor monitor for conscientious office workers, Benecol/Becel for reducing cholesterol, Yotel at Schiphol, Skype, Unsicht-Bar (for eating in the dark), Filter Pen (a straw which purifies polluted water), shoes which generate electricity for GSM and radio, Nikon Coolpix S1000PJ Camera, Perfect Bookmachine, Vitz Vitamin chewing gum, Carbona 2 in 1 Oven Rack and Grill Cleaner, tarmac which can be rolled up like a carpet, fresh orange juice with vodka, Alice internet, TravelChair (a folding chair when travelling), Supersmoker, Twitter, Meridian Sooloos Digital Media System, IKEA house, Procter and Gamble Swiffer Sweeper, Whale tail (propelling system simulating a whale tail), Duo white and brown bread for children, Czeers solar system speed boat, Fire Wire Flexible Grilling Skewer, Coca Cola Zero, Dolby Volume from Dolby, Ideal-payment online, Diesel Flagshipstore, Dove Pro-Age, MyKey by Ford, Pharox lamp, Brondell Perfect Flush for saving water in the toilet, Fishes (durable fish), Design your Heineken, HP Photosmart Premium with Touch smart Web All-in-One Printer, SAAB Biopower Eco clothing, Omo small and powerful washing powder, an automatic paintbrush (Paintpod), Google Android, Vega insurance policy, exotic apple Kanzi and Remington Frizz Therapy Straightening Iron.

The extent to which a product or service can be considered as new varies considerably and is often the topic of discussion. How new is new? This can be looked at from several perspectives but a much-used and significant classification of new products uses three categories:

1. New to the world, for example the first mobile conversation (the USA, July 1946).
2. New to the market, for example Vodafone live! The first UMTS service in the Netherlands (June 2004).[3]
3. New to the company, for example KPN mobile video telephoning with UMTS (May 2005).[4]

What is new for one is not necessarily new for the other. The introduction of a new game for Nintendo DS is not as innovative for either Nintendo or its customers when compared with the introduction of the worldwide, greatly distinguished and popular Wii. Studies have shown that the chance for success increases greatly if the new product or service has additional value for the customer and when it distinguishes itself from already existing competitive products. Many new products which are launched on the market are only 'new to the company' and usually a

---

3   Tjeerd Wiersma (16 June 2004). Vodafone eerste met UMTS-toestellen in Nederland. *Emerce*.

4   www.zdnet.nl/mobile.

variation of, or a successor to, an existing product, or a direct copy of a product from the closest competitor. Research into the introduction of 24,000 new products onto the European market has confirmed this theory. Only 2.2 per cent of all the new products introduced deserve the distinction 'really new'; the rest are 'new' products or, in the terms of the fast-moving consumer goods sector, are 'line-extensions', 'me-too' or temporary 'in-out products'.[5] The lack of real new products often causes many companies to make small modifications to existing products internally which makes it then 'politically useful' to consider them as 'new products'. I am also guilty of this as I used to record each new article number in the ERP-system as an innovation when only the method of preparation or the packaging design had been changed. Well, if your end-of-year bonus is calculated by the number of new products which you have introduced, wouldn't you do the same?

1.3 NEW PRODUCTS ARE ESSENTIAL

New products are essential for a company. Your organisation may well operate in mature markets or markets with slow volume growth and where the life cycle of existing products is becoming shorter. Many reasons have been given for this: the customer has changed, the competition has changed and the world has changed. However, if you don't do anything, new and competitive products will catch up and overtake your products more quickly. A study done by the A.D. Little consultancy has shown that the life cycle of products has decreased by factor of 4.[6] Fifty years ago the average life cycle varied between 12 years (cosmetics) and 24 years (medicine). However, currently it has decreased to two years and eight years, respectively. The change in the behaviour of consumers is also accelerating, as can be seen by the figures mentioned below. These figures illustrate how long it takes to penetrate a target group consisting of 50 million users:[7]

Radio	38 years
TV	13 years
Internet	4 years
iPod	3 years
Facebook	2 years

---

5   Research by Ernst & Young in cooperation with AC Nielsen (ECR Europe, 1999).
6   Robert G. Cooper (2005). *Product Leadership*. New York: Basic Books.
7   Bettina von Stamm and Anna Trifilova (2009). *The Future of Innovation*. Gower Publishing, p. 6.

Nokia is a company which is keeping up well with a fast-changing world. Henry Tirri, Head of the Nokia Research Centre, describes how Nokia stimulates the innovation flow and embraces innovation.

INNOVATION FLOW

Innovation cycles are accelerating dramatically. The speed at which new solutions reach the market can be a matter of months, if not weeks, and this timeframe is continually shrinking as online service organisations embrace a 'beta' culture. The Internet has enabled innovators to share results and garner feedback faster. Feedback from peers, public betas and pilot studies is essential to fuel the accelerated innovation cycle.

Future innovation must also support scale; companies that can scale innovations quickly will succeed by gaining mass-market acceptance almost instantaneously. A willingness to take risks and test ideas fast is vital; we call it the 'fail fast; scale fast' mentality, rooted in a culture of conducting pilots and trials. Often it isn't until you test a product or service that you really understand how customers respond. It is not unusual to see customers using products in unforeseen ways; embracing this can lead to runaway successes.

Nokia Sports Tracker, http://sportstracker.nokia.com/, is one example. Initially designed for runners and walkers, it has been used by everyone from kayakers to motorcyclists. Such unexpected adaptations have prompted Nokia to expand the mandate and functionality of Sports Tracker, conforming to the customers' needs rather than our preconception of what the service should be.

Collaboration also drives innovation forward at a pace that monetary investment alone can never match. Collaborating with leading research organisations globally, Nokia is building an Open Innovation Network to co-create intellectual property and leverage each organisation's insight, expertise and resources. Through research partnerships we maintain a continual inflow of fresh thinking, which ensures we are always challenging established views. This is an integral element of our open innovation philosophy.

Henry Tirri
Head of Nokia Research Centre, Senior Vice President

Source: Bettina von Stamm and Anna Trifilova (2009). *The Future of Innovation,* Gower, p. 32.

Against this background, if you don't do anything, the ability to distinguish your own product portfolio on the market decreases, which will eventually have an irrevocable influence on its distribution, revenue and profit margin. Inevitably this leads to internal crisis moments whereby managers experience the lack of innovation in their own range – moments many marketers have undoubtedly experienced. So have I, and they are moments one does not forget easily. On one occasion, my sales director stormed into a meeting, wound up and red-faced saying: 'Have you heard that Unilever is introducing this new product?' (And he threw a new soup product on the table.) 'I just received it from a director at Ahold. In three months it will be available in more than seven hundred stores. We have to react quickly. This afternoon at three o'clock we will have an emergency meeting with the manager of the research and development department to find out if we can also come up with something.'

If you have ever experienced such a situation, you develop the desire to never 'sit at the back' again. You do not want to have to improvise aggressively or implement small product modifications or simply copy the competition and introduce it with as 'much song and dance' as innovation. No! You want to innovate on a timely basis and become a successful market innovator instead of an unsuccessful follower. You want to look ahead, anticipate and place pioneering and innovative products onto the market; becoming a 'rule maker' instead of a 'rule taker'. Figure 1.1 shows the 10 reasons why it is not only necessary but essential to innovate.

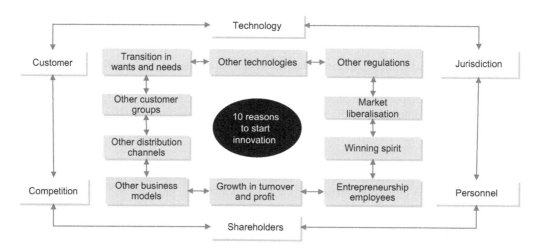

Figure 1.1   Ten reasons to start innovation

You'll note that these reasons are not only from a market perspective, caused by the consumer or the competition, but are also driven by high expectations from shareholders or the financial markets for independent growth which forms an important motive to innovate on time. In addition, new technological opportunities from R&D can be the drive for new products enabling the creation of different business models. What's more, a change in regulations can stimulate innovation. Consider the liberalisation of the energy and postage markets in Europe. This not only led to innovation on the market, but also to a feeling of urgency amongst the current suppliers to create new initiatives in order to restrict the loss of customers to a minimum. Innovation is also a wonderful process from a personnel perspective.

For example, by creating room for the initiative of co-workers within the business strategy, you can enable them to fulfil their own dreams. Google is, for many, an example with their 70–20–10 rule: 70 per cent of the time is spent on the core business, 20 per cent on related subjects and 10 per cent on things you choose yourself. Last, but not least, the achievement of a successful product introduction can give co-workers in the organisation the feeling of elation, both in the sales and marketing department and throughout the whole company; including the co-workers at the call centre, and the administration or the production departments.

1.4 MANAGERS STRUGGLE WITH INNOVATION

The reason why managers struggle with innovation is because they are too far removed from commercial reality. Neal Thornberry, Professor of Management at the American Babson College, explains it as follows:

Marketing presentations take the place of real opportunity analysis. They don't know if they can make it, if anybody will buy it, for how long, at what price and how they will defend it against people trying to steal their market.

Managers struggle with innovation at all levels and in different roles. In the next section seven managers, all wearing a different 'hat', explain, anecdotally, their view on innovation in practice. I am curious as to which hat best fits you.

1. The Despondent Product Manager

'Every problem in my organisation which concerns my product group ends up on my desk. I feel like a rag with a thousand-and-one uses. I hardly have time to pay attention to innovation, and I am happy if I can make time free to accompany the account manager on a visit to a client. I get ideas for new products while jogging during the weekend. In the beginning, I found the idea of innovation difficult as I had no experience and there is no practical training available. So, how do I discover a "hole" in the market and what would be a good proposition? I am learning more about innovation in practice through trial and error. What really gets me down is the ambivalent way in which my bosses approach me. On the one hand they motivate me to develop new products quickly, while on the other hand, every manager above me – right up to the general manager – must have their say about the new concept I present. This causes endless product adaptations and the process takes forever; enough to make me 100 per cent despondent.'

THE DIFFICULT START

2. The Pragmatic Marketing Manager

'We are in a very competitive market, therefore innovation has top priority. I motivate the product managers and support and coach them during our bilateral meetings once a fortnight. Unfortunately, the current turnover is below budget, which puts enormous pressure on the sales department as well as my marketers. Furthermore, extra promotions and product variants which have to be developed quickly always take preference before serious product innovation. In addition, as a result of the disappointing turnover, I had to turn in a part of my marketing budget, and I cannot save on the marketing support of the current "cash-cows", as that would be disastrous. As a result I do not have money available to enter the market with a new product. But, product innovation is still the highest priority.'

3. The Stoic R&D Specialist

'I find real innovation great as I can completely immerse myself in it. I have many ideas but at the moment my desk in the R&D lab is covered with four projects for small modifications to products and six projects around the cutback of the production process for the production managers and engineers with which I am also involved … not to mention the paperwork. As I said I have many brilliant ideas, but I keep them to myself. Many marketers are not open to these ideas as they are more concerned with the theory. I now have the fourth marketer in eight years and they all want to do market research first in order to ask the customer what they want. But customers do not know what they want; we have to create it for them. However, marketers only realise this two years later … '

4. The Procedural R&D Manager

'Many departments, such as engineering, production, purchasing and also marketing, rely on the capacity of R&D. Every marketer wants you to concentrate 100 per cent on their product. If you allow them to, they will constantly make everybody crazy with their new ideas. That's the reason why we have implemented a very good process for innovation, the Stage-Gate process. In this way we can select which project ideas will become an official R&D project and which ones will not. Furthermore, we can follow exactly which project idea is in which phase of development. Preceding these five steps there is a go/no-go moment for the management team, and if it is not a project, then my people may not work on it. In this way we keep control of everything.'

5. The Down-to-Earth Sales Manager

'Simply put, I am all for the business of today and it keeps me very busy. Furthermore, I expect marketing and R&D to come up with new products on time, so that my account managers can go to the customers with a good story. For the moment, I have my hands full with trying to reach the turnover target for this term. Should a marketer come to me with a beautiful new introduction story and research results, then I always ask for some time to reflect. I then test the idea at home with my wife to see if she understands exactly what it is meant for. If she doesn't understand it immediately then the customers won't either, and I do not pursue the idea. It's as simple as that.'

6. The Sound Production Director

'Everybody is talking about innovation. However, looking back over the past 10 years, I dare say that of the 50 new product introductions we had, maybe only 5 were successful. When looking at the production volume, then these products make up only 10 per cent of the volume, but nobody looks back to calculate what these introductions cost. A real fortune! Nobody even asks how much extra turnover it would have earned if, with this money, we had supported the current products more, especially through advertising. I believe marketing and innovation is a playground for young theorists without experience who want to dictate which ridiculous new ideas I have to consider in my factory.'

7. The Divided General Manager

'With regards to innovation I have *zwei Seelen in meiner Brust* (two souls in my chest), as the Germans describe it so well. On the one hand we have a clear focus on the market, a professional innovation process and great people working in R&D and Marketing, but on the other hand I am not yet satisfied with its effectiveness. There are too few really innovative products flowing forth from the innovation pipeline. At one moment there is simply a lack of good ideas and at the next I receive introduction plans for "still unfinished products" which nobody is really waiting for.'

Indeed, I have portrayed these managers as 'characters', but I hope that it brought a smile to your face as well as a flicker of recognition.

1.5 TEN INNOVATION INHIBITORS

Innovation is still a struggle for many organisations; thorough quantitative research done by the Product Development Management Association shows that the share of new product turnover in the United States has decreased in the last 15 years.[8] An important reason is the reduction in 'new to the world' products, and thus to real innovation. The share of these innovations in the product development portfolios of companies has decreased dramatically, from 20.4 per cent in 1990 to 11.5 per

---

8   M. Adams and D. Bolke (2004). PDMA Foundation CPAS Study Reveals New Trends. *PDMA Visions*, vol. XXVIII, July.

cent in 2004,[9] favouring line-extensions and small product modifications. I will not be surprised if this phenomenon is also happening everywhere else.

In my consultancy I experience the tangible struggle which managers have with innovation. Over the years I have discovered 10 factors that cause these struggles, which I call innovation inhibitors:

1. As manager you are much too busy with the current turnover.
2. Because of success in the past you are now trapped in the process whereby old successful formulae are constantly being varied.
3. Dividing the company into business units, market and product groups work against it as real new concepts usually do not fit into any of these definitions and therefore in practice work against rather than with each other.
4. The urgency to innovate is absent and it is only felt at those moments when the competition has already attacked and 'it is hurting' the turnover, market share and profit.
5. Even though considerable market research is done, there is still a lack of insight amongst managers into the motives, needs and problems of the customers – in other words, real customer insight.
6. A structured innovation process is either non-existent or organised so bureaucratically and with so much paperwork that the innovation pipeline gets blocked.
7. Customers are not involved in the innovation process or only get involved at a much later stage.
8. Money, manpower and management support for innovation are not structurally applied but on an ad hoc basis and only on those occasions when it is necessary to 'put out any small fires'.
9. As manager you do not dare to take risks as you fear that one mistake or one ambitious new product which fails might cost you a promising career.
10. At the start of the process, the innovation pipeline is not systematically filled with sufficient pioneering and appealing product ideas.

1.6 THE INNOVATION PROCESS

Many companies make use of the Stage-Gate Innovation Process,[10] which was developed by Robert G. Cooper. The innovation process has been divided into five stages in the original full Stage-Gate model, represented on Figure 1.2.

It offers a blueprint to structure the innovation process from the first idea evaluation until the introduction of the product. Each stage closes with a gateway, which serves as a quality control as well as a go/no-go decision for the management.

---

9   Robert G. Cooper (2005). Your NPD Portfolio May Be Harmful to Your Business's Health. *PDMA Visions*, vol. XXIX, April.

10   Robert G. Cooper (2000). Doing It Right: Winning With New Products. *Ivey Business Journal*, July/August. Stage-Gate is a trademark of R. Cooper and Associates Consultant Inc.

During the past decade many large international companies have implemented this model. However, in practice this model is responsible for many delays in the innovation process, and consequently simplified versions have been developed for less complicated innovation projects. These versions have reduced the number of stages to three (Stage-Gate Xpress) or two (Stage-Gate Lite).[11]

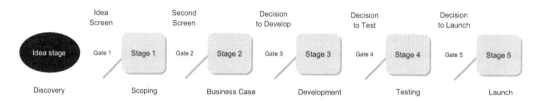

Figure 1.2   The full Stage-Gate innovation process

1.7 THE TRICKY START

The first stage of the innovation process model covers the initial investigation of the innovation ideas. The first gateway in the model asks the question: do we really have to pay attention to this? The model assumes that there are many available and appealing product ideas readily available. However, that is exactly where we miss the boat. Appealing new product ideas do not appear at the exact moment when we need them. The latest international research in *The Economist* shows that almost 60 per cent of companies are not able to generate sufficient innovative ideas.[12]

Ideas for new products and services can come from anywhere: from inside the company through research and development, marketing, sales, the call centre or the online sales department; from top management, the responsible line managers and enthusiastic co-workers. Because interest in 'open innovation' has increased significantly over the last few years, innovation ideas and knowledge can also come from consumers, business-to-business clients, distribution partners, suppliers, consultants, research institutes, scientists and even from competitors. However, in practice, it is still unclear where the innovation ideas should come from, or where in a company new products can be reported or collected and stored. The question about which criteria they should meet is also vague. Do you know, at this moment, who in your organisation has new product ideas or what criteria they have to meet?

As a marketer I was often confronted with a situation where I was in desperate need of something new, knowing full well that there was nothing really new in

---

11   Robert G. Cooper (2008). What Leading Companies are Doing to Reinvent their NPD Processes. *PDMA Visions*, September, 7.

12   The Economist Intelligence Unit (2008). *The Innovators: How Successful Companies Drive Business Transformation*, 10.

the company at that moment. The lack of clarity concerning the beginning of the innovation process led to it being called the 'fuzzy front end of innovation'.[13] The innovation guru, Robert G. Cooper, added a 'discovery stage' before the first stage of his model in order to improve it, as can be seen in Figure 1.2.[14] It is at this stage that ideas are discovered; thus, in advance of any decision to develop a product or service, the start of the innovation process is divided into three steps, with a gateway at each step. However, I consider this phase – from the creation of the idea until a decision is made to develop the product concept – as one unit, with one team and one process. This enables you to gather speed, which is important as the world turns faster each day. From the moment when the idea is created until the decision is made to develop the concept, I use the term 'ideation phase' in order to distinguish it from the idea phase where only the first rough idea is created.

Many organisations spend too little money and time on the front end of the innovation process. Research has shown that companies who spend more time and attention to the ideation phase:[15]

1. speed up the development of a new product;
2. spend a greater part of their effort on product development projects which will lead to successful new products;
3. create a positive influence in the organisation;
4. increase the chance that the product development programme will meet the objectives of the organisation.

A worldwide investigation by the consultancy of Arthur D. Little into the five best practices in innovation shows that effective idea management has the greatest influence on the turnover of new products. It results in an increase in turnover of 7.2 per cent from new products.[16]

The very first phase of the innovation process, the creation of new and appealing product ideas, is therefore of the utmost importance for the further development of the process. Should unsatisfactory or insufficient 'fertile seeds' enter the formal product innovation process, the process might still be good, but nothing will grow from it in the end. According to a recent study by the American Product Development Management Association, in order to put one successful product idea on the market, you need seven new product ideas.[17]

---

13   P. Koen et al. (2001). Providing Clarity and a Common Language to the Fuzzy Front End. *Research-Technology Management*, March/April.

14   R. Cooper, S. Edgett, E. Kleinschmidt (2002). Optimizing the Stage-Gate Process: What Best Practice Companies are Doing. *Research Technology Management*, vol. 45, no. 5.

15   J. Poskela (2005). Uncertainty Management Within Fuzzy-Front-End. TU-22.432 Management of Uncertainty. Helsinki University of Technology, 16 February.

16   Arthur D. Little (2005). How Companies Use Innovation to Improve Profitability and Growth (Innovation Excellence study).

17   R. Cooper (2005). *Product Leadership*. New York: Basic Books.

Table 1.1   The number of new product ideas necessary for one successful product

Phase in the innovation process	Number of new products
Project screening and analysis	7
Business analysis phase	5
Development phase	4
Testing phase	2
Commercialisation phase	1,5
Successful market introduction	1

So, what is really necessary to create successful new product concepts and how do you fill up the innovation pipeline quickly enough with appealing and attainable new product concepts? These are key questions which I will answer in this practical guide for the creation of new product and service ideas, my aim being to 'unfuzz' the fuzzy front end of innovation.

INTERNAL SUPPORT....

2 Success Factors for the Ideation Phase

A discovery is said to be an accident meeting a prepared mind.
(A. von Szent-Gyorgyi, Hungarian doctor)

You must be the change you wish to see in the world.
(M. Gandhi, Indian pacifist)

An idea knocks before it enters your mind.

(Loesje)

2.1 INTRODUCTION

Much can be improved in the innovation process, such as to start with a good ideation approach. In practice there are a few ingredients necessary to generate new product ideas effectively. This chapter will first provide a sketch of what can and does go wrong during the innovation process and thereafter it will provide the success factors necessary for an effective process so that new products and services can be created.

2.2 WHAT'S WRONG AT THE BEGINNING?

Many things can go wrong during the process of creating new products. Figure 2.1 shows the 10 examples in practice. Perhaps it is a 'feast of recognition', which in this case is unfortunate but rest assured, you are not alone.

1. We Don't Know What We Want Regarding Innovation

The invention of new products happens ad hoc, usually at a time when a problem arises or the turnover decreases suddenly or when a competitor enters the market unexpectedly. The question then is – what now? 'Jack Smith, create a list', becomes the creed. At this moment it becomes clear that the existing strategic business plan hardly provides footing or direction for innovation. Do we now prefer to invent new products defensively in order to consolidate our position in the market and so protect the core business, or do we search for new product ideas offensively to develop growth in the market? These are two totally different approaches, and the more simple questions, such as which new product ideas should we use for which market, country, region, product or target group, also play a role. Regrettably, the different strategic plans didn't help me much either, especially at moments when I, as a marketer, had a strong desire for new product innovation. I hope that it is different in your situation. The lack of clear answers to the above-mentioned questions leads to random thought processes, which in many cases are interrupted because the management, after consideration, decide to concentrate on either a different market, product or target group or on another country. When you are suddenly confronted with this during the creative process, it throws a spanner in the works of the creative car which then, under loud protest, comes to a screeching halt.

Figure 2.1   What goes wrong at the start of innovation

2. We Come Up With the Same Thing Over and Over Again

Product ideas are not readily available. When there is a need for it, and at the initiative of a marketer in the organisation, a few people are invited for a brainstorming session. This session usually takes place at the end of a long and tiring day. The people who come together are usually the same group (known as the creative team) but nothing materialises, because when you try and brainstorm with close colleagues nothing new appears. Everyone automatically races towards the same goal; they are irritated with each other's well-known hobbies and the result is that everyone leaves the meeting disappointed. At these moments they all experience an inevitable feeling of failure.

3. We Remain in the Usual Conventions of Our Market

Organisations usually have customer information at their disposal, do regular research into the market and are in contact with customers daily, but this investigative process has become routine. Companies pay more attention to their market shares and on what their competitors are doing on the same market. Therefore, products start looking alike as everyone copies each other's successes which in turn leads to common conventions in the market while the organisation loses sight of what the customer really wants. As a result of this tunnel vision, a 'blind spot' develops in the management from which a new competitor can appear at an unexpected moment with another offer, which might just meet the changing need of the market.

4. The Brainstorming Session is Dominated by Extroverts and the Highest Bosses

In a brainstorming session without expert facilitators, not everyone is given a fair chance. In most cases either the extroverts or the highest bosses dominate it. This is extremely difficult and tactically awkward for the marketing manager who is faced with the problem of leading the meeting. It also applies when his boss has to have the final word in the brainstorm and the rest have been silenced.

5. Coming up with and Evaluating New Product Ideas Goes Haywire

There are brainstorming sessions where everyone can have their say. After all, this is the reason for the brainstorming session, isn't it? However, when you carefully listen to what is being said and build upon the product ideas mentioned by others, the risk is that the ideas are judged immediately. Remarks such as, 'That does not work with us', 'We have tried it before', 'We will never get permission to do that', or 'No, that can definitely not be done', are heard. In reality, these negative statements cause such a mix up so that real creativity does not stand a chance, and a spiral of negativity is created whereby everyone is silenced within a short time as they are trapped amongst all the creativity killers.

6. With Hundreds of Yellow Post-Its on the Wall We Don't Know What to Do Next

Often the person, usually the marketer who is responsible for the innovation itself, facilitates the brainstorming session. Soon product ideas are mentioned and in the end there is a wall full of post-its. But then the process stops, because what next? There might be good ideas amongst them but the question is: how do we create a product idea with a head and tail out of all of this? I must admit that in the days when I was still a manager, I did not have the answer to this question either and thought that I had to find the answers myself, whereby I thanked all the participants for their input and took all the post-its to my office. Here they accusingly stared at me for weeks, until I finally threw them in the dustbin. Thus many things can go wrong in a brainstorming session as the setting up and facilitating of a brainstorming programme is a profession. Fortunately, I learned this later.

7. Product Ideas Remain Vague

Due to the fact that everything in a brainstorming session in the beginning goes so well and creativity is stimulated, new product ideas are expressed in beautiful-sounding marketing jargon. However, beware as this can be a self-made pitfall. For example: 'We are going to make an application whereby we can reach adolescents with trendy virtual mobile marketing', or 'It is going to become a very original product as it appeals to the primitive man inside us because it favours authenticity'. Product ideas in this stage, which can either represent everything or nothing, still have a long way to go.

8. Senior Management is out to Reject Very Innovative Ideas

At the beginning of the innovation pipeline, product ideas are screened. This is the task of the senior management who have the chance to influence the process afterwards. Even though the task really is to innovate, ideas which are considered too far-fetched are removed first, maybe because those present cannot relate to them, leaving the responsible executive managers in a daze. Real innovation was, after all, the intention, wasn't it?

9. The Development Team Puts Everything Back for Discussion

It is great when the decision is made to develop a good and new product idea. Subsequently it is passed on from the product inventors to the product developers – who are usually a multi-disciplinary team under the control of a project leader. It seems strange, but it is usually at this stage when most of the energy disappears from the idea. All the members of the development team now dissect the original product idea as everybody has their own vision as to which direction it should go in. This is normal, isn't it? Of course it is necessary to improve the product idea during the development process, but often the distinguished product idea starts looking more like ideas we have already had, because we can produce something like that. The risk is that you then throw the baby out with the bathwater.

10. Line Management Always Resist Innovative Ideas

In larger organisations, during the development process the product idea has to be 'sold' to the line management on a regular basis because, should the product reach the finish line of the innovation process, they are the ones who will be producing the product and putting it on the market. So while you are waiting for the expected applause, you continue to receive many comments and a pile of questions to which you do not have answers. It is logical that you would ask yourself whether these comments and questions are practical arguments or whether you have become the victim of the feared 'not invented here' syndrome. Maybe it is even a political game. Hence, it can happen that a good new product idea is kept in the freezer for years due to a lack of internal support. The resistance from the line management team can also be caused by the fact that they have more than enough to do with their regular tasks. And if they do not have the time to work on their own ideas then they are not prepared to spend time on the ideas of others which have been forced upon them.

It is possible that you have recognised the above-mentioned situations, but do not despair, for you are not the only one, and luckily in this chapter we are working towards a solution.

2.3 WHO NEEDS AN APPROPRIATE IDEATION PHASE?

Naturally, innovation is not only about trouble and strife as there are many companies which are extremely innovative. According to the Boston Consulting Group, research has shown which companies worldwide are the most innovative, with Apple, Google and Toyota at the top of the list for four consecutive years.

The top 25 most innovative companies are almost totally dominated by companies active in technological sectors such as computers, electronics, the internet or automobiles. Does this mean that large companies which fall in the same category can innovate better than other companies? Not necessarily, as companies in the technological sector can also invent huge failures. Consider the following products which either did not reach the market or stayed on the market for a very short time: Apple, with the unsuccessful Macintosh TV in 1993 – a PC which had a built-in TV-function and cost $2,100; Philips, with their superior Video 2000 which could not compete against the VHS system of Japanese manufacturers in the 1980s; and in the Netherlands – the PPT who failed with the Greenpoint (Kermit) – a mobile phone which was not actually mobile and on which you could not be phoned and only lasted from 1992 to 1999.

When it comes to the innovation process it is important to distinguish those companies which are more technological from those which are less so. For more technological companies, R&D plays an important role as the process is usually driven and developed by new technology from within the company or in cooperation with a chain of suppliers. On average 4 per cent of the annual turnover is spent on R&D, with the most in software (20 per cent), computers and communication (12.5 per cent) and pharmaceuticals (12 per cent). The start of the innovation process is fed by a stream of technological discoveries in conjunction with intellectual rights of ownership. Technological development is a constant drive for the jerky process of innovation. For companies which are driven by technology it is a challenge during the innovation process to change the technical inventions effectively and profitably into a new product concept which is attractive to the customer.

Table 2.1   The top 25 most innovative companies in the world – 2009

Position	Company	Most important reason
1	Apple	Pioneering new products
2	Google	Unique customer experiences
3	Toyota	Innovative business processes
4	Microsoft	Innovative business processes
5	Nintendo	Pioneering new products
6	IBM	Innovative business processes
7	HP	Innovative business processes
8	Research in Motion	Pioneering new products
9	Nokia	Pioneering new products
10	Wal-Mart Stores	Innovative business processes
11	Amazon.com	Unique customer experiences
12	Procter & Gamble	Innovative business processes
13	Tata Group	Pioneering new products
14	Sony	Pioneering new products
15	Reliance Industries	New business models
16	Samsung Electronics	Pioneering new products
17	General Electric	Innovative business processes
18	Volkswagen	Unique customer experiences
19	McDonald's	Unique customer experiences
20	BMW	Unique customer experiences
21	Walt Disney	Unique customer experiences
22	Honda Motor	Pioneering new products
23	ATa&T	Pioneering new products
24	Coca Cola	Unique customer experiences
25	Vodafone	Pioneering new products

Source: Worldwide research amongst 2,700 top executives. Boston Consulting Group

Companies which are not technologically driven have less input from the R&D department. In the food sector, for example, only 0.7 per cent of the turnover is spent on R&D.[1] Often even less is spent on R&D or new business development, and sometimes it is even non-existent. This applies to organisations such as publishers, travel agencies, insurance companies, shops, employment agencies, social services

---

1   R. Cooper (2005). *Product Leadership*. New York: Basic Books, p. 13.

and governmental organisations. If innovation is present in these companies, then it has found a place in the organisational structure resulting in a small department with a small staff consisting of innovation specialists or new business developers who have to report to the management or board of directors. The start of the innovation process is not fed by technological discoveries. It is usually fed by sudden, disruptive developments on the market which causes the start or acceleration of the product development processes within the organisation. Consider the following:

1. Liberalisation of the market:
   - public transport market
   - energy market

2. New competitors:
   - Amazon which started selling books online
   - price-cutter ALDI which started selling personal computers
   - chain stores which started selling insurance policies

3. Dominant trends with client groups:
   - obesity (being seriously overweight) in the food sector
   - 'online social networking' of young people

4. Decreasing market growth:
   - the beer market in Western Europe
   - the postal market in Western Europe

5. New distribution channels:
   - the internet as a direct sales channel
   - out-of-home food market

   In all these cases, the drive for innovation is a serious disruption on the market. Both external (new competitors or dominant trends) and internal factors (loss of market share or loss of profit margin) can cause the urgency. Due to the fact that market urgency develops ad hoc, the innovation process is often not in place or even absent. Less technological-driven companies are also faced with the challenge of starting with the innovation process on time, and to create multiple attractive new product concepts in order to bring sufficient new products or services onto the market quickly. For organisations which react late on disruptive developments in the market, a good ideation phase is essential.

2.4 A GOOD NEW SERVICE OR PRODUCT IDEA

This book addresses the idea of creating new services and products. But what is a new product idea and which criteria should it meet in order to have a chance in the next stages of the innovation process?

The moment an idea 'comes out of nowhere' it is usually seen as playful, rough and idiotic. Generally, it is not more than a fleeting thought, a word or image whereby we experience a 'we-have-to-do-something-with-this' feeling. This is known as an insight, a brain wave, an inspiration, a thought-provoker or an idea. However, it is only a rough diamond as it still has a long way to go, even if you think that it is going to shine beautifully. It is only the start, and though you feel that you have to do something with it, much more is needed for a successful start to the innovation process.

The criteria for a new product idea can be looked at from three different perspectives: the customer, the company and the innovation process itself. As can be seen on Figure 2.2, this leads to eight ideal qualities for a new and good product idea:

1. It is attractive to customers.
2. It stands out in the market.
3. It has the potential for extra turnover for the company.
4. It has adequate profit potential for the company.
5. It fits into the strategy of the company.
6. It is considered feasible.
7. It gives direction.
8. It has internal support.

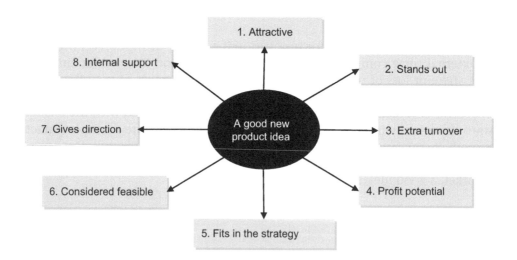

Figure 2.2   Criteria for a good new product idea

It is evident that potential customers have to find the new product idea really attractive. However, there is more to it. The product idea must be clearly distinguishable from, and supply concrete advantages with regards to, the current situation for customers. An attractive and distinguishable new product idea gives the potential customers a concrete reason to change. An innovative product idea will solve the relevant problems of customers or will make something new possible. This not only applies to the consumer market but also to the customers in a business-to-business market. Business services or products often play a huge role in the business processes of customers. When it comes to the decision to buy, many people and departments are involved. As the product becomes more important for the customer with regards to cost or in relation to the primary business process, there will have to be a definite reason for change, especially if the customer wants to switch to something new.

An attractive and distinguishable new product idea which will have to be developed causes many changes within the company. It is therefore important that you are fully aware of the possible changes which will have to take place within your organisation and of the possible resistance to this right at the beginning of the innovation process. Manfred Kets de Vries, Professor in Management and Leadership at the renowned INSEAD, once said: 'The only person waiting for a change is a baby with a wet diaper.' He is absolutely right, because how much are you willing to change? And with this I do not mean as a manager, but simply as a person.

A good product idea is only attractive for an organisation if it is going to bring about a larger turnover and more profit, if it fits into their strategy, and, above all, if it is considered to be feasible. When considering feasibility you should think about the adaptability (internal and external) of the potential product and about the competence of the organisation in order to market the product or service.

To reach this point the product idea must first pass through the innovation process successfully. In other words, a good product idea must also be able to endure elaboration and development during the innovation process. When a product idea is concrete from the start, it will be easier to perform these tasks and it will increase the chance of the product which reaches the end of the innovation process being exactly what was thought of originally, which in itself is a challenge. We have all had the experience of a story which has been passed on from one person to another, and in the end the story has changed completely. One of the greatest obstacles is internal support, yet this is an important condition for the successful completion of the innovation process. Ideally a good product idea is not only supported by the creators, but is fully supported by the development team, the top management and the line management, even if there is some opposition at the beginning.

Vague yet attractive original ideas are a good start to the ideation phase. This is when the brilliant yet unshaped idea develops from a concept into a plan for a new product, which leads on to the form of a mini new business case.

Table 2.2   The development of a good and new product idea

Vague idea	Idea direction	Product concept	Mini new business case
An attractive, vague but original idea which you come up with	An attractive golden thread for a new product or service	The outline of an attractive, possibly feasible, idea worked out with a new marketing mix	An innovative concept elaborated in a plan which is attractive, feasible, substantial and tested with customers

The product idea in the ideation phase is only completed when there is a mini new business case which sparkles like a 24-carat diamond.

The definition of a good and new product idea is:

For the customer and organisation a substantial, attractive, distinguishable and feasible idea for a new product, service or business model, in a specific packaging and with a specific brand name, which is delivered to specific customers with a certain business model through a specific distribution channel.

2.5 FIVE SUCCESS FACTORS

To innovate successfully it is necessary to create, develop and introduce good and new products. The discovery of these ideas, which should be original and distinguishable from existing products, requires creativity. However, the development and introduction of the new product idea in today's business reality also involves a lot of hard work.

The essence of a successful ideation phase is the building of a bridge between the creativity and the daily practice of the management, two worlds which do not tolerate each other easily. It is usually the creative (and sometimes vague) developers, designers, marketers and innovation advisers versus the line managers, who are looking for immediate turnover and profit. There is a love–hate relationship between them because they need each other. On the one hand, the creative outside-the-box thinkers need the management, who are responsible for allowing the product idea to be developed and introduced onto the market, to help their brainchildren see the light. On the other hand, there are the inside-the-box managers who need the creative thinkers (external or internal) to break through the established patterns in the market and in this way create new and distinguishable product ideas for the market of tomorrow. This does not mean that managers cannot be creative or that people who are creative cannot manage, since we all have our strong or weak points.

The bridge between creativity and management rests on five pillars:

1. Urgency and focus.
2. Real customer insight.

3. A fresh look from outside.
4. An effective creative process.
5. Internal support.

Figure 2.3 shows the five success factors. These factors have been further developed into 10 aspects for an effective process for the creation of new products and services and are explained in more detail.

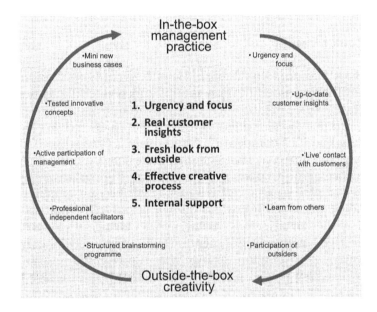

Figure 2.3   Five success factors for creating innovative products and services

1. Urgency and Focus

Recent innovation research has shown that the greatest challenge companies face lies in the internal implementation of the chosen new ideas. The internal resistance against change is therefore the greatest obstacle.[2] This is the reason why urgency is essential both at the top as well as in the line organisation. The urgency decreases the resistance and creates fertile a breeding ground for innovation. Let's take a look at Apple. In 2006, 2007 and 2008 Apple was chosen as the most innovative company in the world. Yet only a decade ago, in the pre-iPod days, Apple found itself in big trouble. At the beginning of 1997 it lost half of its market shares and reported a loss

---

2   The Economist Intelligence Unit (2008). *The Innovators: How Successful Companies Drive Business Transformation*, p. 11.

of more than $700 million.[3] A bad economic climate also highlights that the old solutions do not work anymore, and that intensifies the urgency.

In order to create new products and services effectively it is necessary to know what your goal is and to establish which direction should be taken. For this reason it is important, together with the top management, to establish the focus for innovation which will reflect the company's overall strategy. As the Spanish-Roman philosopher Seneca said: 'If you do not know which harbour you want to sail to, no wind is favourable.' So how will you be able to judge new product ideas if you do not know what you are looking for?

2. Real Customer Insight

Recently a study was done to establish the effectiveness of ideation techniques for product innovation.[4] A total of three groups and 18 techniques at 160 companies were investigated: voice-of-customer (VOC)-techniques (such as ethnography, focus groups and customer visits), open innovation techniques (such as involving start-ups, crowd sourcing and idea competitions) and other methods (such as border vision, patent mining and internal idea systems) were amongst them. Although much attention has been paid to open innovation over the past years, open innovation as the source for new product ideas has not yet become popular. Moreover, the study has shown that open innovation is not yet effective. Methods involving the customer are applied in order to gain new product ideas and produce the best results. The most effective ideation techniques, in the top five, are where the customers are directly involved. It is therefore strange that the research regarding customers is performed by external market research agencies and that the live research is only attended by a single marketing or product manager on occasion. It also seems as if the market research in many companies has become a fixed ritual dance, which leads to the strange situation that, even though much market research is done, in the end there are hardly any insights into the real motives, needs and problems of the customers.

Insight into customer frictions

A customer friction is the difference between what you want or need and what you get (present product performance). Discovering these frictions is a very important source of inspiration for new ideas because customers in the consumer markets or the business-to-business markets only change their own behavioural pattern when a new product brings a better solution, offers possibilities which are relevant and which they really need. Customer frictions are also known as customer insights. In this way you try to find out what is an important theme for the customer, what the

---

3   The Economist Intelligence Unit (2008). *The Innovators: How Successful Companies Drive Business Transformation*, p. 8.

4   Robert G. Cooper and Scott Edgett (2008). Ideation for Product Innovation: What are the Best Methods? *PDMA Visions*, March.

customer really wants as well as what is preventing the customer from achieving it. Once you have identified these customer frictions the creation of an innovative solution is then often simple. Chapter 5 gives a detailed explanation of how to achieve this in practice.

Personal contact with customers

Senior managers do not have much contact with customers. This applies to both business-to-business markets and business-to-consumer markets. In a business-to-business market the daily business is left to the account managers and the senior management only comes into contact with the customer when there is serious conflict or when a new contract has to be discussed. These conversations with the business-to-business customers hardly touch the subject of which strategic issues are important to them, let alone trying to find out the direction of their market in the long term. Strangely, many marketers in the business-to-consumer markets leave the contact with customers to others. Even when I, as a marketer, visited the market research agency, I used to sit behind the one-way mirror, eating sweets, while watching others interviewing 'my' customers. Nevertheless, live or personal contact with customers, whether in the customer's factory or at the consumer's house, has an enormous impact on you. You see where they live and work and you notice the things which motivate them and it allows you to discuss your preconceptions regarding the market. Market research is therefore not enough. The Dutch marketer John Resink described it beautifully: 'If you want to understand how a lion hunts, don't go to the zoo, go to the jungle.' The only condition is that you learn how to look at and listen to your customers without any bias, otherwise the old law of selective perception applies: you only see what you want to see and you are blind to other, maybe more important, aspects.

CUSTOMER INSIGHT

3. A Fresh Look from Outside

'This is how we always do it' is a typical, much-heard innovation killer within organisations.

When creating new products it might be useful to ask yourself whether the old ways which have offered so much safety in the past are still applicable for the future. When you are the only one who 'rebels' against the old ways, you will be the one left with the 'pain'. However, it works best when you allow your colleagues to discover for themselves that the world has changed.

Self-discovery of opportunities

Managers hardly ever visit other companies, organisations or branches to orientate themselves about whether things can be done differently. Yet it is worthwhile to learn from the experience of others. Furthermore, it can be very useful to look outside your own branch, especially to establish what is successful and to then relate it back to your own company. Going outside opens your eyes and you might even discover an application in another sector which can add value to yours.

Involving outsiders

The involvement of people from outside the company during the ideation process is also a form of open innovation and has great additional value. Consider the significance of external specialists who, with their specific knowledge and expertise, can add that which is not available within the company itself. The involvement of outsiders also increases the creativity whereby people will start thinking outside the box.

4. An Effective Creative Process

A structured creative process

The creation of new products, services or business models must be a meticulous and constructive process. On the one hand it is important that the participants start thinking outside the box in order to come up with original – sometimes silly – ideas; this is also known as the divergence phase. On the other hand there is a need for a well-structured process in order to group, select and develop the ideas; this is known as the convergence phase. In this way the creative process ends with concrete concepts for innovative products and services.

Expert independent facilitator

To be able to facilitate a structured creative process is a profession through which many pitfalls can be bypassed. An expert and independent facilitator, who can keep the process on the right track, is essential. This person leads the group with a 'soft' hand in the right direction in order to achieve a 'hard' goal and only where necessary allows for side-tracking. Furthermore, independence is necessary for a neutral approach towards all participants so that should anyone, whether a junior product developer or the top manager, deviate from the rules or try to inhibit the brainstorming agreements, he can be dealt with immediately. During the past few years independent FORTH innovation facilitators have been trained and certified by me. In Appendix I you find an overview with seven professional facilitators who can help you. For a recent list, please check www.forth-innovation.com.

5. Internal Support

The internal resistance against change is a huge obstacle. The lack of support is also an important cause as to why the fuzzy front end of innovation sometimes drags out endlessly. Right from the start of the ideation phase I usually try, in three ways, to get things going within the organisation.

Managers and specialists involved

If you haven't come up with the idea yourself, then it is no good? This applies not only to your colleagues but also to you! Therefore, allow the line managers and specialists to participate in the ideation process at the front end of the innovation pipeline. And it pays off. Furthermore, restrict the passing on of ideas from one to another to the minimum. Is it not better to keep the same ideation team from the idea to the developed product concept?

Tested product concepts

The essential question is: 'Is the innovative idea attractive to the customer?' It is important to establish this as soon as possible and not to wait until the testing of the product or service at the end of the innovation pipeline. The first opinion of the customer will not only serve to establish the attractiveness and the distinctiveness of the new product idea, but also increase the support of the top and line management because you can base its attractiveness on the test results with customers.

Concrete mini new business cases

A new product idea is not only a creative product but it must also comply with all the regular business criteria. Does it have (extra) turnover potential? Does it have profit potential? Does it fit into the company's strategy? And, of course, the 'Bob the builder' question: can we make it? These questions are answered, as far as possible, during the ideation phase of the innovation process. A common way in management practice is the business case where I then choose a mini variant which complies with all uncertainties in the earliest phase of the innovation pipeline.

The above-mentioned pillars, on which the bridge between creativity and management practice rests, form the foundation of the FORTH innovation method for creating new innovative products and services. This method will be described in the next chapter.

2.6 DILEMMAS IN THE IDEATION PHASE

The characteristics (already described) of an effective way in which to create new products were created not only through my own experience but also by others who have applied the innovation method through experimenting, doing things differently and then maintaining the improvements in the approach and adjusting that which was not so good. In this way I have been continuously confronted with some very pertinent questions or dilemmas from myself, from customers and other innovation facilitators. The following five questions complete the success factors described in this chapter.

Can an Expert Approach Not Achieve More than a Team Approach?

Is it not possible to create better ideas with a small group of experts than with a group that includes also internal managers and co-workers who are not innovation specialists? The obvious answer could be yes. However, what is the use of brilliant product ideas if there is no support in the organisation, or when, during the first selection process, the ideas are rejected because of the 'not invented here' feeling? When internal 'non-experts' (who also play a role in the development and introduction process) participate in the invention of their own innovations, it creates an enormous positive energy with co-workers and colleagues, and therefore creates speed, which is visible and helpful, further down the line. Surely you want to make your own children yourself? You will also be amazed at the creativity which is released by your own colleagues. For this reason I support a team approach, solely for the support and for the important role which the experts, internally or externally, play. This should be obvious.

Should the Top Management Control or Let Go?

The board of directors are usually those who assign the task internally (internal client). Do you then give the top manager the opportunity to control the thought process or must he let go? Usually I ask the senior management to do both. Even though the internal client is involved in the approach regarding aspects such as the innovation goals and team formation, it would be unwise to give them rigid control of the content at such an early stage of the ideation phase. At a later stage in the ideation phase you give them more control over the content of the process because you need their support for the development of the right product concepts into mini new business cases. In practice, the internal client gets a 'wild card' at decisive moments throughout the ideation process.

Are We Going to Search For Revolutionary or Evolutionary Product Ideas?

Which product idea is the best to search for – revolutionary or evolutionary? Clayton Christensen,[5] Professor at the Harvard Business School, distinguishes between sustaining and disruptive innovations. According to him, with a sustaining or evolutionary innovation strategy, you search for new distinctive products for the top of the existing market. It's all about new products which can be sold at a higher margin. This is the most common strategy which all players on the market follow as it is visible in the endless stream of product improvement which raises the whole sector to a higher level: more services, more features, more luxurious, nicer, quicker and so on, and of course at a higher price. Consider the development of supermarkets (Ahold), petrol stations (Shell), aviation companies (Air France/KLM). They are all good examples.

With a disruptive or revolutionary approach the search for innovative ideas is jerky. There are two types: the 'bottom-of-the-market innovations', which jump to the bottom, and 'new market innovations', which take a step to the side. When all suppliers in the market follow an evolutionary innovation strategy, it creates a hole at the bottom of the market. 'Bottom-of-the-market-innovators' focus on customers for whom high quality is not that important. The new concepts then jump into the hole and with the low-cost business model they serve their customers in a different but cheaper way. Consider the examples of the Lidl supermarket and EasyJet.com who are new at the bottom of the market. New market innovations are focused on the creation of new markets and on changing non-users into users. The new products can now, due to technological development, be sold for much less or can be made simpler in order to be attractive to a larger number of customers. Another good example is TomTom. Existing manufacturers of navigation systems focused their sales strategy on the automobile industry. From the start TomTom considered route planners as consumer electronics and thereby handled completely different criteria for the product, such as that they should be mobile, easy to operate and cheap. The first TomToms were more than less the price of the route planners of the regular competitors and in this way they opened a new market: the consumer market for route planners.[6]

An organisation should search for real 'new-to-the-world' innovations as this dramatically increases the chances for success. Of course the type of innovation on which you should focus is also dependent on the current role of the market and the characteristics of your company. If you are an established player in an existing food market, with low potential for growth, such as Unilever, then you have to dare to go for unique 'new-to-the-world' innovations. However, if you are a relatively small

5   C. Christensen and M. Raynor (2003). *The Innovator's Solution*. Boston: Harvard Business School Press, p. 34.

6   Elsevier, 17 December 2005, p. 38.

newcomer in an enormous growth market, then I can imagine that you first want to conquer the market with new and improved versions. This choice will be discussed in Chapter 4.

Do We Have to Tackle Ideation on a Small or Large Scale?

Of course you can come up with a new product idea on your own, as an idea always starts in the mind of one person. However, you could also create products and services with the whole company. The first is on too small a scale and the second on too large a scale. On the one hand the ideation of new products should be on a large enough scale in order to create variety, mobilise experts and gain internal support. On the other hand it should be on a small enough scale in order to facilitate an effective brainstorming process and keep the process going at the right tempo.

When is the Right Moment to Ideate New Products and Services?

The completion of the innovation process – from the idea to introducing it on the market, takes about 18 months. However, in 25 per cent of cases the time to the market takes more than two years. As already mentioned, in a non-technological organisation the start of the product development process is usually caused by a sudden, disruptive development on the market. Therefore, anticipating a change in the market is very important in order to react at the right time. Even though you notice the holes in the roof during winter, it is better to make alterations during the summer. The ideation process can only succeed if the company has the financial and mental space in order to do this. If the board of directors and co-workers are under a lot of pressure you should think twice before starting an ideation project. If the organisation is in the middle of a re-organisation process, everyone will be busy with 'their position'. In a crisis it is always all hands on deck for the business of the day, with no priority for innovation. It is best to wait until the dust has settled.

According to Bert Paalman, previously member of the board of directors of Bührmann-Tetterode for the packaging sector, it is the art of the top management to challenge the management and co-workers to the development of innovations under the motto: good can be better!

The creation of new products and services can be best linked to the strategic process. When the strategic planning is well rounded with the company's ambition and focus, it is the perfect time to start the ideation phase for creating the concrete innovative ideas to realise these ambitions. As the ideation phase produces three to five new concepts it is sufficient to start a company-wide ideation project for real innovations once a year. The co-workers' effort should also be focused on the quick delivery of the new product concept in order to keep the time-to-the-market as short as possible. In larger companies it is advisable to carry out multiple ideation projects for different business units of the regional organisations, especially when these organisational branches are active on different markets, busy with other activities or situated in different regions.

In this chapter the success factors for the creation of new products and services have been discussed. The bridge between creativity and management practice rests on five pillars. The next chapter will discuss the FORTH approach of the ideation phase, which in practice is built on these five success factors.

HE-HO! LETS GO!

3   The FORTH Innovation Method

What makes the desert so beautiful, is that the source is hidden somewhere.
(A. de Saint-Exupéry, French pilot/poet)

It doesn't make a difference to the mountain from which direction you approach it.
(Japanese proverb)

Genius is one percent inspiration, ninety-nine percent perspiration.
(Thomas A. Edison, American business man and inventor)

3.1 INTRODUCTION

In the previous chapter we discussed the success factors necessary to create new products and services. The solid bridge between creativity and management practice rests upon five pillars and it is upon these pillars that I base my method for the ideation phase which I call FORTH – an acronym found in the first letter of each step: Full Steam Ahead, Observe and Learn, Raise Ideas, Test Ideas and Homecoming. This method, used for the creation of new products and services, was developed in practice and has been used successfully in not only business-to-business markets but also business-to-consumer markets over the past five years. Companies who have successfully implemented this method are insurance companies, producers of medical appliances, employment agencies, companies facilitating conferences, educational institutions, manufacturers of bicycle seats for children, producers of fresh foods, publishers, social services and governmental organisations.

The FORTH method consists of a journey in five stages. First, I will explain why I have used this figure of speech, and give an outline of the five stages. Thereafter the different roles of the people necessary for the creation of successful new products will be discussed. Finally, the chapter ends with a description of the 'hard' and 'soft' qualities necessary for the journey.

3.2 GOING ON A JOURNEY

When new product ideas do not appear automatically, you have to go and search for them somewhere else. You go hunting for new inspiration and for good and new ideas. Why then do I compare this search to a journey?

I hope that you will be able to recognise yourself in the following situation which has often happened to me. You live in your own country all your life, yet you don't really know it. While racing along the highways, you visit a few places daily, others never. But there is so much more to see. However, you only realise this when you receive friends from abroad who visit your country for the first time. Together with them, I in the Netherlands for example, will visit Delft, Drenthe and Zeeland to see the old porcelain, the blossoming moorland and the impressing Delta works. And then I am impressed (again) by the culture, the landscape and the enterprising spirit of this small country.

This experience can be directly transferred from your private life to your job: in your own market you also race over highways where you daily see the familiar things, the things you like to see. That might be one of the reasons for the need for creating new and different products you now experience. That is why it is better to look and listen at different places in the market to become aware of and break through your own rigid routine. Therefore you should go on a journey. Because when you go on a journey you usually have the time to engage in something for which you don't usually have time in the hectic day-to-day life. You do things you don't normally do. Have you visited the old church or museum in your neighbourhood? No, well neither have I. But I do that when I go on a journey, when I am open to new things. We are consciously going to use this idea when we start creating new products and services. We are going to search for sources of inspiration which we can apply in the process later in order to create wonderful new product ideas. So you visit your own customers and the customers of your competitors and you take a look at the different applications of your product in reality in different (business) market sectors. Just as the Netherlands has many foreign places, there are many different markets – markets adjacent to your own market or markets for the same products in other countries or on different continents. It is enormously helpful to go and discover these things as it brings you out of your comfort zone and opens up the world to you.

In order to characterize the process for creating new products, I gladly use the example of a journey as it has so many similarities with the many voyages of discovery in the past. Previously, as hunters or farmers, we only went looking for food or new land when we have run out of food or the land has become infertile. Actually, you only searched for the adventure when it was really necessary. This happens in all organisations that have to innovate. Real urgency is only experienced when the current market is saturated. Furthermore, many discovery voyages in the past lasted for many years due to unexpected setbacks such as an unknown illness, tropical storms or mutiny by the crew. The average time for the development process of a new product (18 months from idea to introduction), follows a similar pattern. Many ships also perished along the way. On one of the voyages of Magellan, four of the five ships did not return, but the ship which survived came back with enough spices to pay for the expedition and to even make a profit. Is this much different from the process of innovation? From the seven new developed product ideas only one product enters the market successfully; the remaining six perish along the way. Sometimes the explorers also thought that they had landed on a small island, but it proved to be an enormous continent afterwards. This was the case with the Vikings who discovered north America long before Columbus. You can compare this with the development of SMS-services of mobile telephones. This application was originally developed and positioned on the business market, but it did not take off. When young people caught on to the idea of SMS*ing* as a modern, and cheaper, way of keeping in contact with each other, it became a gigantic worldwide market in a very short period of time with more than three billion users! Another similarity is that innovators, just like explorers, will be remembered for a long time. I am curious as to who of the following people will be the most famous in a hundred years' time: Steve Jobs (founder of Apple) or Columbus (who discovered America)?, Sergey Brin and Larry Page (founders of Google) or Edmund Hilary (first man to reach the top of Mount Everest), Bill Gates (founder of Microsoft) or Neil Armstrong (first man on the moon)?

3.3 THE FORTH METHOD IN FIVE STAGES

The FORTH method is a journey in five stages:

1. Full Steam Ahead
2. Observe and Learn
3. Raise Ideas
4. Test Ideas
5. Homecoming

Figure 3.1 represents this method for the ideation phase and it also shows the correct position it takes during the innovation process: at the beginning of the process after management has made the decision to actually go ahead and develop a new product. The FORTH method is a complete method for the creation of new products from the idea to a mini new business case. In other words, the FORTH method is a practical approach with which you can successfully pass through the discovery stage and the first two steps, with one team and in one go, shown in the model of Cooper (Figure 1.2, Chapter 1), bringing you from the first idea for the product or service until it is developed into a mini new business case.

The five success factors for generating new product ideas, discussed in the previous chapter, can all be found in these five stages. The choosing of the innovation focus happens immediately during the first stage: Full Steam Ahead. Here you choose the destination and you determine the innovation task. During the second stage, Observe and Learn, you discover and understand what the potential target group considers to be important and with what they struggle the most. It is very important that during this stage not only do you start looking at things differently but you also start listening differently. Furthermore, this stage allows for another important condition necessary for the generating of new ideas: a period of incubation – in other words time to allow the idea to hatch. When you take on a challenge it usually takes a while before you start thinking of solutions. Not only are you consciously busy with it, but also subconsciously, and sometimes an idea can enter your mind at a time when you least expect it, such as in the shower, or while on holiday or while

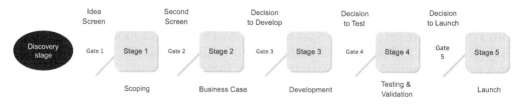

The original stage-gate innovation process (see chapter 1).

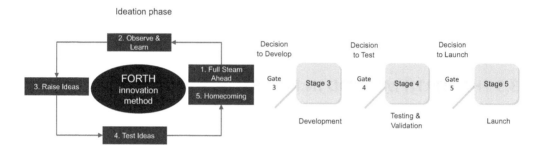

Figure 3.1   The FORTH innovation method as part of the innovation process

jogging. Usually, while you are busy doing something which happens 'without thinking', you have room mentally in which ideas can surface and it pops into your head. This is not surprising when you realise that conscious thinking happens at 60 bits per second, whereas subconscious thinking happens in millions of bits per second.[1] Therefore, by allowing for a discovery phase right from the start, an incubation period creates the possibility of discovering the challenge given in the first stage and the development of the product or service idea in the next stage, Raise Ideas. Acquiring insight into the customer's needs and the opportunities available, as well as 'outside-in' thinking and an effective, creative process are all part of this stage. The new product idea is now practically created and developed into a product concept. The last two stages of the journey concern the testing of the effectiveness of the product and the obtaining of support. During stage 4, Test Ideas, the newly developed product concepts are tested with the potential target group. During a follow-up workshop the negative aspects, expressed by the customers during the market research, are amended. In the final stage, Homecoming, the most attractive and tested product concepts are substantiated with market insights, and turnover, profit and malleability are estimated. As a mini new business case it is then presented to the management, who by this time are dying of curiosity as to what the journey has produced.

---

1   I. E. Oden (2006). Beslissen: Waarom u uw gevoel moet volgen (maar niet altijd). *Psychological Magazine*, January, 14–20.

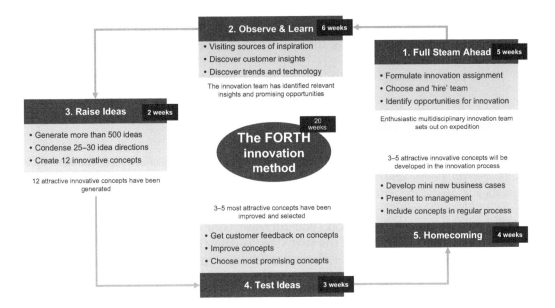

Figure 3.2   FORTH: method for creating innovative products and services

I have learned from experience that the FORTH method lasts about 20 weeks, and for the participants in your company, approximately 15 weeks from the kick-off workshop. However, be aware that before the process can begin, essential conversations in the organisation are necessary to decide whether the FORTH method is going to be used. The start to the ideation phase needs, especially in larger organisations, a good introduction. This is necessary for two reasons: firstly, many people and departments are involved; and secondly, the subject of innovation can sometimes be very sensitive as someone will be held accountable for the fact that there are no good and attractive product concepts in the pipeline. Furthermore, the time needed for applying the FORTH method also depends on the scale of the innovation task. Should the number of target groups, countries or continents increase, the process needs extra time, especially during the stages Observe and Learn, Test Ideas and Homecoming. You should therefore understand that a worldwide, uniform and qualitative concept research done on a few continents takes longer than three weeks and is also more complex than the same research done in one country only. The same applies to the making of a mini new business case. Can the process be done in less than 20 weeks? If necessary, then of course! If something can be done in 20 weeks, it can also be done in 16 weeks, on condition that everyone makes sufficient time available. However, there are disadvantages. My experience with the FORTH method taught me that if you take too little time to observe and learn, the participants gain less inspiration, which causes fewer pioneering ideas in the development stage. Furthermore, I have learned that if you shorten the time in which to develop the mini new business cases from four weeks to two or even one, you risk losing sight of important issues such as whether the idea is feasible or not. Unfortunately, this will only be discovered in the next stage of the development process.

In the next section the main features of the five stages are discussed.

3.4 FULL STEAM AHEAD

Men wanted for hazardous journey. Low wages, bitter cold, long hours of complete darkness. Safe return doubtful. Honour and recognition in event of success. (Advertisement to recruit men for a polar expedition. E. Shackleton, British explorer)

When you go on an expedition, you increase your chances of success by being well prepared and that is why the first stage in the creating of new products is so important. Figure 3.3 shows the themes, activities and the intended results of the first stage. At this time you make four very important decisions:

1. What is the innovation assignment?
2. Who is the internal client?
3. Who would make the ideal ideation team?
4. Which opportunities are chosen to be explored?

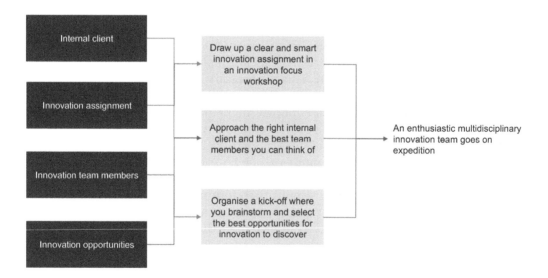

Figure 3.3   Stage 1: Full Steam Ahead

Innovation Focus Workshop

At first you have to determine a definite aim and direction. At the same time, together with those who are going to judge the product concept at the end of the ideation phase, you have to decide which criteria the product has to meet. It is a good idea to hold a separate meeting, the innovation focus workshop, at the beginning. At this meeting, not only are the line managers, innovation manager or manager of New Business Development who are directly responsible, present, but also the project leader (on behalf of the ideation team) and the facilitator. The innovation focus workshop has only succeeded when you have collectively formulated a concrete innovation assignment and can start putting an ideation team together.

Putting Together an Ideation Team

The two important decisions that have to be made at this stage determine how your ideal team will be put together. The bigger the team, the greater the diversity and the greater the chance of coming up with wild, foolish and pioneering product ideas. However, there is a limit. The maximum size of the team is determined by the number of participants with whom, as one team, you can go through an effective brainstorming process. The maximum number of participants in this stage is limited to 12–14 people. Through experience I have discovered that 14 is the absolute maximum, made up of 12 internal FORTH team members with the option of bringing in two outsiders for the brainstorming process. How much time the process demands depends upon the role of the team members. I usually distinguish between two roles: core team members and the so-called extended team members. A core team member goes through the whole process very intensively. This demands, from the start, a period of about 25 days in 15 weeks, or a third of the available time spent at work, but it can vary during every stage. Extended team members experience the process less intensively, mainly only the highlights. They are, for example, the internal client, other members of the board or managers. From them, the FORTH method requires approximately seven days in 15 weeks from the start.

Make sure that you choose a well-balanced internal team of 12 people. There are a few aspects which should play a role in your decision. It is very important to consider the relationships between:

- participants according to expertise and support;
- participants with various skills;
- participants from internal departments, business units and national organisations;
- other aspects which might have an influence on the innovation assignment, such as:
  - the relationship between male and female;
  - the relationship between young and old.

KICK-OFF!

The third important decision at the start is the choice of the best people for the ideation team. This decision is actually quite simple: always choose those who have a passion for the assignment and who possess the right qualities. A specific assignment always requires special people. However, they are usually those with the least time available and therefore do not get permission from their managers to participate – but it is only a matter of convincing them. Always be creative and persistent in the putting together of the team as the journey can get rough. In order to create new ideas you need people and only with the best people can you get the best new product and service ideas. The extra time you take in order to put together the best team will pay off in the long run.

Organising a FORTH Kick-Off Workshop

After the innovation assignment has been determined and the team has been put together, you have to organise a FORTH kick-off workshop. I usually implement a full-day programme whereby, together with the internal client, the project leader and the ideation team, we strive to achieve three things. Firstly, a good personal introduction is important to break through existing ways and to allow the participants to get acquainted in a creative way. Secondly, the team has to get acquainted with the content of the innovation assignment. In this respect the director or chairman of the board of directors or the branch manager has a huge role to play, especially when it is about innovations for a specific branch. It is their task to emphasise the urgency of the innovation assignment, to explain the innovation assignment and to reach an agreement after amendments have been made. Thirdly, it is very satisfying when you have determined, with the help of an excellent pre-analysis and some creative techniques, the possible innovation opportunities for the ideation team. This is done very practically by asking questions. Where are the greatest opportunities with regards to the innovation assignment? Which potential customer groups are we going to visit? Which customer groups, experts, organisations or companies will be a significant source of inspiration? How are we going to approach them? Chapter 4 includes a practical checklist for the kick-off workshop.

The duration of this process, until you have reached the kick-off stage, takes about five weeks. Chapter 4 explains the above-mentioned activities during the Full Steam Ahead stage, in more detail. At the end of the first stage your enthusiastic, multidisciplinary team will be ready to go on an innovation expedition.

3.5 OBSERVE AND LEARN

A true voyage of discovery does not exist in the observing of new landscapes only, but in learning how to look at it differently.
- (M. Proust, French writer)

The essence of Stage 2 is to start viewing things differently, to detach yourself from your own existing thought patterns about the market, and to gain new and fresh impressions. The core team members each explore a different innovation opportunity and start to discover the market and the target group. They link their progress to each other and to the extended team members in Observe and Learn workshops. Figure 3.4 describes the themes, activities and the intended result. During this stage a new and renewed learning process is developed in three ways:

1. Which trends and technology can we take advantage of?
2. Who is the customer and what frictions are they struggling with?
3. Which innovation opportunities offer promising perspectives?

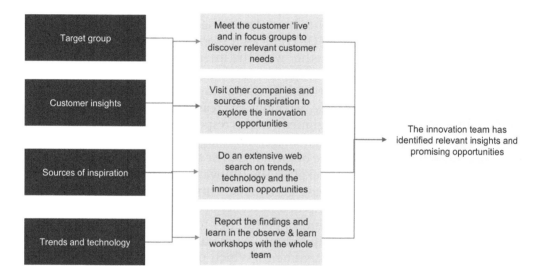

Figure 3.4   Stage 2: Observe and Learn

Exploring Trends and Technology

During the Observe and Learn stage it is not only educational but also meaningful to start exploring the different trends and technology which play a role in the domain, theme or markets of the innovation assignment. In this way the team gets an overall view of what is going on and promising trends and technology can be traced and given a role during the brainstorming sessions in the next stage.

A Live Meeting with the Customer and with Focus Groups

The fundamental question is: who are the customers and what are they concerned with? During the first stage it has been established who the target group is, but in this stage you meet with the customer personally. Within the organisation the available market research poses a good starting point, as you can start with the question, 'What do we learn from this?' The 'decision-making unit' should also be identified, as they are the officials who will make the decision whether to buy and or use the product and therefore have an influence on it.

In the FORTH method, during the Observe and Learn stage, we have been using two very effective voice-of-customer techniques. Meeting the customer in person and finding out the frictions of the customer, with the help of focus groups, is most effective when wanting to create new product ideas. This has been confirmed by a recent (2008) American study concerning ideation techniques.[2]

For both the business-to-consumer and the business-to-business markets it is of the utmost importance to know how the product is being used or which role it plays in a specific production process. The current behaviour of customers and the visible difficulties experienced create an excellent source of inspiration. In their regular jobs, not all ideation team members have had the opportunity to speak to customers. However, in this stage all core team members and extended team members will pay a visit to customers. In this way they will not only read about it in the market research, or see them in the focus group, but also get their own personal impression of the customer, their concerns and experiences, and in addition the members can also observe the customer closely.

You can observe wild animals in the zoo, but this is comparable to market research – an easy start. However, a safari in Africa makes an unforgettable impression, far better than visiting any zoo. This also applies in this situation because personal contact with the target group creates fertile soil for new product ideas. It is also important to identify and visit different types of customers (non-customers, ex-customers, small customers, major customers) in as many market sectors as possible. Chapter 5 includes a very usable model. The innovation assignment also gives direction. Visits to customers are done alone, or in pairs, after good preparation.

The focus groups are a type of qualitative concept research whereby a group of customers are interviewed by the facilitator. The core team members only listen and observe closely. Directly after the interview they discuss the situation and the needs and frictions concerning the target group. Due to the fact that often more than one target group is mentioned in the innovation assignment, it means that a focus group is necessary for each target group. In Chapter 5 you will find a practical plan on how to identify customer frictions.

Visits to Sources of Inspiration to Explore Innovation Opportunities

All innovation opportunities must be explored by the core team members. They have to make contact with the selected sources of inspiration during the kick-off workshop and then visit them individually in order to explore the direction. In

---

2   Robert G. Cooper and Scott Edgett (2008). Ideation for Product Innovation: What are the Best Methods? *PDMA Visions*, March.

this way they search for the best practices in other companies and for valuable experience from other people or companies. Their experiences are discussed in the Observe and Learn workshops when they can inform the core team members and the extended team members of what they have discovered.

Organising Observe and Learn Workshops

The members of the core team go on 'a hike' for six weeks wherein they have to not only get new impressions but also capture them, even digitally. During this time the facilitator organises four Observe and Learn workshops where the core team members can share their experiences with each other and the extended team members. Under the guidance of the facilitator and during the last Observe and Learn workshop they then choose the most promising innovation opportunities and customer frictions. These will then be placed under the spotlight during the brainstorming session in the next stage. This also applies to favourable trends and technologies.

   The process described above is very intensive and lasts six weeks. During this process the participants start getting new and different product ideas which they carefully record in an idea booklet. In Chapter 5 the activities during the Observe and Learn stage are described in more detail. At the end of the second stage the ideation team have already discovered promising and relevant customer frictions and innovation opportunities.

3.6 RAISE IDEAS

A pile of stones stops being a pile of stones the moment a single man looks at it and in his mind's eye he sees the image of a cathedral.
• (A. de Saint-Exupéry, French pilot/poet)

This stage constitutes the *pièce de résistance* of the FORTH method. It consists of a two-day new product brainstorming session and a concept development workshop. The brainstorming session is where the new product ideas are actually prepared and developed into a product concept. These product concepts are then further developed during the concept development workshop. The acquired customer frictions, the involvement of outsiders and an effective creative process are all part of the third stage. It is the creative peak of the journey.

Organising a New Product Brainstorm

The new product concepts are developed during a two-day new product brainstorming session which takes place in a suitable external brainstorming location. The brainstorming session is led by the facilitator and supported by a cartoonist – more about this at a later stage. Both the internal members as well as the outsiders participate. The group consists of a maximum of 14 people. It is a carefully developed creative process in nine steps which was developed in my brainstorming consultancy. The process starts with the introduction. As all the internal participants already know each other from the kick-off workshop, it is still necessary to have a personal introduction in order for the outsiders to get acquainted with them. After discussing the rules which will apply during the two-day brainstorming session, the innovation assignment now takes place first. In the second phase the participants are once again inspired by the customer insights, the investigated innovation opportunities and the trends and technology which were discovered in the Observe and Learn stage. However, the outsiders are confronted with this information for the first time.

After a creative warming-up-of-the-mind session, the generating of new product ideas is in full swing. At last the participants can, after six weeks, get rid of their new product ideas in a spontaneous 'brain dump'. The outsiders will bring new ideas and will inspire the insiders and vice versa. In the divergence phase which follows, the participants, with the help of different brainstorming techniques, are led outside the box. In this way many new and original product ideas are generated – 500 or more ideas are not unusual. Subsequently, the convergence phase starts. All new ideas are condensed into 25 or 30 idea directions. The participants choose the 12 idea-directions with the most potential and develop these into idea mind-maps.

Day two starts with the participants being divided into four small groups to develop the idea mind-maps into concrete new business concepts. Well-prepared formats help them to develop all the relevant aspects of the new product or service. Furthermore, the participants add an image and create a sphere to their ideas with the help of pictures, photos and cartoon sketches, and create a mood board. After three sessions of one hour each, 12 concept boards are ready. The participants now present their concepts during a short presentation and the concept boards are improved with additions from the group. The concept boards are then evaluated individually by each participant and their evaluation must be based on all the criteria established in the innovation assignment at the beginning of the journey. Both reason and feeling play a conscious role during the evaluation and, based on this, the product concepts are ranked in order of attractiveness. During the completion of the process all developed product concepts are discussed in order of attractiveness and it is not uncommon that, at this point, a spontaneous 'wow' feeling develops. The participants end the new product brainstorming session with a preview on the concept development workshop, weary, but extremely satisfied.

The Concept Development Workshop

In the next stage the product concepts are tested by the target group. However, the product concepts must be presented in an appropriate way and for this reason the FORTH method has added a one-day concept development workshop. At this workshop the concept boards from the new product brainstorming sessions are quickly converted into two-dimensional product sketches and descriptions, which characterise the concept well and in a language which the target group can understand. The core team usually performs this task.

Chapter 6 describes the setting up and implementation of the new product brainstorming session as well as the development workshop in more detail. At the end of the third stage the ideation team have developed 12 attractive and practical concepts for innovative products or services.

3.7 TEST IDEAS

We did not do what the customer wanted. We did something better.
- (T. Hoff, Intel)

How attractive are the new product concepts and how much do they really stand out? A justifiable question and that is why it is good to reflect on the developed concept, especially after the euphoria of the brainstorming session. Figure 3.5 shows the themes, activities and result of this stage.

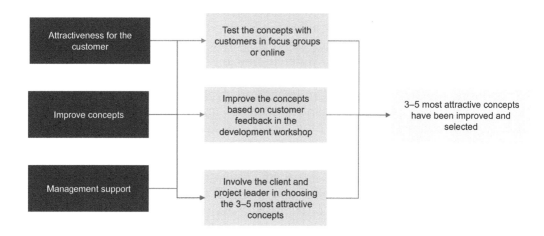

Figure 3.5   Stage 4: Test Ideas

Doing Qualitative Concept Research

How attractive are the new product concepts? You have created them yourself and therefore you are terribly enthusiastic about them. However, it is well-advised to ask the customer's opinion about it as well. In this way you receive useful feedback about the possibilities and feasibility of the product concepts which can help in improving or changing the product concept in the current ideation phase. Should the opinion of the target group be mostly negative, then it is better to try to stop the concept at this early stage rather than spend much energy on it later during the innovation process. There are exceptions, but more about that in Chapter 7.

The attractiveness is directly tested in the target group. Qualitative concept research can happen quickly not only on a small scale, but also at the same time in different countries or on different continents. The indicative character of the qualitative concept research during the ideation phase is no problem. The main reason for the concept research is to get insight into why the customers find the new product concept attractive or not. For the testing of concepts in the business-to-business target groups the preference is individual in-depth interviews. During the interview the new concepts are presented one by one to individual respondents and this can be done at the customers' work place or in a research room. Group discussions with six to eight customers are also an excellent form of testing the consumer products. A good independent market researcher will not allow individual opinions to be outweighed by a few extroverts, whom you will always find in a group. The core participants of the ideation team can follow the individual interview live and the advantage is that they find new inspiration and improvements immediately. During the qualitative concept research the negative aspects are also pointed out, but then that is what it is meant for.

Adjusting Negative Aspects

The first reaction of potential customers on the new product concepts often offers good suggestions for improvements. For this reason, directly following the qualitative research, an improvement workshop in order to develop the negative aspects is held. During this workshop the results of the concept research are presented and through a brainstorming session the core team members, as well as the extended team members, find ways in which to adjust the negative aspects. At the end of this improvement workshop a choice is made as to which three to five concepts will be developed into mini new business cases in the next stage. Also, a 'match' is made between the chosen concepts and the core team members who will be responsible for its development.

The activities mentioned above (the qualitative concept research and the improvement workshop regarding the negative aspects) take place over a period of three weeks. Chapter 7 describes these activities during the stage Test Ideas, in more detail. At the end of this second last stage the ideation team has tested 10 to 12 attractive new product concepts and have chosen three to five which will be developed into mini new business cases.

3.8 HOMECOMING

Dogs bark at what they do not recognise.
• (Heraclitus, Greek philosopher)

In the final stage of the FORTH innovation method you return home with your tested product concepts as souvenirs, which you now present to the organisation. The themes, activities and the result of the final stage are presented on Figure 3.6. The attractive new product or service concepts with enough support now fill the innovation pipeline. This stage is the climax of the journey.

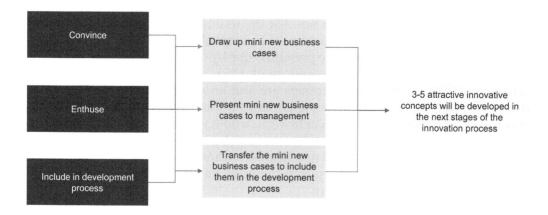

Figure 3.6   Stage 5: Homecoming

Drafting Mini New Business Cases

During this stage the new product concepts are further developed by applying the criteria regarding turnover, profit, feasibility and whether it fits into the organisational strategy. On this basis the ideation team presents three to five new product concepts, which will actually be developed. It is also important that the concepts are presented in a recognisable and convincing way. An excellent way, taken from the Anglo-Saxon business world, is the business case: a clear, commercial, professional and financial base for new initiatives or new investments. I call it the mini new business case. Mini, because in this phase it is still only developed on the surface. New, to distinguish it is a business case regarding a new concept rather than, for example, an investment. The advantage of drafting mini new business cases for the ideation team is that they become aware of the fact that not only creative aspects, but also commercial, professional and financial aspects contribute to the decision to include the new concepts in the innovation process. In addition, it increases the power of your persuasion because you have based the attractiveness of the concept on strategic, commercial, professional and financial indicators.

Holding Presentations for Line Management

It is very important to get those who have not been working closely with the FORTH innovation method enthusiastic about the concepts. For those who have 'stayed at home' it is often nice to not only see the mini new business cases but also to get insight into the creative FORTH process which preceded it. An 'outside the box' presentation of the creative process, in the form of a guided tour in their own 'innovation room', is usually a good start to get them involved. Next it is important to present the mini new business cases of the chosen product concepts to the group of line managers who will make the official decision as to whether the product will be developed or not (Gate 3: decision to develop).

Transferring of the Knowledge, Experience and Participants

The ideation phase ends with the admission of the new product concepts into the innovation process. In larger organisations a new team is set up for the product development phase as it requires different skills and abilities. I strongly suggest that you transfer the knowledge and experience gained with the creation and development of the product concept to the development team. It is also advisable to allow a few participants of the ideation team to continue working in the development team who are now responsible for the realisation of the concept. These participants already know the history and background of how the concept came into being and which characteristics played a role in the choice of these products. In the development team they fulfil the role of 'concept guards'. So after the decision has been made to develop the new product concepts, a transfer workshop can be organised to not only transfer the responsibility from the ideation team to the development team but also to secure the 'soul' of the concept.

The three activities in the last stage last about four weeks. Chapter 8 gives greater clarification on the Homecoming. At the end of this, the fifth and last stage, the ideation team have completed their task. Their journey has ended. Three to five attractive product or service concepts with enough support enter the innovation pipeline and can be developed further.

RETURNING

3.9 DIFFERENT ROLES

The ideation team creates room for six different roles: the project leader (leader of the expedition), the facilitator (the guide), the core members, the extended team members and the outsiders. In addition there are the sponsors: those who do not participate in the ideation team but are very important for the ideation phase, such as the general manager or the chairman of the board of directors, the top manager responsible for the end product and the managers who will decide which product ideas will actually be developed later on in the innovation process. Following is a description of each role and of the most important requirements necessary in order to create new products or services successfully.

1. The Internal Project Leader (the leader of the expedition)

The internal project leader is the face of the project, responsible for the smooth running of things and for achieving the result: three to five mini new business cases on the date agreed upon. The project leader can either be a commercial line manager for whose business unit, market or product group the innovation assignment is being performed, or the innovation or new business development manager who at the commission of the board of directors must lead the ideation phase group. He/she is responsible and will work closely with the internal or external facilitator during the ideation phase. The project leader also has the total financial budget for the journey at his/her disposal. As project leaders are so much involved they need to have the ability to motivate, enthuse and be able to be strict when someone wants to cross the line. The time involved during the 20 weeks amounts to 40 days.

Table 3.1   Other leaders of expeditions

When?	Who?	What?
1495 BC	Hatsheput	Discovered the 'Point', currently Somalia
323 BC	Alexander the Great	Conquered Small Asia and India
948 AD	Erik de Rode	Discovered Greenland
1001 AD	Leif Erikson	First European in north America
1299 AD	Marco Polo	Discovered the way to China and Asia overland
1460 AD	Prince Hendrik	Travelled along the west coast of Africa
1487 AD	Bartolomeus Diaz	Discovered the most southern point of Africa
1492 AD	Christopher Columbus	Discovered central America
1498 AD	Vasco da Gama	Discovered a sea route to India
1502 AD	Amerigo Vespucci	Discovered north and south America
1519 AD	Ferdinand Magellan	Sailed around the world

Table 3.1 *Concluded*

When?	Who?	What?
1530 AD	Francisco Pizarro	Conquered the Inca kingdom
1596 AD	Willem Barentsz	Discovered a sea at Nova Zembla
1608 AD	Henry Hudson	Discovered the coastline of north America
1642 AD	Abel Tasman	Found Tasmania and New Zealand
1779 AD	James Cook	Discovered New Zealand and the Pacific Ocean
1871 AD	David Livingstone	Explored central Africa
1909 AD	Robert Peary	First to reach the North Pole
1911 AD	Roald Amundsen	First to reach the South Pole
1912 AD	Robert Scott	Second to reach the South Pole
1953 AD	Edmund Hillary	Reached the top of Mount Everest
1969 AD	Neil Armstrong	First man on the moon

Source: Voyage of Exploration (www.mediatheek.thinkquest.nl)

2. The Facilitator (the guide)

The innovation facilitator is an expert in the application of ideation techniques, supervision of creative workshops and in the drafting of mini new business cases during the ideation phase. Preferably the facilitator has gained experience in line management. Although the facilitator can be someone from within the company the preference still goes to an external person as they can force a breakthrough more easily. Do not take the role of the facilitator too lightly as not everyone who has attended a basic course in creative thinking can be an experienced facilitator. In paragraph 3.10 more detail about the role of the facilitator will be given. If you are considering using the FORTH method on a regular basis then you should also consider training internal facilitators for this purpose. The time involved during the 20 weeks amounts to 30 days.

3. Core Team Members

The internal core team members are recruited on the basis of their specific expertise, their personal skills and from the perspective of good balance within the team. They are involved with the content and they participate in all stages from beginning to end. The time expected from them amounts to 25 days during the 20 weeks, a quarter of their time spent at work. The time varies during each stage. The investigation during the Observe and Learn stage and drafting the mini new business cases requires most of their time.

4. Extended Team Members

The internal extended team members are recruited on the basis of their position, experience and overview. The internal client can also be an extended team member who participates in the ideation process. Extended team members are usually managers from higher ranks who either directly or indirectly have an interest in the ideation project. During the 20 weeks, the time expected from them amounts to seven days, a tenth of their working time, calculated from the kick-off workshop.

5. Outsiders

The outsiders are recruited with a specific goal in mind, determined on the one hand by the content of the innovation assignment and on the other hand by their skills and special expertise. The external participants are only involved in the Raise Ideas stage, in other words during the two-day brainstorming session and the concept development workshop.

6. Sponsors

In order to ensure the success of the FORTH innovation method it is of the utmost importance to have the support of the general director, chairman of the board of directors, the top managers who have the final responsibility, and the managers who in one way or another have to make official decisions regarding the innovation process. The start of this process requires, especially in larger organisations, a good run-up to ensure that these managers openly support the process. Perseverance from the sponsors and their indispensable support is essential in order to get the cooperation of the department managers to 'free up' their co-workers for 25 days (during 15 weeks, calculated from the kick-off workshop), in order to participate in the ideation team. This applies especially to business units and departments who are not affected directly at the start of the FORTH method.

3.10 THE ROLE OF THE FORTH FACILITATOR

The facilitator does not only supervise the complete FORTH process in all its stages but also functions as the partner and confidant of the project leader of the ideation team. A good facilitator is very important and should not be underestimated.

HARD AND SOFT CHARACTERISTICS OF THE JOURNEY

UNDERESTIMATING THE SUCCESS FACTOR OF THE FACILITATOR

The name of our agency is self-explanatory: FLEX/theINNOVATIONLAB. As an industrial development agency we are concerned with the development of new innovative consumer products, packaging and professional products on a daily basis. We also actively apply various brainstorming techniques. We are critical users of these kinds of methods. This leads to the fact that we are sometimes not satisfied with our results. We, the participants, can also be disappointed when we are not guided by a well qualified person during the brainstorming session which then leads to poor results.

I was invited by a client to participate, as an outsider, in a two-day new product brainstorming session with an international party as participant and as observer. There were many participants and the ambition was large: the development of various totally new product concepts. The background of the participants was diverse – from marketing, sales to new production. The great thing about the session was that the facilitator was able to involve all the participants actively for two days. The various brainstorming techniques were not unknown, but the combination and the way in which these techniques were used, was very convincing. For two days a high energy level was maintained: a condition necessary for a successful session, which in reality hardly ever happens. The facilitator was never vague about the subject matter as he had great insight. With this he created a good balance between the abstract and the concrete. The new product brainstorming session created a well-defined concept with which the client could work directly. Personally, I have experienced this procedure differently in other companies.

Finally, I, as an outsider, am very positive about the method followed and I would like to see all development projects start in this way. I believe that the role of the facilitator is still an underestimated factor in the success of the method.

Jeroen Verbrugge
Director
FLEX/theINNOVATIONLAB

The FORTH process consists of the innovation focus workshop, the kick-off workshop, the four Observe and Learn workshops, a two-day brainstorming session, a concept development workshop and an improvement workshop, with four days to draw up mini new business cases and a presentation to the management. In order to facilitate all these meetings effectively, it demands from the facilitator the following three aspects:

1. application of creative think techniques in the most effective way;
2. monitoring all participants enthusiastically and involving them in the process, and

3. monitoring the group in the light of steering the innovation assignment in the best possible and feasible direction.

This demands a great deal of skill from the facilitator, especially at those meetings where the whole group is present. Beware of the many pitfalls which befell me. Together with the FORTH facilitators, whom I trained in 2010, we have compiled a list of 25 personal tips which will help you to facilitate the FORTH process successfully.

PERSONAL TIPS TO BE A SUCCESSFUL FORTH FACILITATOR

1. Choose the way of working which suits you best.
2. Know yourself well, and how you come across to others, so that you can act upon that and always stay genuine and be yourself.
3. Be open to ideas or suggestions from the group to adapt the process. Do not always try to keep to the programme you have set.
4. Give the opposite energy to the group. If the group is too busy/active: be calm. If the group is too calm, be more active and energetic.
5. Time box. Make sure everybody knows what the time limits for different assignments are. Always have a clock available, whereby you and the participants can see how much time is left.
6. Always explain what you are going to do and why. People come with different expectations and information and want to know what is going to happen. Explain what brainstorming techniques are and give examples of what is expected at the end.
7. Give everyone the same colour post-its and pen so that it does not stand out whose idea it is and it will not influence the choices.
8. Always write legibly. This is a rule which is often broken!
9. First check with the project leader, who knows the participants better than you, before dividing them into teams.
10. Choose appropriate music to create the best atmosphere (lively, energetic, calm, relaxing).
11. Make sure it is enjoyable. Fun promotes good results.
12. Take control of the process and not of each individual, as everyone needs some space. Expect the unexpected, as it doesn't always go the way you've planned it.
13. During disagreements in the group, follow your own instinct, opinion and feeling. Remind them of the agreement to be respectful towards one another.
14. Give credit where appropriate, stimulate, motivate and enthuse the group publicly.
15. Apply a time limit, especially when someone takes their time, by indicating: 'You have one minute left – give us the three most important points'. If necessary use a timer.

16. Let the group do the work. For example, ask them for their help by letting them count the number of stickers on the concept evaluation board. In this way everybody stays involved and busy.
17. Keep the pace going, otherwise it becomes too long-winded and boring. Always be one step ahead and make sure that you apply the next technique immediately.
18. Ask the group for help if you are not sure how to carry on. This is powerful and effective because even the facilitator does not know everything.
19. Always treat everyone with respect but be sure to point out things of which you do not approve.
20. Pay attention to the body language of the participants.
21. Constantly check what the groups are working on so that, if necessary, you can guide them.
22. Allow people to choose which innovation opportunity, idea or concept board they want to work on. If you allow them to do this then they can choose not only that which they have a passion for but also what they have knowledge of which will lead to good results.
23. Be present, but not obtrusive. Trust in the quality of the group and allow them to work independently. Intervene only when it is really necessary.
24. Give the project leader and the client a 'wild card' during the selection process, as in this way you also make the division of roles clear.
25. Preparation, preparation, preparation.

3.11 PROPERTIES OF THE JOURNEY

In this chapter we have discussed the different stages of the FORTH innovation method. The managing of the ideation phase of the process is the managing of paradoxes, obvious opposites. The journey knows both hard and soft properties. The most important characteristics of the five stages have been summarised in Figure 3.7. Although it involves hard work, it is neither a beach holiday nor an endless trek through the jungle hoping to get to the end. It is an expedition – purposeful and adventurous – even though you sometimes tread on unknown territory. The good news is that all FORTH expeditions have returned home successfully. Furthermore, all participants have described it as an unforgettable journey. Experiencing the journey is for many just as important as reaching the destination successfully.

In the next chapter we start with Stage 1: Full Steam Ahead.

Hard properties	Soft properties
Specific smart innovation assignment	Common travel destination
Clear evaluation criteria	Off the beaten track
Clear, tightly directed process	Inspiration from other sectors
Five defined stages	Searching for the customer's soul
Customer insights are recorded	Space to be silly
External experts are involved	Group formation and team building
Purposeful creativity	Results in shared vision
500 ideas	Mutual trust and appreciation
12 concepts boards	Fun
Customers test the concepts	Team members feel really proud
Senior management participates	Lots of energy for the next step
The expedition always returns	
Mini new business cases	
3–5 new concepts fill the innovation pipeline	

Figure 3.7   The hard and soft properties of 'the journey'

DEPARTING

4 Full Steam Ahead

You cannot discover new oceans unless you have the courage to lose sight of the shore.

(Anonymous)

A journey of a thousand miles starts with one step.

(Confucius, Chinese philosopher)

The only way to discover the limits of the possible is to go beyond them into the impossible.

(A. Clarke, English writer)

4.1 INTRODUCTION

You never start a professional expedition unprepared, as good preparation not only increases the chances of success but also creates priorities and the will to succeed. That is why this first stage is so terribly important. This chapter illustrates how you can challenge the management to start the FORTH method and how you, together with top management, can formulate an assignment during the innovation focus workshop. It also shows how you can put together the correct ideation team with internal and external participants. This, the first stage of the ideation phase, lasts about five weeks. At the end of the five weeks you will have an enthusiastic, multidisciplinary team ready for the innovation challenge.

4.2 IN ADVANCE

Reasons to create new products can appear from both inside or outside the organisation. External reasons to innovate can arise from spotting a trend which has made much impact, changing legislation regarding market liberalisation or the shifting needs of the customer which have been noticed by the accounts management. Moreover, a new competitor (or the threat of one) or a newly introduced and promising product (or the threat of one) from a competitor can increase the urgency for innovation within the organisation. In addition, the reasons can appear from within the organisation in that the R&D notices a new and promising technological application for which they have just received right of ownership, or the initiative can come from a top manager who wants to realise the immediate and independent growth of the turnover and profit.

What is important for the 'feeling' of the ideation phase is to understand which reasons led to innovation and to point out where the initiative came from. If the initiative originates from the top management with the purpose of attacking the changes in the market and to show independent growth with new developed technologies, then it is a skill to persuade the rest of the organisation. If the initiative originates from the middle management, who are constantly surprised by innovations from competitors, then it is also a skill to convince top management of the importance to prioritise and to innovate.

For a good ideation phase it is important to know, in both situations, who the interested parties are and who has the responsibility within the company in order to get the necessary support before the start. In the build-up towards a structured way in which to create new product ideas, public commitment and support from the sponsors at top level can be used effectively to create and enlarge enthusiasm for the innovation challenge within the company.

4.3 INNOVATION FOCUS

This stage concerns the establishing of the purpose and the innovation direction. In the FORTH method it is done collectively in an innovation focus workshop with the managers concerned as well as with those who will lead the FORTH method.

The agenda has four main points:

1. The innovation assignment and the criteria for evaluation.
2. The participants of the ideation team.
3. The planning of the FORTH innovation approach.
4. The time and money spent.

Checklist 1, at the end of the chapter, contains a concept programme and tips for the establishing of the purpose of the innovation focus workshop. In order to determine the assignment, an answer should be given to the following question: what type of new products, services or business models do we want the ideation team to actually create? This will lead to the question as to what kind of innovation your company is looking for. Figure 4.1 provides help with the answer to this question. Following the previously mentioned classification of Christensen, I distinguish between evolutionary and revolutionary innovations. Table 4.1 gives 15 examples.

With evolutionary products you are searching for new products or services which will allow for growth in the market as well as growth of your position. So the innovation focus lies on attractive, new and distinguished product concepts:

- for the same users;
- for the same region or country in which you are working;
- for the same distribution channels;
- according to the same business model.

You are searching for the next generation in the product portfolio. These kinds of evolutionary product concepts usually lie at the top of the market and are directed at better product performance. This is typical of the big market players who want to both allow for growth on the market but also protect their share. A good example is Hansaplast Liquid Protect of Beiersdorf, a liquid plaster which allows for faster healing and can be removed more easily than the traditional brown plasters.

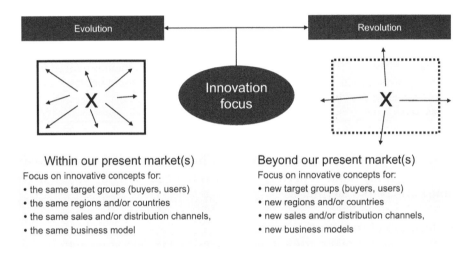

Figure 4.1   The innovation focus

Table 4.1   Fifteen innovations

Revolutionary 'bottom'-innovations (with a new business model)	Evolutionary 'top'-innovations (in the same market)	Revolutionary new market innovations (aimed at non-users)
Skypephone Free mobile calls via internet with other mobile Skype phones.	**Hansaplast Liquid Protect** A liquid plaster which allows for faster healing and which can be removed more easily.	**Yotel** Affordable small hotel rooms, behind customs at airports, for taking a rest or to freshen up.
IKEA-house BoKlok: a complete house for €150,000 from IKEA, that you don't have to build yourself.	**Vitz Vitamin chewing gum** A chewing gum, from Davitamon, full of vitamins to chew yourself healthy.	**Barcoo** To scan the barcode with your Smartphone to get all the information: cheapest prices, durability, test information.
RealtyBid.com a live internet auction site to sell your house without the use of an estate agent.	**Becel pro-activ** Becel-products (Benecol), for bread, which actively decreases the cholesterol level in the blood by 10 per cent.	**iBood.com** An online shop which offers only one product for sale per day.

Table 4.1 *Concluded*

Revolutionary 'bottom'-innovations (with a new business model)	Evolutionary 'top'-innovations (in the same market)	Revolutionary new market innovations (aimed at non-users)
SimPC A simple, easy-to-use computer for €799 exclusive for a service subscription of €10.75 per month.	**Fishes** Fish products, caught in a sustainable way, for supermarkets.	**Wii Fit** Health game from Nintendo for a completely new adult target group.
Easy-formulas All 17 (by now) 'easy companies' by Stelios, such as: easyJet.com, easyCar.com, easyCruise.com.	**Philips Wake-up Light** A new-generation alarm clock based on light intensity.	**Brennels** Clothing produced from stinging nettles.

If you want to create a new market, you have to work on revolutionary new products. For a really modern product the focus must not only be on attractiveness, but it must also be pioneering:

- for the group of non-users;
- for other regions or countries, in which you are not operating yet;
- for other distribution channels;
- according to another business model.

Different and much talked about! This is the golden thread in your search or to say it in a more trendy way: 'You are looking for a totally different family instead of for the next generation.' Firstly, there are revolutions at the bottom of the market and it is usually the newcomers to the market who, as outsiders, are amazed at what is happening in the market and who develop these types of innovations. With a different business model they unleash a revolution at the bottom of the existing market and in doing so attract large numbers of new users. Consider the following examples: all the easy-formulas (17 already) by Stelios, such as: easyJet.com, easyCar. com, easyCruise.com and RealtyBid.com where you can join a live auctioning of houses without an estate agent. In this way everything is cheaper.

Secondly, there are revolutionary new market innovations, whereby new technology is applied to create new markets. Consider the new, free-of-charge Smartphone application Barcoo which started in Germany. When you scan the barcode of a product with your Smartphone then you immediately receive useful information such as the cheapest price, how durable the brand is and how much it scored with consumer tests. Another example is Nintendo's Wii Fit. This health game opens up to a totally new target group who is much older than the regular 'gamers' of Nintendo.

Determine therefore collectively with the management whether the FORTH method will concentrate on evolutionary new products or services at the top of the market or on revolutionary new products or services at the bottom of the market or on revolutionary products or services for a completely new market.

4.4 CLEAR EVALUATION CRITERIA

The next step is to determine the evaluation criteria for new product ideas. If the management has not decided on this yet, then it helps to ask some questions. In practice you will go a long way with the following eight questions:

1. Turnover. How much turnover must the new product concept realise during the next three years or, if new products will cannibalise existing products, extra turnover to be realised?
2. Profit margin. What profit margin should the new product concept realise?
3. New. Should the new concept be new to the market, new to the country or new to the world?
4. Attractive and pioneering. How attractive and pioneering should the new product concept be to the target group?
5. Talk of the town. To what extent should the new product concept be the talk of the town among potential customers?
6. Positioning. To what extent should the new product concept fit into the current brand positioning?
7. Producible. To what extent are we obliged to make the new product concept ourselves (with our own manufacturing facilities)?
8. Strategic fit. To what extent should the new product concept fit into the strategy of the organisation?

In discussion with the management, you can collectively formulate which criteria the new product ideas must meet as well as determine a quantitive ambition level for the turnover and profit criteria.

4.5 CONCRETE INNOVATION ASSIGNMENT

It is essential to start the journey with a good and concrete innovation assignment. This forces the top management from the start to be concrete about the market/ target group for which the product idea must be developed and which criteria these new concepts must meet. This forms the guidelines for the ideation team when they are underway. Once the innovation focus and the evaluation criteria have been chosen, then it is easy to formulate the innovation assignment with the help of the following six questions:

THE INNOVATION ASSIGNMENT

1. Why? (reason or purpose)
2. Who? (target group)
3. Where? (distribution channels, countries, regions or continents)
4. What? (evolutionary or revolutionary concepts)
5. When? (intended year of introduction)
6. Which? (criteria which the new product concepts should meet)

The output is now a challenging innovation assignment from the board of directors or the management to the ideation team, wherein the purpose, direction and expected results are established. It is also important to know who will decide whether the new product concepts will be developed. Below, you find an example of a concrete innovation assignment from the FORTH AGRO-practice of AB Oost, which is a cooperative employment and posting agency for the agriculture and business sector with 4,500 co-workers in the Netherlands.

EXAMPLE: INNOVATION ASSIGNMENT

In order to stay in the market in the future as an efficient partner with regards to the supplying of temporary and full time jobs for the agricultural market, we have to link up closely to the top of the agricultural market. The challenge is to develop new or renewed attractive but simple products with regards to labour (in the broadest sense of the word) for farmers and nurseries in our working area. We direct ourselves in the first place to the top 10 per cent of companies as far as size in greenhouse farming, dairy farming and pig farming. The new, renewed product should have a potential turnover of €2.5 million per year per product, three years after its introduction, with a profit margin of 5 per cent of the turnover. Ideally these new products should link closely to those aspects AB Oost are currently good at, such as farm care, posting and the posting of EU co-workers. Our aim is to create three new products this year. The assignment for the AGRO innovation team is to present three mini new business cases on the 25th of June which meets all the above mentioned criteria.

Checklist 2 gives six criteria with which the innovation assignment can be tested. The most important criterion is that the assignment should be challenging enough to give the team positive energy in order to accept the challenge. Should you have doubts, test it personally with a few people prior to presenting it to the ideation team.

4.6 THE RIGHT IDEATION TEAM

The next important step during this stage is to choose the members for the ideation team.

Determining the ideal size of the ideation team is contradictory. The bigger the team, the bigger the diversity, the greater are the chances for breakthrough new product ideas. However, the number of participants is limited by the maximum number with which you can brainstorm effectively. In reality I choose a maximum of 14 participants (excluding the facilitator). My experience has shown that this is the maximum number with which you can have an effective 'brain dump' during a new product brainstorm.

For an effective ideation team you need people who are enthusiastic, who will take responsibility, who will create support, who possess a fresh new outlook and the correct expertise in order to create new product ideas, which will meet the criteria of the innovation assignment. The criteria whereby potential participants should be chosen are:

1. Their enthusiasm and drive. Find participants who are enthusiastic about the theme and who are driven to innovate. Their unrestrained energy and passion will rub off onto the group.
2. Their responsibility and support. These aspects are closely linked. You usually include participants whose work relates to the innovation assignment which then causes internal support. For example, if you include the marketing manager because it concerns the market for which he is responsible, it automatically creates support in his department.
3. Their knowledge and expertise. You include participants in the team because their knowledge and expertise about a specific area are essential for the successful execution of the innovation assignment. Consider the following aspects: the creation of the product concept, knowledge of the customer, product development expertise, knowledge of technology, financial experts or those with knowledge of the production processes.
4. Their fresh new outlook and skills. You also choose outsiders to complement the internal team especially during the Raise Ideas stage. The advantage is that an outsider can bring in something extra or different. Be sure to check during the Full Steam Ahead and Observe and Learn stages where there is a need for reinforcement so that the team can be successful. For example, the level of creativity, knowledge of a specific market, technological or designing skills. Should the assignment include products whereby the product and packaging design is very important, it might be a good idea to include a designer from a design agency. During the two-day new product brainstorming session drawings of new product ideas and packaging which are produced on the spot can add to the inspiration of the team.

Figure 4.2 shows the composition of the team. Make sure that you have a good balance from the above-mentioned perspectives. Within an organisation there is still the traditional contrast between the 'commercial' and the 'techies'. This might be making fun of the situation a bit, but I have often experienced that what the 'techies' can make, the commercials cannot sell and what the commercials can sell, the 'techies' cannot make. This is why it is so important to sufficiently include both in the ideation team. I know for a fact that they can make the FORTH journey together and as professionals they also know very well that they need each other.

In order to compose an effective ideation team of 14 members, you can use the following ratio as your starting point:

- eight internal core team members (including the project leader)
- four internal extended team members
- two outsiders (only during the stage Raise Ideas)

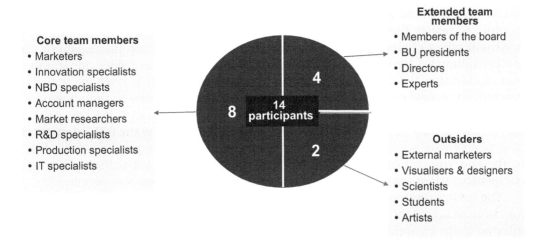

Figure 4.2   The innovation team

The proposed FORTH team therefore consists of 12 internal participants who will go through all five stages of the FORTH process and two outsiders who will be added to the team during the Raise Ideas stage. It is obvious that the outsiders should handle the information which they receive regarding the product concepts which are being developed as confidential. At the end of the chapter you can find an example of how a concrete composition of a FORTH team was put together in the case study, FORTH New Mobility Services of Univé.

The creating of a team is extremely important especially for the team leader and the facilitator. When creating a team it is important to keep in mind that the whole expedition should not only start the journey together but also return together, 15 weeks after kick-off. The required time for the internal team members varies from seven days for the extended team members to a maximum of 25 days for the core team members:

- Ideation team leader: 30–40 days
- Facilitator: 25–30 days
- Core team member: 20–25 days
- Extended team members: 7 days
- Outsiders: 3 days (Raise Ideas stage)

During the innovation focus workshop the choice for the internal participants is made in collaboration with the management. Choose the best people for your ideation team. This should always be done. Often the best people are those with the least time and might not be given the permission from their managers to participate. However, stand firm and stick to the motto: 'If I am responsible for the result, then I should also have the authority to use the means I believe necessary in order to realise the result, which includes choosing my team.' Be creative and persistent when choosing a team and use the support of the top management. In my consultancy I have learned that when the top management does not support you in choosing the best people for the ideation team, then it is a sign that the innovation process does not have the highest priority. It is better to then postpone the project. To create new products you need people and only with the best people do you get the best new product ideas. Of course you can follow the FORTH method with people who are less qualified but then you won't get any good product ideas. In the end you can only be successful in a competitive market with professional competitors when your best innovations are developed by your best people.

The invitation to participate is the task of the internal client (top manager) who functions as an extended core member in the ideation team. It is a good idea for the internal client to approach the team members personally after which the ideation team leader should have a follow up discussion in order to get acquainted and to go through the innovation assignment and planning. In this way you ensure that the participants know what they have agreed to and they can commit themselves to the rigid planning which makes great demands on their agenda.

Apart from the ideation team leader and the facilitator no other roles are given to the participants. They each bring their own specific skill and expertise and their input is equal. This is different for the internal client and the project leader who, in collaboration, will have to make the final decision at a specific time. Research has shown that an effective team consists of a few characteristics. For your inspiration, here are the success factors for winning teams by Dr Meredith Belbin, renowned expert in team roles.

WINNING TEAMS

Meredith Belbin has been doing scientific research regarding team effectiveness for many years. The conclusions regarding the success factors are based on well over 100 experiments with management teams at the Administrative Staff College in Henley (England). The results of the experiments can give you food for thought when selecting your own ideation team members. Belbin discovered the following factors which can have an influence of the success of a team:

1. The team leader

A successful team leader is a patient, impressive figure who instils respect and who has an eye for the qualities of the team members and knows how to utilise them. In reality he always works with the most talented team members and never works against them.

2. The presence of a creative and intelligent team member

Successful management teams always have team members who are creative and smart. Creative team members who are only moderately smart perform badly due to the fact that they cannot realise their own credibility within the team. According to Belbin this applies to management teams with six people. In my opinion it is advisable to include creative as well as smart team members for the ideation team at the starting phase of the innovation process.

3. A reasonable spreading of intellectual capacity

It seems as if a team whereby the intellectual capacity of the members is different work better together than a team which has a more uniform intellectual capacity.

4. A diversity of personal characteristics

With different types of members the possibilities within the team grow. The destructive friction which develops between two or more members who are competing for the same role restricts these possibilities.

5. Dividing the responsibilities according to personal characteristics

Belbin discovered that a winning team consists of members who have been given tasks and responsibilities which fit well with their abilities and personal characteristics. It will be good to consider the role of especially the team leader and the facilitator in the ideation team.

6. An eye and compensation for the imbalance in the composition

Weaknesses in the team can be compensated with self-knowledge and by doing something about it. With the FORTH method we can compensate by the choice of the outsiders in the third stage.

Source: R. Meredith Belbin (2005). *Management Teams: Over succes- en faalfactoren voor teams.* The Hague: Academic Service.

A recent study done in the Netherlands, has shown that only 40 per cent of the companies involve customers when it comes to generating ideas at the beginning of the innovation process.[1] Companies provide two reasons for not involving the customer. Firstly, they are cautious in case good ideas filter through to the market. Secondly, 25 per cent believe that the customer does not really know what he wants anyway. I am a great believer in involving customers in the innovation process, but not to make them permanent members of the ideation team. That does not mean that customers cannot be a good source of inspiration. On the contrary, the involving of customers in the ideation process has much value in practice. This also happens in the FORTH method, not with the development of the product ideas but during the stage which precedes it. During the Observe and Learn stage effective voice-of-customer techniques are used, in order for the members of the ideation team to gain some experience of how things work in practice. They will search for new customer insights themselves. Most of the customers also like to cooperate in research and interviews, especially in business markets.

4.7 THE FORTH KICK-OFF WORKSHOP

When the innovation assignment has been determined and the team have been put together, you invite the team members for the FORTH-kick-off-workshop. This workshop has three objectives:

1. Getting to know one another, the challenging innovation assignment and the FORTH innovation method.
2. To make mutual agreements regarding the journey.
3. To brainstorm and choose the best innovation opportunities and sources of inspiration which will be visited during the Observe and Learn stage.

This workshop usually lasts for one day. As FORTH facilitator I have found that it is a good idea to meet with the core team the evening before the workshop, where you can meet and share personal experiences. This should be done at the venue where the kick-off workshop for the next day has been organised. It is possible that the members have had negative experiences at the start of a development process in the past which can then hamper the fresh start of the FORTH method. Should this be true then it might be a good idea to add it to the kick-off agenda and discuss it at the beginning of the workshop. An excellent technique for how to do this can be found in 'The Dustbin' (see Appendix II: Thirty Brainstorming Techniques A.5). Checklist 5 will also provide more help with the composition of the programme.

During the kick-off workshop there are three essential activities which affect the effectiveness of the process: getting acquainted, discussing the innovation assignment and generating and choosing the innovation opportunities with the

---

1   Twynstra, The Bridge (2005). *Innovatiemonitor*, 11.

accompanying expedition goals for the stage Observe and Learn which starts directly after the kick-off-workshop.

Getting Acquainted

When you work for a large organisation it is almost impossible to know all the people. It is therefore essential to be able to get acquainted with each other. This can be done very freely and creatively. Appendix II – Thirty Brainstorming Techniques – gives three creative ways in which the ice can be broken. A good introduction of the innovation assignment is also crucial. When this is done by the general manager, who informs the team that the mission is important for the company and that they can rely on his/her support, it carries more weight, especially when the manager is open to questions and criticism.

Generating and Choosing the Innovation Opportunities for Innovation

After the kick-off workshop the core team starts observing and learning. The question is where and with whom do you start as there are so many ways to go. In the FORTH method the realising of the innovation assignment always takes priority. That is the reason why during the kick-off workshop the opportunities for innovation must be generated and we choose the opportunities which have the most potential in the light of the innovation assignment. An opportunity can be anything. I usually define it pragmatically as a theme, topic, technology, trend, area or target group which provides the best opportunities to realise the innovation assignment. During the kick-off workshop the innovation opportunities are collectively generated in a brainstorming session in two ways. Depending on the innovation assignment, you choose a perspective of a specific theme. Firstly, you look at it from the point of view of the target group and you try to place yourself in their position, after which you brainstorm on the basis of the question: 'Which questions and problems do the target group experience with this theme?' In the next step you approach the answers from step 1 from your own organisation and brainstorm for concrete opportunities based on the question: 'Which innovation opportunities are produced by these questions and problems surrounding this theme?' In the case study FORTH New Mobility Services of the Dutch insurance company Univé (at the end of this chapter) you will find five concrete examples of innovation opportunities. From all the innovation opportunities the group then choose those with the most potential to be developed in the next stage: Observe and Learn. Each core team member then chooses the innovation opportunity which they prefer. In other words if you have seven regular core team members you choose seven innovation opportunities. The eighth core team member, the project leader, does not actively participate in this decision due to the pressure of coordinating the whole process.

Generating Expedition Goals for Each Innovation Opportunity

When you have chosen seven innovation opportunities, the question arises: 'From whom can we learn the most with regards to these opportunities?' Each participant at the kick-off workshop then writes as many as possible interesting and concrete expedition goals on a flip-chart with one page for each opportunity. This includes, for example, names of experts, contact persons at organisations who excel in this, interesting existing concepts to investigate, websites where you can get more information and inspiring places to visit. When everyone has had the chance to contribute their ideas to the opportunity pages which were passed around, the core team member, who has adopted the innovation opportunity, reads the information and discusses the concrete input from the others. With this, the kick-off workshop draws to a close and after ending the day with champagne and good wishes for a successful journey, the core team members can start the journey immediately.

Four more practical tips taken from the practice:

1. Together with the facilitator, it can be useful to draw up a so-called FORTH departure document. In this document suggestions for the innovation assignment, the core team members and extended team members, the characteristics of the FORTH method, the provisional planning and the amount of time involved for each participant can be mentioned. This document can be used during the innovation focus workshop with the internal client and thereafter it is an excellent discussion point with the potential participants at the start of the FORTH process.
2. Provide the ideation project with a clear and recognisable name and slogan. The innovation assignment usually ends up as a long piece of business text. Try and give the innovation assignment a more inspiring form by choosing a striking slogan which resembles the core of the innovation assignment. Another idea is to make a colourful mind-map or mood board of the innovation assignment. In order to improve communication and to create the correct perception of the innovation project internally, it also helps to give the FORTH innovation project an appealing name; for example, the FORTH Mega-Brand-Extensions, the FORTH New-Client-Groups or the FORTH New-Mobility-Services.
3. Create a special FORTH innovation room within the organisation. This will become the central place from where the team will hold the Observe and Learn workshops as well as develop the business cases. After a while this room will be filled with photographs, impressions of customer visits, flip-chart pages of innovation opportunities, customer friction boards and concept boards. This will also create curiosity, in a pleasant way, with other workers in the company which causes the innovation to be experienced by more than just the FORTH team members.
4. Provide the participants with an 'idea notebook'. As soon as someone is asked to participate, and especially after the Kick-off and during the Observe and Learn stage, ideas start entering their mind which they can then write down. This also

allows them to be open-minded, because as soon as they have written down an idea, they are open to more ideas. These notebooks play an important role during the brainstorming session in the third stage.

4.8 PITFALLS

Reality is full of pitfalls. Ten pitfalls for the Full Steam Ahead stage have been described below, followed by some advice on how to handle them should you recognise them in your own company.

1. Innovation is not the Correct Solution

The average time taken to complete the process whereby a new product has been developed amounts to 18 months. There is also a 50 per cent chance that the product will fail. Should the profitability of the company be in danger, don't innovate. First reduce costs over a short period of time and only innovate when there is no struggle regarding the continuity of the company. However, do not postpone the innovation process for too long as you might just be wiped out by the competition.

Reaction: Do not proceed with the FORTH method.

2. Managers do not Support the Process One Hundred Percent

Should you notice that during the run-up or the innovation focus workshop the managers do not support the start of the ideation phase, it is better to discuss it immediately. It is the role of the chairman of the board to challenge the management for complete support. Should the FORTH method not get enough support, it is better to stop the process. The most awkward situation is when everyone confesses support, yet the internal participants are constantly opposed by their own managers, so allow this to be discussed immediately. If this happens the chance of co-workers stopping halfway through the process due to pressure from the manager becomes greater.

Reaction: Discuss it immediately. Where there is constant doubt do not start with the FORTH method.

3. The Innovation Assignment Continues to be Vague

During the innovation focus workshop you are not successful in determining a clear and concrete innovation assignment with the managers.

Reaction: Do not proceed when you establish that the assignment does not provide enough direction. Arrange a follow-up meeting and try to reach as many managers in the meantime. As project leader you can also present a concept innovation assignment.

4. The Top Management is not Involved in the Ideation Phase of the Innovation Process

You notice that the top management is not directly involved with the ideation phase but has delegated it to one of the managers from the business unit or the staff organisation. This is not unusual in larger companies and it should not create too many problems especially if the authority to start the innovation project has also been given to the other manager. However, if the top management are involved with the choice of concepts at the end of the ideation phase it is important that they have agreed to the innovation assignment and evaluation criteria.

Reaction: Check the support of the top management before the innovation assignment.

5. The Board of Directors does not Allow Certain Business Units to Participate

Due to the pressures on businesses today the board of directors might decide that the sales department are not allowed to participate.

Reaction: Check if there are solid grounds for this or are they busy playing a political game. If you discover that the sales department has been deliberately prohibited from participation just to allow them to boycott the process later, do not continue. You will serve the interest of the company if you allow it to escalate now, rather than being involved in a defensive battle at the end of the ideation phase.

6. The Board of Directors Ignorantly does not Allow the Best People to be Chosen

It becomes clear during the innovation focus workshop that you, as ideation team leader, cannot rely on your first choice for participants.

Reaction: It is possible that when it comes to choosing the right people, other aspects take priority and the urgency to innovate is not high enough yet. But do not start the process with the B team. Suggest that you start the FORTH method six months later, as the urgency and the willingness to use the best people might have increased by then.

7. The Ideation Team Leader does not Have Enough Authority within the Company

You notice that the team leader does not have enough personal authority in the eyes of the participants and their managers.

Reaction: Discuss this immediately, first with the project leader personally and then with all other parties concerned. A FORTH journey is always stressful and the leader of the ideation team must have a strong personality which is acceptable to the participants, the board of directors and other managers.

8. There is Resistance to the Involvement of Outsiders

During the selection of the participants there are strong doubts as to whether outsiders can actually contribute more.

Reaction: Try to find the reason for this way of thinking. It could be the fear that they might take a look at what is going on in your company; the fear that the confidentiality might be affected, or even a matter of extra cost involved. With regards to confidentiality you can come to an agreement.

9. The Chairman of the Board does not Have Enough Time and Sends a 'Second Rate Substitute' to the Kick-Off Workshop

Reaction: Confront him or her directly. Innovation is either important or not; it is not just of little importance. That is not enough.

10. The General Director is not Involved Enough and Sets the Wrong Tone at the Kick-Off

Reaction: What a shame! Try and save what can be saved. Prevention is better than cure. Make sure that the general director is briefed well in advance, if he/she comes. You can even write the speech for them. There is only one message: 'What you are going to do is really important for us and you can rely on my support.'

4.9 CASE STUDY: FORTH NEW MOBILITY SERVICES: FULL STEAM AHEAD

Previous History

During a meeting with the top management of Univé, one of the biggest insurance companies in the Netherlands, the wish to create value for their customers was one of the most urgent discussion points. They did not only want to continue to insure cars in the traditional way but wanted to add real value for their customers, which are members of their cooperative. This was the result of a preceding comprehensive strategic plan whereby the world of car insurance was investigated over a long period. Jan Dijkstra, the director of the Business Unit (BU) Indemnity Insurance, was well aware that his BU was not strong when it comes to innovation. For this reason he contacted Bart Schouten, who was just appointed as manager of Innovation at group level. He requested some assistance as he knew that 'real innovation cannot be realised with a lack of time and creativity'. Bart searched for the right way in which to approach this situation. During his holiday he read the Dutch version of this book. The FORTH innovation method appealed to him because of its structured and practical approach. This led to a meeting with Gijs van Wulfen and together they made an appointment in Assen, where the BU Indemnity Insurance is housed.

After the meeting between Gijs van Wulfen, Jan Dijkstra and his internal advisor, Jan van Raalte, a decision was made to have a follow-up meeting in which they would construct a concrete innovation assignment, the FORTH approach and the best team. Everyone left the meeting with some homework to do. The second meeting was held in October when the innovation assignment, the concrete approach and the planning and composition of a good FORTH team were discussed. In November Bart Schouten and Jan Dijkstra presented this to the management team of the BU Indemnity Insurance, where it was received well. The board of directors of Univé was also informed about the FORTH initiative of the BU Indemnity Insurance in November. Due to the nature of the assignment it was called the FORTH New Mobility Services project. Jan Dijkstra, as the internal client, personally approached the participants which he had in mind for the FORTH team in November, to ask if they would help him. Directly afterwards, Bart Schouten who, in the meantime, was appointed the project leader of the FORTH New Mobility Services, contacted the participants individually to discuss the approach, the planning and the time needed for the project.

Stage: Full Steam Ahead

The reason for the innovation project of Univé was due to a real threat from within the market. The market for private car insurance is very competitive which leads to a decrease in the price and profit erosion on the one hand and on the other it offers chances for new mobility concepts. Should Univé do nothing they run the risk of being overtaken on both sides and with that lose the independent access to the customer. To continue in the top three with a grade A product and to become a market leader in price and performance, Univé wanted to develop new distinctive and additional products or services with regards to the mobility needs for the three current important customer segments in the private-car-owner-market in the Netherlands. Univé wanted to do this not only from the interest of its present customers: the members of the cooperative.

Innovation Assignment

The following innovation assignment was determined:

We want to develop three new (not available in the Netherlands yet), distinctive and additional products/services in the form of mini new business cases which will realise 200,000 clients three years after its introduction. They will contribute, directly or indirectly, to the profit margin of Univé Indemnity Insurance and the rest of the company. It is important to note that Univé consists of 30 independent regional insurances. Both existing and new sales channels can be deployed for the new products or services. The proposed additional products/services will not affect the current car portfolio and fit well within the strategy of Univé as well as BU Indemnity Insurance. They should also contribute to strengthen the brand Univé. The aim is to introduce the new products and services within one year.

The FORTH Innovation Team

The best team can be approached from various angles:

- Who are the experts?
- Who are the workers who 'will go the extra mile'?
- Who has shown that they can think creatively?
- Whom do we need for the support?

The search for and finding of the best people to participate in the team is not always straightforward. Although most people realise the importance of the assignment, there are still some obstacles to overcome before the best FORTH team is set up. The problem is due to time and priority as the best people are usually the busiest. His intense involvement, his charisma and his personal approach, allowed Jan Dijkstra, the internal client, to assemble many participants, and their bosses, for the project.

The FORTH innovation team consisting of 13 people was made up of:

a) A core team:

1. Bart Schouten (Innovation Manager Univé and FORTH project leader)
2. Jan van Raalte (Internal Innovation Manager Univé BU Indemnity Insurance)
3. Johan Buigholt (Commercial Team Manager Univé BU Indemnity Insurance)
4. Wim Brouwer (Team Manager Univé Compander)
5. Joop Kluin (Director of Univé Stellingland)
6. Aletta Dokter-Eiten (Marketer BU Indemnity Insurance)

b) Extended team members:

1. Jan Dijkstra (Director BU Indemnity Insurance and internal FORTH client)
2. Luc Lievers (Head of Commercial Management Regio+)
3. Willem Bos (Business Analyst BU Indemnity Insurance)
4. Jan Willem Bolhuis (Product Manager BU Indemnity Insurance)
5. Ruud van der Wal (Manager Sales Support Univé Stad en Land)
6. Robert de Ruiter (Director Univé Regio+)
7. Cock Meerhof (Innovation Manager Univé; joined during the last Observe and Learn workshop)

Gijs van Wulfen was the FORTH innovation facilitator who guided the ideation process.

The FORTH Programme

In Table 4.2 you find the programme that was drawn up at the start. It gives concrete insight into all the activities of the FORTH New Mobility Services, the division of roles between the core team members and the extended team members as well as the investment of time by the participants.

Table 4.2   The FORTH programme

Activity	When	Who	Explanation	Time invested core team (in days)	Time invested extended team (in days)
Kick-off workshop	18 and 19 December (one and a half days)	All participants	Team session 18 December from 16.00 to 22.00 and kick-off the next day: introduction of assignment and choosing of innovation opportunities.	1.5	1
Discovery approach and insight training	10 January (one day)	Core participants	Discovery approach made concrete and training of a half a day in how to gain insight with customers.	1	0
Connecting with customers and other sources of inspiration	Between 11 January and 12 February	Core participants	Gaining insight with customers and getting inspiration from experts.	6	0
Observe and Learn workshop 1	22 January (morning)	Core participants	Sharing knowledge and experience.	0.5	0.5
Observe and Learn workshop 2	29 January (morning)	Core participants	Sharing knowledge and experience.	0.5	0.5
Observe and Learn workshop 3	5 February (morning)	Core participants	Sharing knowledge and experience.	0.5	0.5
Observe and Learn workshop 4	12 February (morning)	Core participants	Sharing knowledge and experience.	0.5	0.5
Two-day brainstorming session	15 and 16 February (overnight stay included)	All participants and two outsiders	Two-day brainstorming session where through various methods the development of concrete concepts are realised.	2	2

Table 4.2 *Concluded*

Activity	When	Who	Explanation	Time invested core team (in days)	Time invested extended team (in days)
Qualitative market research	Week 10	Core participants	The developed concepts are investigated qualitatively with customers.	1	0
Improvement workshop	15 March	All participants	Based on the result of the research the concepts are further developed.	1	1
Writing of various MNBCs	Week 10–14	Core participants	Mini new business cases are developed based on all the input.	8.5	1
Progress meeting MNBCs	28 March (morning)	Core participants	Discussion of progress and problems.	0.5	0
MNBC-presentation to the FORTH group	5 April	All participants	Various MNBCs are presented and discussed.	1	1
Final concepts handed in	13 April	Project leader	Delivering the presentation to the Innovation Board of Univé.	0.5	0
Estimated number of days				25	8

Shortly before the Christmas holidays the FORTH New Mobility Services started. This sent an important and positive signal to the company and it was important for Jan Dijkstra as it was a pleasant topic of conversation at the New Year's reception.

Unfortunately, a bleak Best Western hotel, Hotel Hiddingerberg, was chosen for the kick-off workshop. This happens when you personally do not inspect the venue first. However, the disadvantage of being directly next to the A3 motorway was immediately changed into a positive advantage: FORTH New Mobility Services is starting with a view on driving cars …

Getting Acquainted With the Core Team

Despite the lack of atmosphere in the hotel, the evening where everybody got acquainted before the kick-off workshop had much value. As is common in larger companies it seemed that most core team members met each other for the first time. With the Bunch of Keys (see Appendix II Thirty Brainstorming Techniques) I allowed the core team to get acquainted. With the help of the Belbin method regarding team roles they gained insight into the role of each core team member.

While studying the profile of the team we came to the realisation that the 'natural creativity' was under-represented and we decided to compensate for this by keeping it in mind when choosing the outsiders for the brainstorming session. Furthermore we decided to add the creative innovation manager, Cock Meerhof, as an extended team member. We concluded the get-together with a meaningful discussion of how we were going to treat each other in the team.

The Kick-Off Workshop

The following morning, 19 December, the kick-off workshop was attended by all the team members, core as well as extended. I asked all members to bring a photo of their own car to the meeting. The introduction, with the help of their photo, broke the ice and directly focused their minds on the topic of the kick-off: New Mobility Services. The identification of the possible innovation opportunities which will be discovered in the next FORTH stage – Observe and Learn – was done with the help of role play. There are three target groups on which Univé wanted to concentrate and in three groups we imagined and asked ourselves the following questions:

1. What do you consider important about your car?
2. What do you struggle with when choosing, selling/buying, driving and maintaining your car?

Inspired by our own input we brainstormed possible innovation opportunities for Univé concerning New Mobility Services. With this, the following five innovation opportunities were chosen by the group to be further developed in the Observe and Learn stage:

1. Car purchasing support.
2. Links to other types of transport.
3. A guarantee for mobility.
4. Private leasing.
5. Sponsored transport.

For each of the five innovation opportunities there was a brainstorming session about people, organisations and/or companies who have the best practice and from whom Univé can learn something. In this way an expedition plan was developed for each innovation opportunity. Finally, each team member 'adopted' an innovation opportunity. After the champagne each member, with their innovation opportunity sheet, entered the Christmas spirit.

Just before leaving the meeting, the project leader Bart Schouten arranged three further aspects which were going to stimulate the contact between one another within the team. He created a format for a digital FORTH newsletter which they would receive on a regular basis during the FORTH journey. A special FORTH project website was made where all the participants could give and receive information.

Furthermore, he would arrange for a FORTH innovation room within the already fully occupied building of the BU Indemnity Insurance in Assen. In this room the Observe and Learn workshops, as well as the drafting of the mini new business cases in the later stages, would be held.

4.10 PRACTICAL CHECKLISTS

CHECKLIST 1: INNOVATION FOCUS WORKSHOP

Four objectives:

1. To determine the innovation assignment and the evaluation criteria for new product or service concepts.
2. To choose the internal participants for the ideation team.
3. To collectively discuss and come to an agreement regarding the FORTH approach, planning and costs.
4. To gain the support and assistance from the top management.

The innovation focus workshop is a meeting with higher management at which they make the decisions regarding the start of the FORTH method.

Duration

A meeting of four hours is sufficient, provided that the company has a clear vision on innovation, that innovation is on the management agenda regularly and that the workshop is well prepared. If innovation is only in the beginning stage or only appears on the agenda on an ad hoc basis, then it will be better to allow for two meetings.

Location

Choose an inspiring external location which has a connection with the assignment; for example, at the discount supermarket Aldi (if it is about the bottom-of-the-market revolution); in a university (if students are the target group) or in the conference room of Facebook (if it is about new online products or services).

Participants (four–six)

- the manager responsible for innovation (CEO, Chairman of the Board, Business Unit Manager)
- the member of the board and manager concerned
- the intended ideation team leader
- the facilitator of the FORTH process

Scenario

There are four points on the agenda:

1. Innovation assignment and evaluation criteria.
2. Participants of the ideation team.
3. Planning for the FORTH approach.
4. Time and costs.

Tip: Together with the facilitator, create a so-called FORTH departure document for this meeting. This document should contain the suggested innovation assignment, suggestions for the core and extended team members, provisional planning and the duration for each participant. This will accelerate the meeting considerably.

CHECKLIST 2: THE INNOVATION ASSIGNMENT

Possible components of the innovation assignment (six Ws):

1. Why? (purpose or goal)
2. Who? (target group)
3. Where? (distribution channels, countries, regions or continents)
4. What? (evolutionary or revolutionary concepts)
5. When? (intended year of introduction)
6. Which? (criteria which the product concept must meet).

Verify that the innovation assignment complies with the six U-SMART-criteria:

1. Utterly challenging. Has the assignment been formulated in such a way that it transfers positive energy to the ideation team?
2. Specific. Does the assignment give clear direction?
3. Measurable. Can the expected concrete results be described as measurable?
4. Acceptable. Are the assignment and the objectives acceptable?
5. Realistic. Are the assignment and the objectives realistic?
6. Towards the deadline. Is the time in which the assignment has to be realised, clear?

Tip: Use analogies from other companies to liven up these challenges.

An example of a bottom revolution:

*   How can we obtain an easyJet or Aldi position in this branch?

An example of a top revolution:

*   How can we get a TomTom or Senseo effect in this market?

An example of a new market revolution:

*   How can we become the Wii or Google of this sector?

CHECKLIST 3: THE IDEATION TEAM

For a good ideation team you need people who are willing to take responsibility, create support, have a fresh outlook and have the right expertise in order for the innovation assignment to succeed. Possible core and extended team members can be considered for the team due to:

1. Their responsibility and their support

Include participants in the team because the innovation assignment connects with their responsibility or because they can create support within the organisation. These aspects are usually closely related. It can, for example, be the:

a) Product manager
b) Market manager
c) Marketing manager
d) R&D manager
e) Sales manager
f) Account manager
g) Area manager
h) Business unit manager
i) Director
j) Staff (innovation) specialist
k) Managers involved in the decision-making process whether to include new product concepts in the innovation process
l) Co-workers active during a later stage in the innovation process
m) Managers whose department will later develop, buy, produce or sell the new product concept

2. Their expertise

Include participants because their knowledge and expertise are essential for the successful implementation of the innovation assignment. This can be:

a) Expertise in creating new product concepts and designing them
b) Marketing and communication expertise
c) Knowledge of the region, market or target group
d) Knowledge of product development
e) Knowledge of ICT
f) Financial expertise in the making of business cases
g) Knowledge of internal production processes
h) Knowledge of suppliers and possible partners

When putting together a team, always keep the balance of the team in mind. As a starting point you can make use of the following suggestion that an effective ideation team should have a maximum of 14 participants and can consist of the following members (including the ideation team leader):

- the eight core team members;
- four internal extended team members because of their direct responsibility or support;
- two outsiders, during the Raise Ideas stage because of their fresh new outlook.

There is often an overlap between participants which you select because of their responsibility and expertise. The above mentioned global arrangement will have to be adjusted to the department, the organisation and the assignment.

CHECKLIST 4: TIME AND OUT-OF-POCKET COSTS FORTH PROCESS

Table 4.3   Estimated maximum time for internal participants of the FORTH process

Number	Role	Number of days	Total number of days
1	Ideation team leader	maximum 40	40
7	Rest of core team members	maximum 25	175
4	Extended team members	7	28
12	Total		243 days

Note: based on the assumption of an external FORTH facilitator.

The total out-of-pocket costs for the FORTH process depends on the following factors:

- Is there a paid internal or external FORTH innovation facilitator? There are certified external FORTH innovation facilitators trained (see Appendix I). The daily rate varies between €1,500 and €2,500 (excl. VAT).
- Are the outsiders being paid for their efforts? When you involve advisers, you have to consider a daily rate of a minimum of €1,000. Anything below this is a give away price.
- Travel and accommodation costs vary considerably depending on the luxury of the chosen location for the FORTH Kick-off workshop and the two-day brainstorming session. The cost can vary between €5,000 and €15,000 for a luxurious location.

Based on the experience gained in practice, the total out-of-pocket cost for a professional FORTH project with an external FORTH facilitator is €100,000. This is compiled as follows:

- External FORTH innovation facilitator (30 days)   €60,000
- External web search (3 days)   €3,000
- Focus groups and customer visits   €9,000
- External locations and overnight stays   €10,000
- Outsiders Observe and Learn stage (2×3 days)   €6,000
- Cartoonist brainstorming session (2 days)   €2,000
- Qualitative concept research   €10,000

   Total   €100,000

The cost therefore amounts to approximately €100,000 if you want it done professionally. It is a good idea to relate this cost to the challenge of the innovation assignment. For AB Oost, for example, the ideation team returned with three mini business cases with an annual turnover potential of more than €2.5 million, three years after introduction. The cost justifies the means also when it comes to developing new products.

CHECKLIST 5: FORTH PROGRAMME KICK-OFF WORKSHOP

Three objectives:

1. Getting acquainted with each other, the challenging innovation assignment and the FORTH approach.
2. Mutual agreements regarding the journey.
3. Brainstorming and choosing the innovation opportunities and sources of inspiration to visit during the Observe and Learn stage.

Location

An inspiring external location. Ideally you choose a venue with a link to the innovation assignment.

Programme

Table 4.4   Getting acquainted and teamwork for FORTH

Time	Phase	Topic	
16.30	Arrival	Coffee and tea	
17.00	Getting acquainted	Round of introductions	Facilitator
18.00	Challenging projects	Your most challenging project and your own personal style	Facilitator
20.00	Informal	Dinner	

Table 4.5   Kick-off workshop core and extended team FORTH

Time	Phase	Topic	
		Arrival and coffee	
09.00		Welcome by the internal client and reason for urgency	Internal client
09.05	1. Introduction	Internal Client introduces facilitator Facilitator explains the programme Mutual agreements	Facilitator Facilitator

Table 4.5 *Concluded*

Time	Phase	Topic	
09.15	*2. Getting acquainted*	Introduction	
09.40	*3. Current situation*	Presentation about the situation on the market and the position of the company	Project leader or internal expert
10.10	*4. Strategy company/ BU*	Relevant sheet about the vision for the future	Internal client
10.25	*Break*		
10.45	*5. Assignment*	Innovation assignment in the spotlight Buy-in of the team/re-formulating	Project leader Facilitator
11.45	*6. Approach*	Explanation of the FORTH process	Facilitator
12.15	*Lunch*		
13.00	*7. Outside-in*	Customer needs and friction are worked out in four groups Four groups present the frictions to each other	Facilitator
14.45	*Break*		
15.00	*8. Innovation opportunities*	Brainstorming innovation opportunities based on the innovation assignment Choose opportunities with most potential	Facilitator
16.00	*9. Making plans for the expedition*	A short brain dump for each opportunity towards the expedition goals: websites, people and companies to visit Selecting the goals for the expedition Commitment of the team and client	Facilitator
17.00	*10. Conclusion*	Project leader and internal client close the meeting Expedition drink: champagne on a successful ending	Client

DIVING INTO THE MARKET

5   Observe and Learn

The fish is the last one who will discover water.

(Anonymous)

To gain customer insights, we must understand that we are prisoners of what we know and what we believe.

(Mohanbir Sawhney, Kellogg School of Management)

In a side street you often find the most wonderful things.

(Loesje)

5.1 INTRODUCTION

In the second stage, the FORTH team leave the premises; they literally and figuratively go on a discovery expedition which will lead them to their own innovation opportunities, customers, trends and technology. They acquire new impressions by observing and talking to the target group. The purpose of this stage is to gain inspiration from different sources and to let it rub off on them. At the end of their expedition they choose the most valuable innovation opportunities, customer frictions, trends and/or technologies. These are then used as a source of inspiration in the brainstorming session during the next stage. The Observe and Learn stage lasts for six weeks and also functions as incubation time in order to integrate the experiences in their subconscious whereby new product or service ideas are created.

5.2 IN SEARCH OF INSPIRATION

Innovation is about breaking through patterns and discovering new combinations. To be able to innovate means to be able to learn from others. For this reason it is important not to keep on looking for inspiration from behind your desk, but to go and search for inspiration and new insights elsewhere. This is easier said than done. As a marketer I used to have great difficulty in going out. I used to promise myself endlessly that I would go to the customers, to observe and to learn in order to touch the right nerve. While I was working at the soup manufacturer Honig I promised myself to go the supermarket to observe how people bought. Also while I was working at the sweets factory Red Band Venco and didn't then have children of my own, I promised myself to visit school grounds. However, I always had enough business excuses, meetings and emails to 'escape' from doing so. Once, three product managers and I actually took the step and on a Wednesday afternoon, we went on our 'market outing', to the movies to watch Disney's Aladdin with hundreds of screaming children. I can therefore imagine that you in your job hardly have time for this, but I do not have any sympathy with that. It is crucial to visit customers. Regard the Observe and Learn phase of the FORTH method as your opportunity, with your colleagues, to throw yourself into the market.

A visit to a customer is not the only way to get inspiration. A visit to another organisation or company brings the same results and is educational too. How did you approach the target group? How do things work in your branch? Why are you so successful? While exploring innovation opportunities (more about this in Section 5.6), you learn much through only a few conversations with others about their experiences.

You can only break through patterns in the market if you break through your own patterns: if you can't change, how can you expect it from others? So, get up and go!

THE CREATION OF NEW IDEAS

It sometimes seems as if ideas develop spontaneously, but this is only pretence. This is only because it is not always possible to establish the reason for the idea; it is also nearly impossible to establish when exactly an idea developed. According to Plato there is no such thing as having a new idea. What often looks like a new idea is only the recognition of an existing idea or a new application of an existing concept. From this viewpoint, the 'newness' of an idea is only the experience of newness as it happens with the discoverer of the idea. A more modern belief is that a new idea develops when someone discovers a new combination, classification or application of an existing idea. An idea can also lie dormant for a long time before it sprouts. It then transfers itself from the subconscious to the conscious, known as the moment when someone 'gets' an idea. At this time it can be that the idea is not more than a 'gut feeling', or a feeling that there is 'something'. 'The right circumstances' will imply a specific situation whereby a change occurs and a natural process makes it possible for the idea to be discovered. A new combination, classification or application is created.

Source: Gijs Verrest. *Groeistuipen van een idee*. www.cocd.be

The inspiration compass on Figure 5.1 will help the ideation team to find the right sources of inspiration. The compass represents four closely linked directions. The first, and most effective, source of inspiration is the customer. Observing, listening and talking to customers seem a bit scary in the beginning but gives an enormous amount of energy and valuable insight afterwards. Trends form the second source of inspiration. Identifying and translating trends ensures that you can look ahead in a constructive way and also allows you to become aware of what is happening in the market. The third source of inspiration is technology. New technology is the main source of inspiration when it comes to cars, telecommunication, electronics or computers. Even in non-technological driven markets, it can be a significant source of inspiration – for example, to broaden your knowledge about the rapid and continuous developments regarding the internet and communication technology and the quick changes it brings about in society. The last source of inspiration has already been chosen during kick-off. It is the promising innovation opportunities. During this stage each opportunity is explored by one core team member. Below is an explanation of the named directions for inspiration.

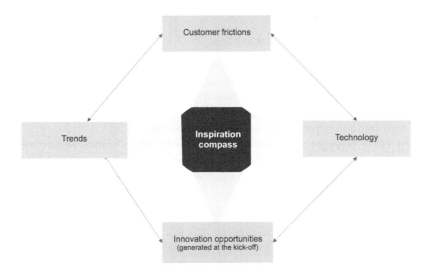

Figure 5.1   The inspiration compass (developed in cooperation with Richard Stomp)

5.3 DISCOVERING CUSTOMER FRICTIONS

As is known from recent research, meeting with the customer in person and discovering customer frictions with the aid of focus groups, are probably the most effective sources of inspiration when it comes to inventing new product ideas.[1] This has also been my experience with FORTH innovation projects over the past few years. During the Observe and Learn stage the core and extended team members all visit customers independently. Furthermore, the core team are present at the focus groups where, under the guidance of the facilitator, relevant customer frictions are brought to the surface. A customer friction is familiar to a customer insight. A customer insight is defined as a 'fresh and not-yet-obvious understanding

---

1   Robert G. Cooper and Scott Edgett (2008). Ideation for Product Innovation: What are the Best Methods? *PDMA Visions*, March.

of customers that can become the basis for competitive advantage'.[2] It is a very popular term used in the recent innovation literature. For this reason companies such as Procter and Gamble are employing anthropologists.

INSIGHT INTO CUSTOMER INSIGHTS

A customer insight is a fresh and not-yet-obvious understanding of customers that can become the basis for competitive advantage.

This definition suggests several characteristics:

1. It is a not-yet-obvious discovery. Insights seem logical in hindsight, but they are not obvious before they are discovered.
2. It is a unique and fresh perspective. If you want to have different conversations, you must have different voices. And if you want to see different things, you must look through different eyes and with different lenses.
3. It rarely emerges from quantitative research. While market research produces oceans of data and information, it rarely produces much consumer insights.
4. It is often rooted in an observed anomaly. In uncovering insights, it is important to heed the saying: 'Always ask why'.

Source: Mohanbir Sawhney. Insights into Customer Insights. www.defyingthelimits.com

---

In other words it is about a new and unique insight which forms the basis for competitor advantage. In my opinion, this is too general. In cooperation with innovation colleague Richard Stomp we formulated the following definition of what we call a customer friction:

A customer friction is a (re) discovered relevant need, urge or wish from a specific target group in a recognisable situation, which is not sufficiently satisfied and which you can use as a relevant basis for a new distinctive product concept.

In short – the difference between what somebody wants and what he can have.

Why do we focus upon discovering frictions, struggles or irritations that business customers or consumers experience? My experience as a marketer has taught me that both consumers and business customers do not change their behaviour easily. People are actually 'creatures of habit' and are not inclined to change. Yet they are the people to whom we want to introduce new products or services. It can only work if the new product or service actually is attractive to them and solves an existing and relevant friction. In this way you make something possible which they have not been able to achieve but really want to. This is the reason why we

---

2   Mohanbir Sawhney (2001). *Insights into Customer Insights.* [Online]. Available at: www.defyingthelimits.com

go looking for frictions in the target group during the Observe and Learn stage by observing, listening and interpreting for ourselves. The participants do this during the Observe and Learn stage in two ways: by visiting customers and by attending focus groups.

1. Visiting customers

The purpose is to get the internal participants from behind their desks and to immerse them into the market through personal contact with real customers. The trick is to find the right people to do this. Figure 5.2 shows a model which can be of help. The choice you make must relate to the innovation assignment. It is obvious that with an assignment for evolutionary top innovations you have to visit critical, regular or large buyers and users. For revolutionary innovations you will try to find non-buyers, ex-buyers and critical buyers, to find out why they have stopped purchasing the product or why the current product does not appeal to them. In a well-formulated innovation assignment the target group should be clearly defined.

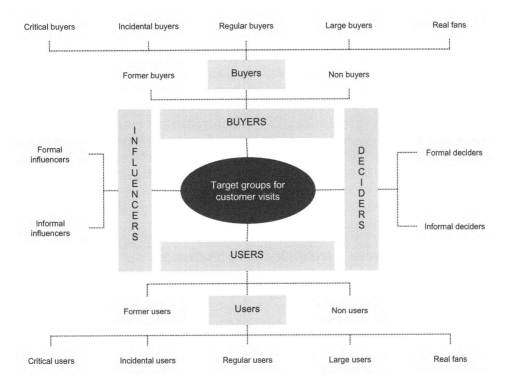

Figure 5.2   Target groups for customer visits

Based on what you want to find out and from whom, you try to find the best location where you can observe the behaviour of the customer and where you can get into contact with them. Choose a user area, where the customers feel relaxed and can show their usual behaviour – for example, at a petrol station, at home, during the interval at the movies, in a shop or café, mobile phoning while walking, at the computer, in the sports canteen or in the school playground. The question is: when is the right moment? Choose this very carefully. Different times of the day can also be tried if you believe that it will bring about a different result.

There are a few reasons why visiting a customer should be done in pairs. Firstly it gives confidence to the participants and secondly it is practical when recording experiences, which is usually done on film or with digital photographs. Afterwards, it can be viewed again and you can also present it to others during the Observe and Learn workshops where you share your experiences with the whole FORTH team.

It is also advisable to consider a strict casting. The cameraman/woman must try to capture the behaviour of the customer discreetly in order not to disturb them. Ensure that with the observation you also 'mirror this with the target group'. In this way they will feel at ease and you increase your chances of seeing real behaviour. When you have an appointment with consumers, approach it naturally, wear your jeans and jumper and should you have lunch or dinner with them, go into the kitchen afterwards (help with the dishes if necessary). After your visit, immediately discuss what you have observed and what has caught your attention.

It demands much from you as the participant to carry out such a customer visit. In fact you should learn anew how to observe and listen so that you can register exactly what is happening. There is specific training for customer observation which you can follow with the ideation team: together with other participants you learn how you can (again) look at the behaviour of people with an open mind. Customer insights are 'hot'. Many new specialised consultancies which can help you are popping up like mushrooms. There are also consultancies that specialise in training before going on a visit to customers. At the end of the chapter, Checklist 6 provides some practical tips for customer visits, with special attention paid to customer visits in a business-to-business market.

2. Discovering Customer Frictions in the Focus Groups

Discovering customer frictions in the focus groups is a very effective technique. In the FORTH practice we usually invite six to eight people for the focus group in a place where there are good facilities for the core team to be able to join in. While the FORTH facilitator leads the group discussion the core team members observe the discussion via close circuit TV or from behind a window. The subject is defined by the innovation assignment. The facilitator tries to discover:

- What do you want, what keeps you busy or what do you find important?
- With what are you struggling? What have you come up against?

It is important to keep on asking: Why? How come? Can you tell us more about it? It is quite remarkable to see how people open up.

After the two-hour discussion, the core team members, together with the facilitator, start dissecting the customer frictions mentioned. It is important to remember that it is not only about what has been said but also about what has not been said. Through this collective discussion and interpretation each focus group leads to about ten customer frictions. However, they are not always relevant to the innovation assignment. An example of a customer friction is described below.

EXAMPLE OF A CUSTOMER FRICTION

Name: Permission horror

Target group: People who have plans to build or renovate

Customer situation:
I have been living in the same house for 15 years. The children are growing up and the house is becoming fuller. In the morning we have to squeeze into the bathroom.

Need of customer:
I am considering some renovations but I was told that I need permission from the local council.

Customer friction:
I have heard so many contradictory stories from friends and neighbours regarding the local council and the building inspection and now I am not sure how best to apply for the permission.

A focus group is organised for each target group. It is not uncommon to produce almost 30 customer frictions from three target groups, as in the example of the innovation assignment for FORTH New Mobility Services of Univé. At the end of the chapter you will find the top three customer frictions in the case study FORTH New Mobility Services.

Due to the fact that online tools for qualitative research have developed much in the past years, it gives interesting possibilities to get customer insights online. These internet tools are very practical, especially if the target group includes people from all over Europe and/or other continents.

INSPIRING INSIGHTS BY TAKING AN ONLINE LOOK AT THE CONSUMERS AT HOME

There is a whole range of qualitative online tools with which the consumer challenges us to take a look into their lives and to share their behaviour, motives, needs and emotions. Through inspiring assignments they are invited to share their story.

The online research is used to get hold of the 'problems' which the consumer experiences with a product, to show their habits in the product field and to make online observations: when, how and why they use a specific product or service.

The output of this discovering journey can be designed in three ways:

1. An online profile through pictures and words

The consumer receives pictures of different brands, activities, products, hobbies, TV programmes, magazines and so on.

They are asked to click on the pictures which represent them the best. Thereafter they see an overview of all the pictures they have chosen on one screen. They are then asked to describe the image of themselves which they have created through the pictures. This leads, even for the consumers themselves, to unexpected insights.

2. An online mood board

The consumers are invited to express their feelings and emotions regarding the category, product or brand by making an online mood board. The pictures have been arranged in certain categories (such as emotions, situations, atmosphere and so on). They can determine how many pictures they want to place on the mood board and can also enlarge or reduce the pictures.

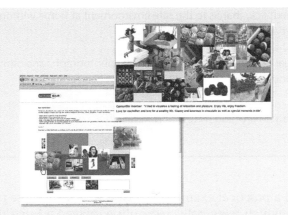

Subsequently they are asked to express, in their own words, what is important to them and with a marking tool they can show the most important subjects. This automatically provides a list of priorities.

3. Photograph diary

To get a better insight in the use of the product, we ask the consumers to take photographs of themselves, their family and their living conditions as well as how they use the products (to prepare a meal, for example). This gives an excellent insight in the daily life of the consumers and how they use the products.

What do online tools produce?

- Consumers share their experiences, feelings and motives.

- Honest feedback, thanks to the safe environment at home without the intervention of an interviewer or moderator.
- Many and deep consumer insights.
- More visual output such as mood boards, photographs and short films.
- Quicker and cheaper than traditional research.

Jaap Vessies
Business Unit Manager NPD and Innovation Research
Metrixlab

Below you find a practical example of a new and distinctive product where the customer insights, which were collected online, played a huge role. This research formed the foundation for the 'me-time' magazine *Flow*, which Sanoma Publishers launched in the Netherlands in November 2008. And it is a great success.

ONLINE QUESTIONS WITHOUT QUESTIONING: INNOVATION CASE *FLOW*

About a year before the introduction of the magazine *Flow*, I as the developer at Sanoma received the concrete task to develop a magazine concept that would capitalise on the growing health market. Desk research produced stacks of useful figures and insights. However, while analysing these reports I still had the feeling that there was more to it, that health is for both the researchers and the respondents a topic where subjective assumptions and socially acceptable answers could be a huge pitfall. After all, health is always associated with sport, balanced eating, and prevention and cure.

For a new product in the competitive magazine market, the existing research data and methods were not enough to produce a distinctive concept. It was necessary to expose the underlying need. I had to do something else, but how? I did not want to use a questionnaire, as it wouldn't bring the deeper meaning to the surface and I didn't want a qualitative interview session as the results would not be concrete enough to deviate from the original assignment.

Questions without questioning

When you are looking for the deeper meaning, the spirit of the time, it is important to question without questioning. From my experience with brainstorming techniques I know how much creativity and opinion you can get from people. While examining a few co-creation cases I saw how you can brainstorm with large groups online. I realised that in this way I could combine the qualitative and quantitative research not only because you can literally count the number of pictures but also by applying possible semantic techniques whereby you can process qualitative open questions in a quantitative way. Furthermore, it produces interesting quotes and the result is visual.

The most important aspect was not to mention the word 'health' during this research. For this reason we spent much time with formulating the brainstorm theme. This resulted in an online research whereby hundreds of respondents where asked to brainstorm around the theme 'to feel good'. In only one week they expressed their feelings and thoughts online in three steps through mood boards, diaries, card grouping, word associations, statements and irritations. I wanted the respondents to decide for themselves at which moment they found it relevant to mention the word 'health'.

The real need

The research showed that more can be generated when the focus is not on health, as health usually has negative associations such as 'have to' and 'illness'. Women saw health more as a basic condition, almost a necessary evil, to be able to do and maintain things. Based on this research I could prove that health was not the opportunity in the growing market but that the potential lay in 'time for yourself'. This time is necessary to re-charge so that you can give again, because 'to be able to give to others' was a very important indicator to 'feeling good'. However, to make time for yourself and to rest once in a while is still considered egotistical and this is totally forbidden for these women. Other key elements around this theme were: 'work towards solutions'; 'not pedantic'; 'can' instead of 'must'; 'positive'; 'comforting' and 'genuine' instead of 'pretentious'. 'To exercise' did not appear in the top 10 of the needs mentioned!

It was in-depth research and a few respondents reacted spontaneously after it was completed with: 'mentally it was a stiff research, but I hope that it has given others as much food for thought as it has given me', and 'a research which opens your eyes'.

This online research was the first phase in the development process which eventually led to producing the magazine *Flow*. *Flow* is a 'me-time' magazine aimed at women between 30 and 45 who have a busy but good life. It is a modern magazine with surprisingly different kinds of paper and creative extras. It also contains completely different columns which distinguish it from other women's magazines. It has five permanent sections: Feel Connection, Spoil Yourself, Live Mindfully, Simplify your Life and the *Flow* Mini Book.

The follow-up steps in this innovation project were also tackled differently from what is usually done at Sanoma with the main purpose that it should be distinctive in all aspects, like magazine design, organisation, launching and business model. Each aspect has an interesting innovation story. *Flow* was launched in November 2008.

Anita Mooiweer
Head of Business Development
Sanoma Publishers

5.4 EXPLORING TRENDS

Trends also produce inspiration for new product or service ideas. Roothart and Van der Pol distinguish between three types of trends: micro-, maxi- and megatrends.[3] Micro-trends are market trends. They are developments within a specific market and have a lifespan of zero to five years. An example of a micro-trend is the emergence of real-life soaps on TV. Maxi-trends are all about the development of the wishes, needs and behaviour of consumers. Their lifespan is longer: five to ten years. An example is the search for authenticity. Megatrends are social developments which go beyond the level of the individual consumer. They are broad social trends with a lifespan of 10 to 30 years and an example is the continual individualisation.

The most interesting source of inspiration for new products or services is future market trends. The challenge lies in anticipating new products for the market based on these trends. However, to look for and discover these market trends you have to look far ahead, and then convert the megatrends into maxi-trends (what does this mean for the consumers and companies?). And then convert the maxi-trends into market trends (what does it mean for my behaviour in the market?). The market trends derived in this way can be an excellent source of inspiration for new product ideas. The ten crucial consumer (maxi) trends for Trendwatching.com described below can form an effective starting point.

TEN CRUCIAL CONSUMER TRENDS

1. *Business as unusual.* Forget the recession: the societal changes that will dominate 2010 were set in motion way before we temporarily stared into the abyss.
2. *Urbanity.* Urban culture is the culture. Extreme urbanization, in 2010, 2011, 2012 and far beyond will lead to more sophisticated and demanding consumers around the world.
3. *Real-time reviews.* Whatever it is you're selling or launching this year, it will be reviewed 'en masse', live, 24/7.
4. *(F)luxury.* Closely tied to what constitutes status (which is becoming more fragmented), luxury will be whatever consumers want it to be over the next 12 months.
5. *Mass Mingling.* Online lifestyles are fuelling and encouraging 'real world' meet-ups like there's no tomorrow, shattering all clichés and predictions about a desk-bound, virtual, isolated future.
6. *Eco-easy.* To really reach some meaningful sustainability goals this year, corporations and governments will have to forcefully make it 'easy' for consumers to be more green by restricting the alternatives.

---

3   H. Roothart and W. Van der Pol (2203). *Van trends naar brands.* Deventer: Kluwer, p. 11.

7. *Tracking and alerting.* Tracking and alerting are the new search, and 2010 will see countless new info list services that will help consumers expand their web of control.
8. *Embedded generosity.* Generosity as a trend will adapt to the zeitgeist, leading to more pragmatic and collaborative donation services for consumers.
9. *Profile Myning.* With hundreds of millions of consumers now nurturing some sort of online profile, 2010 is a good year to introduce some services to help them make the most of it (financially), from intention-based models to digital afterlife services.
10. *Maturialism.* It will be even more opinionated, risqué, outspoken, if not 'raw'; you can thank the anything-goes online world for that. Will your brand be as daring?

Source: www.trendwatching.com. One of the world's leading trend firms, trendwatching.com sends out its free, monthly Trend Briefings to more than 160,000 subscribers worldwide.

To help you with the conversion of trends, Checklist 7 gives a convenient trend list. Should the innovation assignment demand it, organise a special trend workshop during the first week of the stage Observe and Learn as no visits to any sources of inspiration have been planned yet. Relevant trends can serve as a source of inspiration for new product ideas during the new product brainstorming session in the phase Raise Ideas.

5.5 EXPLORING TECHNOLOGY

Besides customers and trends, technological developments can also serve as a source of inspiration. In a technologically driven company it is usually the reason for the creation of new commercial applications. However, it can also be an important source of inspiration for non-technological companies or markets. Technology influences our behaviour. Consider the influence that Information and Communication Technology (ICT) has had on our behaviour over the last decade. We can always be in contact (wireless) with almost everybody, use the internet as a quick means of communication or sales and the concentration of the media to an 'all-in-one' iPhone type: music, photos, TV, telephone, agenda, email and so on. With the introduction of the iPads and E-readers we have become even more digital. ICT has influenced many traditional markets such as newspapers, insurances, travel agencies, toys and music.

Good insight into technological development can be found worldwide and in specific fields. You do not have to invent it yourself and it is recommended that you make use of the available knowledge of technologically orientated organisations, wherever they may be. You will find technological resources in your own country as well, such as Technical Universities, research centres linked to the government or research organisations linked to larger technological groups such as Nokia, Philips, IBM or Vodafone.

So get into contact with market leaders such as Microsoft, IBM or Cap Gemini or other companies who are involved in the 'best practice' in the timely anticipation of new technology regarding their product or service portfolio.

5.6 EXPLORING INNOVATION OPPORTUNITIES

During the kick-off workshop, innovation opportunities were selected and concrete sources of inspiration were mentioned in order to get inspiration. Each innovation opportunity was adopted by one core team member who then contacted the selected source of inspiration and visited them in order to explore the opportunity. In this way he/she searches for 'best practices' of different companies as well as valuable practical experience gained by others. Shortly after the kick-off it can be useful to hold one core team member meeting where each team member presents their expedition plan to the others. You will find that some team members often have a measure of resistance or hesitation when it comes to contacting a company they do not know. This is normal. Offer them a helping hand by preparing an introduction together. My experience has shown that managers of other organisations are usually more than willing to meet you. The Observe and Learn stage of six weeks is relatively short and you have to insist that they make appointments quickly, otherwise they will not succeed before the brainstorming session starts.

A brilliant and rapid start can be made by making an extended worldwide web search for each innovation opportunity. You will help the core team members enormously when you provide them with this search. Personally I always make use of a professional Flemish web searcher, Marc Heleven of 7 Ideas. In this way each core team member receives a presentation, a week after the kick-off workshop, about what is currently happening in the world regarding his subject, theme or domain. Below you find seven tips for a really innovative web search.

TIPS FOR A REALLY INNOVATIVE WEB SEARCH

How can you quickly find ideas, inspiration and innovation opportunities on the web? Stop searching and find with these seven tips right away the most unique and relevant websites.

1. Offline preparation

Do not start to Google right away. You better take a blank sheet and prepare your web search meticulously:

- What are the five to seven key terms of my query?
- Search not only in English, and translate the most important key words in three languages (use Google Translate).

- Imagine the perfect page that answers your question. What is the ideal answer? Use this literally as the search term.

2. Use all of Google

Behind the 'sober' home page of Google search are hundreds of extra search options.

- Always use Google Advance and select desired language, country, file type, date.
- Search using at least three keywords and use quotation marks as words belong together.
- Google has many special channels. Explore your query also in Google images, scholar, video, news, blogs, directories.

3. Solo brainstorming

You are now in the middle of your query. Time to just abandon it. After all, you are looking for something that you do not know – and therefore you cannot ask Google. So do your best to come up with ideas yourself and hope that you find your evidence on the web. Make a list of more than 50 new product or service ideas about your query. The crazier the better. Then go in search of these imaginary products. You'll immediately go to sites you would not believe.

4. There is much more than Google

Time to leave Google. Because Google only displays a fraction of the web. An ideal starting point is http://www.browsys.com/finder/. You will find many well-classified search engines (general, images, videos, news, social, files, reference, academic). Immediately you notice that you can search across various formats.

5. Search in other languages

Install the Google toolbar. This allows you to instantly translate foreign language sites to English. The translation is not perfect but gives enough on what it is about. Are you looking, for example, for food innovations or gadgets? Search in Japanese. So imagine beforehand which countries may have considerable expertise or experience in your innovation opportunity. And explore the web in the subsequent languages.

6. Deep web search

A lot of information is not traceable directly through Google. There are various sources (large databases, libraries, archives) that you need to search directly. You should therefore search (via Google) for main sources around your problem, and then explore these sources one by one with your main keywords. You can search deeper by multiplying smart. Say you have a very well hidden source around your query. Search Google and you will find out who is talking about this site. You probably find another good source. Then, if you combine the two sources into Google, you'll probably find a third and fourth. And if you combine all four sources, you will discover a site where someone has already gathered all around your query.

7. Find ideas from other sectors

Three tips to combine ideas from other worlds with your theme.

- RSS feeds: subscribe not only to sites around your own professional field but also subscribe to a dozen other sectors or areas of interest.
- Find a (non-)related sector or industry where the innovation rate is higher than in your domain. Check if you can translate these innovations to your sector. For example: how to avoid queues at the supermarket? Then go looking around for all the innovations in reducing traffic jams on the highway.
- Make a list of the 10 most innovative companies. Imagine how these pioneers would innovate around your subject. For example: how would Nike innovate public transport? How would Virgin design a new mobile phone design? How would Cirque du Soleil renew the catering business?

Marc Heleven
Professional Web Searcher
www.7ideas.be

The feedback of the visits regarding innovation opportunities can be done in a simple format. The core team members relate back to printed sheets, one for each visit, with answers to the following three questions:

1. What have I seen/heard?
2. What has caught my attention?
3. What can we learn from this?

The progress of each innovation opportunity will then be discussed during the Observe and Learn workshop. By sticking all the feedback reports on a large innovation opportunity sheet, you see the results of the discovery grow. If everybody takes photograph of the person they have spoken to, that will give it an even livelier image.

5.7 FEEDBACK FROM OBSERVE AND LEARN WORKSHOPS

The members of the core team go hiking for six weeks. Through this they get new impressions and record them, digitally. While they are away, the facilitator organises four Observe and Learn workshops of half a day each, preferably in the innovation room. During these workshops the core team members can share their experiences with each other as well as the extended team members. It is very important that you ask each member to 'wait with their judgement' and to make sure they do. The moment one starts to judge, it will not work; you stop discovering and you go back to the paved and smooth roads of before.

During the six weeks you will also notice that the innovation room starts filling up with innovation opportunity sheets, more than 30 customer friction boards, feedback through photos of the customer visits, trends and new technologies. At the last Observe and Learn workshop the ideation team, under the guidance of the facilitator, choose the most promising innovation opportunities and customer frictions. At this time I usually give the internal client a wild card. The chosen innovation opportunities and customer frictions are set under the spotlight during the brainstorming session in the next stage. This also goes for the most favourable trends and technologies. In this way they all serve as concrete 'idea triggers'. Checklist 8 provides you with a programme for the Observe and Learn workshops.

During the Observe and Learn stage the participants have enough time to allow their experience in the market to sink in and to think about it quietly. From the moment that the innovation assignment has been given, the subconscious is working and many ideas will come to mind. This is great as the participants can write these ideas in the idea notebook which they received at the kick-off workshop and it ensures that no product idea is lost during this phase.

5.8 PITFALLS

It is possible that you will come up against obstacles because there are many pitfalls in the practice. Below you will find five of these obstacles which you might encounter during the Observe and Learn stage, followed by some advice on how to handle the situation.

1. Participants Hesitate to Make the Call for an Appointment

Members who are less outgoing find this quite difficult especially when they think they have nothing to contribute and are only going to collect information.

Reaction: Try to remove their fear. In practice people usually enjoy talking to other people who are only listening and not contributing.

2. Participants Find Talking to Customers Scary but Want to Admit It

Many team members have never spoken to customers and they probably do not even feel a connection with them. This is understandable, especially when you, as a product developer aged, say, 25, have to visit the top manager (aged, say, 58) of a business client. Or the opposite; when you as the production director (aged, maybe, 55) have to go to a community centre to observe how young people associate with each other.

Reaction: Calmly go through the 'Tips for customer visits' (Checklist 6) with the whole team. It might also help when you give the participants the chance to visit customers in pairs. I have found that the comment 'they are also just people', has helped much. Furthermore, there is special training available where you can learn how to observe the customer in the best way.

WHAT'S HOT?

3. Participants Cancel just before the Workshops Start

There are sometimes internal participants who cancel beforehand, usually because of a too heavy workload or due to pressure from their management.

Reaction: When you know that this is happening, discuss it with the participant and his manager. If you do not react now, it will happen constantly. Others might follow and that will influence the quality of the process (and the results). It is a good idea to collectively set up some rules during the kick-off workshop, one of which should be that if you participate you go all the way, and that goes for the management as well. If not, they let the group down. Only ask for support from the top management when it is really necessary.

4. A Few Team Members are Wondering Where All This is Leading

During the Observe and Learn workshop you might notice from their closed attitude that some participants believe it is all going too slowly. Apart from that, they are not even allowed to pass judgment.

Reaction: For managers who in their hectic work environment have to make decisions constantly it is not easy to sit in a session where they are not allowed to judge. If this concerns one individual, talk to him or her separately. However, if there is more than one, discuss it in the group. Probably someone who is enthusiastic enough will convince the others of the usefulness of it all.

5. They are Already Coming up with Ideas for New Products

During their visit to the customer and the Observe and Learn workshop, many product ideas develop spontaneously.

Reaction: This is great. Ask the participants to write them in their idea notebook which they received during the FORTH kick-off workshop. Tell them to keep it by their bedside or to take it with them to the bathroom, as many a good idea arises there. In the next stage during the brainstorming session all notebooks and ideas are laid out.

5.9 CASE STUDY: FORTH NEW MOBILITY SERVICES: OBSERVE AND LEARN

Before Christmas I contacted Marc Heleven and asked him to do a worldwide search for interesting initiatives of the five chosen innovation opportunities. The core team members were able to download it at the beginning of January. Shortly after New Year, Bart circulated the first digital newsletter in order to keep the FORTH project at the forefront of their minds.

Core Team Meeting

For the first time since the kick-off, the core team met again on 10 January. For every innovation opportunity we discussed their plan of action. In this way the core team members were given a little push over the threshold. For the innovation opportunity: 'links to other types of transport', core team member (Aletta Dokter) made appointments with the following sources of inspiration:

1. Schiphol (Amsterdam Airport)
2. OV 9292 (Public transport)
3. Department of Health and Social Security
4. Q-Park (Parking)
5. The councils of large cities
6. Martin van Arendonk (internal Univé)
7. NS (Dutch Railway)

I then gave a short insight training. I explained in a practical way how you can discover frictions by customers, as they will have to do this themselves during the three focus groups in the coming weeks.

Individual Customer Visits

Besides examining innovation opportunities the core and extended team members must visit two customers at home to look for insights with regard to new mobility services. Most of the team members admitted that this was a scary thought. Not everybody has the courage to visit people, despite the attempts from Bart and me to spur them on. However, later these visits became an unforgettable experience. At the four Observe and Learn workshops everyone gave an account of their visits.

Focus Groups

The innovation assignment is directed at three customer segments. For each segment a focus group is organised with six people from each target group. The purpose of these focus groups is to find out what frictions the customers have regarding new mobility services. The three focus groups took place at three different places in the Netherlands where Univé is well represented. From the Univé database a random sample was selected, personally phoned and invited for the three panels. In practice a very intensive job.

Table 5.1   Focus groups

Focus group I	Focus group II	Focus group III
Six customer types: green (calm and sensible)	Six customer types: yellow (neat and social)	Six customer types: red (enthusiastic and pleasant)
Hotel Assen	Hotel Wientjes	Golden Tulip
15 January 18.00–21.00	1 February 18.00–21.00	6 February 18.00–21.00

After the group discussion the core team members generated, between 21:00 and 22:30, as many relevant customer frictions as possible. These frictions were written on so-called friction boards. A video recording of each focus group was also made. With this, the frictions could be shared at the Observe and Learn workshops with the whole FORTH team present. That is, if the video recordings had succeeded. Unfortunately, the personnel of the video company were not very professional in the formatting of the video recording, as was evident at the first focus group in Assen, when the recording failed.

Four Observe and Learn Workshops

For four weeks in a row the results of discovery experience was submitted at the Observe and Learn workshops where all participants, also the extended members, were present. By doing this every week workshops also served as a motivation for the core team members to get on with their explorations. The Observe and Learn workshops also had an inspiring function for the extended team members. These took place at the FORTH innovation room at the office of Univé in Assen. The discovery from the previous week was shared in a fixed format: What did I see or hear? What caught my attention? What can we learn from this? Important to remember is that during the discovery and submitting it is necessary to delay judgement. There are some practical team members who have problems with the length of the Observe and Learn journey. They find it very difficult to delay their judgement for such a long period of time. They would rather, when they get an idea during the Observe and Learn stage, start working on it immediately. But that is why they have an idea notebook which was given to them at the kick-off workshop. Rather quickly, during the Observe and Learn phase, the FORTH innovation room starts breathing an atmosphere of new mobility services. Often other co-workers of BU Indemnity Insurance took a look during their lunch break as the innovation room was strategically chosen next to the canteen!

During the six weeks of the Observe and Learn stage there was an important swing in the perception. After the submission of the elaborated web search and after the first discovery conversations by the core team, a feeling of 'there is actually so much' developed. With this came the doubt as to whether Univé could add anything more. However, in the three focus groups, so many customer frictions regarding new mobility services were revealed that in the last two Observe and Learn workshops the feeling changed to 'there are actually many opportunities'. At the last Observe and Learn workshop the team decided to take all five innovation opportunities to the brainstorming session. They had the impression that each innovation opportunity could become fertile ground for good ideas. Twenty-seven customer frictions were revealed in the three focus groups. The team chose seven which, in the light of the innovation assignment, they believed to have the most potential for coming up with good innovative solutions in the brainstorming session.

The top three customer frictions were:

1. Name: Fear to negotiate

    Target group: 80 per cent non-negotiators

    Situation: I buy another car from a garage or private person.

    Need: I do not want to pay too much, and I want a fair price.

    Friction: I do not dare to negotiate.

2. Name: No alternative

    Target group: Economical drivers

    Situation: I drive a car but it really costs too much.

    Need: I would like to drive more economically.

    Friction: Current economic alternatives such as car sharing, car rental, Greenwheels or public transport does not meet with my needs.

3. Name: Moral objections

    Target Group: The majority

    Situation: I know that driving a car is bad for the environment.

    Need: I do not want to lose the freedom of owning a car.

    Friction: I am troubled with more and more moral objections.

On 12 February we ended with the last workshop in the stage Observe and Learn. It was a stage which demanded much energy from the participants but also a stage from which they received much energy and inspiration. Everyone was looking forward to the brainstorming session three days later.

5.10 PRACTICAL CHECKLISTS

CHECKLIST 6: TIPS FOR CUSTOMER VISITS

The ways in which the ideation team with innovation assignments immerse themselves in the business-to-business market and the business-to-consumer market are different. In the business-to-business market there are fewer customers and often only a few who are really important for your company. Target groups in business-to-consumer markets are (hundreds of) millions of people. This has an effect on not only the preparation but also the execution of the visits to customers. The preparation for the business-to-business market will be more complex internally as you will have to consult the account or sales manager in the line organisation (make sure they are part of the ideation team).

Tips for talking to the customers

Why?

- The purpose of the Observe and Learn stage is to get internal participants from behind their desks and to immerse themselves in the market by making personal contact with real customers. Customer visits are not optional. Discuss with the ideation team what the real purpose is for the visit to a customer and the best way to approach it.

What?

- Determine with each other what you want to find out through these customer visits. Draw up a list of questions which you want to be answered.

Who?

- Based on what you want to find out, determine who will be the best customer to visit. Users or non-users of the product or service? Customers who are loyal buyers or critical ex-buyers? Figure 5.2 can be of help.

Where?

- Based on what you want to find out and from whom, you try to establish the location where you can observe the customers' behaviour and come into contact with them. Find a user area where the customer is at ease and can show their usual behaviour. For example; the petrol station, home, during the interval at the movies, in a shop or café, mobile phoning while walking, at the computer, in the sports centre or in the playground?

When?

- So when is the best moment? Choose this carefully. Different times of the day can also be an option if you believe it might affect the results.

Which?

- Which internal participants are going on customer visits? Everybody of course, even the extended team members. This can be done in pairs. The advantage of pairs is that it gives confidence and it is more practical when you want to record the experience. This is preferably done on film with a digital camera which can be used to show the other members during the Observe and Learn workshops. It is also important to establish a strict role division as the cameraman/woman will have to record the customers' behaviour in such a way that they do not feel uncomfortable.

How?

- In advance
  - Choose customers from whom you expect to learn much through their behaviour and use.
  - Make it clear that you are using the information for a small scale investigation.
  - Be discreet and don't over emphasise the visit, as it can be annoying.
- During
  - Ensure that during the observation you 'mirror the target group'. This will make customers feel at ease and enlarges your chances of seeing their real behaviour. When you have an appointment with a customer, do it informally by wearing your jeans and jumper. Should you enjoy lunch with them, go into the kitchen afterwards (and help with the dishes if necessary).
  - First observe. Look at how they use a product, for example, mobile phones, or how they prepare, for example, foodstuffs. Which actions do they perform? What do they do in practice? Observe and listen well.

Then question. Why? Why? Why? Talk about their behaviour in a pleasant manner so that they do not clam up. It is not an inquisition, but rather a conversation.

  - Record: ensure that you record the behaviour as well as the conversation on film. This will help you to observe more closely and afterwards you can share it with the other team members.
  - Take a small gift which you can give at the end. It is always nice.
- Afterwards
  - Directly after the meeting, discuss with each other what you have seen and noticed. At the Observe and Learn workshop you can show the film and inform the rest of the team.

Tip: Follow customer-observation training. Learn (again), together with the other ideation team members, how you can look at the behaviour of people with an open mind. There are consultancies that specialise in this type of training.

Tips for conversations with business customers

It will be useful to read the above mentioned tips for conversations with customers. There are a few specific aspects relating to visiting business customers to which I would like to draw your attention:

- Inform them of your involvement in an idea phase for new products and that the conversation has no commercial purpose. Make sure that the account manager does not accompany you but keep him well informed. This should be done not only in advance but also afterwards if feedback is necessary.
- Analyse the company process and specifically choose the parts which you want to observe more closely.
- Choose the people whom you want to observe and with whom you want to have an informal conversation. Make it clear that it is a visit where you are only coming to look, listen and talk to co-workers.
- Tell them that the visit is very important to you personally and that you will appreciate it if they can make time for you.
- Discuss confidentiality immediately. Do not over emphasise yourself (even if you are the CEO of a company).
- Try to influence the conversation in such a way that you do not just get to see snippets of presentations or other corporate promotional material. Should they ask you to take a look at their newly released promotional company film, then be human and say: of course!
- Do the visit in pairs. In business this is normal. As already mentioned, it gives confidence and helps with the recording of the experience. Use a film camera or digital camera so that you can watch it again afterwards and also use it to show the rest of the team during the Observe and Learn workshops. It is important to allocate roles as the cameraman/woman must try to record the customers' behaviour in such a way that they do not feel uncomfortable.
- When you visit the business customer during the day or at their office, dress appropriately, such as in a suit or blue overalls. The overalls are just in case you have to spend the day with a mechanic. In a car together with representatives or mechanics you always find out the most, but don't adopt a specific role. Just be yourself.
- Take a look at where, how and who works with the product. Ask questions at the work place (if possible).
- Observe and listen well.
- Be spontaneous and keep on asking questions.
- Why, why, why?
- Take a gift with you (if it fits the policy).
- Always send a thank you note.

CHECKLIST 7: USEFUL TREND LISTS

Ten global megatrends (Richard Lamb)

1. Time-On-Demand
2. Safety Web
3. Time for sale.
4. Interactive Society.
5. Twinning.
6. Quality of Life.
7. Pure Communication.
8. More Mobility.
9. Experience Industry.
10. Pull Economy

Source: http://www.trendwatcher.com/

Ten megatrends

1. *Emotional Scapes.* Modifying daily routines, returning to the 'child' you never stopped being, hedonism.
2. *Brand Extensions.* Brands stepping outside their traditional boundaries, creating styles, spaces.
3. *Sensory.* Recapturing the sensory world from all sides and in every environment, the connection of the inner and outer selves.
4. *Back to the Past.* Returning to styles, lifestyles, cooking, personal care ... from the past.
5. *Gender Complexity.* The feminisation of society, the unisex universe, the nouveau man.
6. *Family Complexity.* Restructuring of the traditional family unit, singles, gays, 'DINKs'.
7. *Consumption Experience.* Multi-spaces, services that go beyond shopping, leisure within shopping, social marketing.
8. *Age Complexity.* Kids who want to be grown-up and grown-ups who want to be younger, the third generation and its second wind.
9. *Egonomy/Customisation.* Personalisation within globalisation, the margin between what's culturally acceptable and personally differentiating.
10. *Income Complexity.* Targets with high purchasing power that defend anti-luxury standpoints, those with a lesser purchasing power but are seduced by luxury.

Source: http://intrendsmagazine.files.wordpress.com

Ten strategic technologies (Gartner)

1. Virtualisation
2. Business Intelligence
3. Cloud Computing
4. Green IT

5. Unified Communications
6. Social Software and Social Networking
7. Web Oriented Architecture
8. Enterprise Mashups
9. Specialised Systems
10. Servers – Beyond Blades.

Source: http://www.urenio.org

Eight important consumer trends

1. *Status Spheres*. A variety of lifestyles, activities and persuasions, which can be mixed and matched by consumers looking for recognition from various crowds and scenes.
2. *Premiumisation*. According to trendwatching.com it will be about the premiumisation of everything and anything. In other words, no industry, no sector, no product will escape a premium version in the next 12 months.
3. *Snack Culture*. This embodies the phenomenon of products, services and experiences becoming more temporary and transient; products that are being deconstructed in easier-to-digest, easier-to-afford bits, making it possible to collect even more experiences, as often as possible, in an even shorter timeframe.
4. *Online Oxygen*. The idea that consumers need online access as much as they need oxygen.
5. *Eco-Iconic*. Over the past few years, the ECO trend has moved from Eco-Ugly (ugly, over-priced, low performance alternatives to shiny 'traditional sphere' products and services) to Eco-Chic (eco-friendly stuff that actually looks as nice and cool as the less responsible version) to Eco-Iconic in 2008: 'Eco-friendly goods and services sporting bold, iconic design and markers, that help their eco-conscious owners to visibly tout their eco-credentials to peers'.
6. *Brand Butlers*. Instead of stalking potential and existing customers (which is not very 2008), why not assist them in smart, relevant ways, making the most of your products and whatever it is your brand stands for? Remember, giving is the new taking.
7. *Make It Yourself*. With (in particular younger) consumers having come to expect to be able to create anything they want as long as it is digital, and to customise and personalise many physical goods, the next frontier will be digitally designing products from scratch, then having them turned into real physical goods as well.
8. *Crowd Mining*. When co-creating, co-funding, co-buying, co-designing, co-managing anything with 'crowds', the emphasis in 2008 will move from just getting the masses in, to mining those crowds for the rough and polished diamonds. How to do that? Shower them with love, respect and heaps of money, of course.

Source: http://www.trendwatching.com

Fifteen mentality trends

1. The Inevitable Metrosexual Question: Where is the Cowboy in Me?

2. Globalisation's Shift to the East.
3. Cool Wonderlands Evolve into Human Pearls.
4. Living in Stress Society.
5. The Inevitable Rise of Experience Economy.
6. Roots and Wings.
7. Give Me Narratives.
8. Coloured Mood Management.
9. Discount Cool.
10. Secrecy, Please.
11. Cool Creators of Cool.
12. Manipulating Media Society.
13. Empower Me.
14. The Better World.
15. Dolphins in the City.

Source: http://www.scienceofthetime.com

CHECKLIST 8: OBSERVE AND LEARN WORKSHOP PROGRAMME

What?

A feedback session of three to four hours with the core and extended team members to view and listen to each other's experiences of visiting sources of inspiration, customers and focus groups. During the last Observe and Learn workshop (3 or 4) the three top innovation opportunities and the top five customer frictions are chosen. During this stage in the idea phase no product or service ideas are generated yet, so postponing judgement is the order of the day.

Programme:

*   Opening by the project leader (what's new?)
*   Progress of the six–eight innovation opportunities (everyone gets a turn)
*   Feedback of the customer visits (everyone gets a turn)
*   Feedback of customer frictions from the focus group:
    *   Look at parts of the discussion on film fully.
    *   Allow each core team member to explain a few friction boards.
*   Closing by the project leader.

AT THE NEW-PRODUCT BRAINSTORM

6   Raise Ideas

Creativity is mainly destruction: the breaking down of old insights, views, ideas or feelings in order to come up with something new.

(P. Picasso, Spanish artist)

If at first the idea is not absurd, then there is no hope for it.

(A. Einstein, scientist and inventor)

The impossible is often the untried.

(J. Goodwin)

6.1 INTRODUCTION

The development of new product or service concepts forms the *pièce de résistance* of the FORTH innovation method. It is the creative peak of the journey and consists of a two-day new product brainstorming session and a concept development workshop. The new product brainstorm is actually a journey within a journey. It is what the participants have been working towards: a short, intensive process of two days where the new product or service ideas are actually created and developed into product concepts. Personally I find this stage the most exciting as the question arises, 'Will you manage to create really new product or service concepts with the ideation team?' It is a carefully constructed, creative process in nine steps which I have developed in my innovation consultancy. The brainstorming session is led by a facilitator, with the help of a cartoonist. An extra stimulus during this stage comes from the outsiders who will also participate. In this chapter the programme for the new product brainstorm is discussed in more detail. I will also pay attention to a good brainstorming location. A week after the brainstorming session the product concepts will be further developed at the concept development workshop, after which they will be ready for the market research in the next stage.

6.2 BRAINSTORMING: HOW DO YOU DO IT?

Everybody is creative. This might surprise you as possibly you do not think of yourself as creative, or others might even have told you that you aren't. I wonder what you were like as a child. All children are enormously creative. In a child's world everything is possible ('Daddy, there is a crocodile under my bed!'). However, over the years we have been taught much but sadly also untaught. At school we were taught not to go outside the lines, but to stay inside; we have been taught to keep our noses out of other people's business and we have been taught not to ask the awkward why questions with which grown ups have so much difficulty.

In these ways we have lost much of our childlike curiosity, open-mindedness and imagination, exceptional creative characteristics which we can use so well when we have to create new product ideas. We all still possess these characteristics, although they have been lying dormant for so long, and with which you are now going to do something. During the new product brainstorming session you are going to make a huge demand on your own creative talent.

The spiritual father of the brainstorming technique is the American Alex Osborn. In 1941 he, together with his colleagues, created the brainstorming technique and developed it further. He is also one of the founders (and the 'O') of the still worldwide-renowned advertising agency BBDO.

However, brainstorming is difficult. You have probably read about it in Chapter 2 and maybe experienced it in reality. Many little things can go wrong which can have huge consequences. But enough has been said about this. The frame below gives a summary of the dissertation *How the Group Affects the Mind: Effects of Communication in Idea Generating Groups*. In it you will read that ever since the 1950s it has been known that when you work alone you can come up with more and better ideas than when you work in a group. This also applies to the size of the group, as the larger the group the less effective it is.

BRAINSTORMING WITH MORE THAN TWO PEOPLE IS NOT EFFECTIVE

Many people believe that to brainstorm in a group works better than individually. However, ever since the 1950s it has been known that the opposite is true: people come up with more and better ideas when they work alone than when they work in a group. Furthermore, the size of the group also plays a role as the larger the group, the less effective it is. According to research the reason is that the thought process of group members is disturbed by the communication within the group. Yet communication does not only have negative effects, as group members can also stimulate each other and in certain circumstances groups can function effectively as well.

The greatest problem in brainstorming groups is that there is usually one person at a time talking. The result is that the group members often have to wait for the person to finish which leads to the disruption of their own line of thought. They are then not able to expand on their own ideas as their thoughts are continuously interrupted by the words of others. Apart from that they have to follow the discussion in order to contribute when there is an opportunity. This demands attention through which the group members cannot concentrate on their own idea production. These effects are so strong that people in face-to-face groups often generate fewer ideas than the individual working on their own.

It is also possible to exchange ideas via notes or computers. As the group members can write or type at the same time, they do not have to wait for each other. This kind of exchange has, under the circumstances, little stimulating effect in that the ideas of others lead to new associations. The reason why the stimulating effect is so small is that the group members react on the ideas of the others and give too little attention and thought to their own. Communication also has another positive effect as without communication people quickly get the impression that they are running out of ideas and they stop devising new ones. Should ideas be exchanged then they get the impression that there is still a possibility for new ideas and they continue going, which eventually leads to higher production.

The research suggests two ways in which to make group sessions more effective. Firstly, it is recommended that the ideas are exchanged without having to speak out aloud. The ideas of others must be available the moment you need them, in other words, when your own line of thought does not generate any more new ideas. Secondly, the group can be divided into pairs. The advantages of working in pairs are that you do not have to wait that long for the other person, you have immediate access to the stimulating ideas of the other and a relatively high perseverance.

Source: Bernard Nijstad (2000). Summary of the thesis: *How the Group Affects the Mind: Effects of Communication in Idea Generating Groups.* www.cocd.be

Why then do I recommend a two-day new product brainstorming session with 14 participants? Luckily we have had other insights into brainstorming after the 1950s. In those days it was acceptable that everyone who participated could spontaneously shout out their ideas, which led to chaotic situations whereby individual thought process was constantly interrupted. Furthermore, most participants in large brainstorming groups had to wait a long time before they could unload their ideas, which caused ideas to disappear before there was a possibility to even mention them.

For this reason, and after much experimentation, the brainstorm approach in our new product brainstorming session is done differently. With the generating of new ideas the participants first get the opportunity to do this in silence. They write their ideas on a post-it – each idea on a separate post-it. The facilitator then 'harvests the post-its'. In addition to this they ask the participants to read their product ideas out loud. This has a very stimulating effect on the others as they are encouraged to keep on listening to each other and to elaborate on the ideas themselves. The positioning of the participants in the room also has a stimulating effect as they are sitting in a horseshoe formation (without tables) and can see each other clearly. In this way the idea of one participant is a source of inspiration for the other. Brainstorming in this way usually leads to, after the first spontaneous brain dump, hundreds of post-its on the ideas wall. As participant and facilitator it gives you a great feeling.

6.3 THE NEW PRODUCT BRAINSTORM

Figure 6.1   Creativity is a choice not a gift (© Bart Knegt)

The two-day new product brainstorm demands thorough preparation from both the facilitator and the ideation team leader. This preparation starts as soon as the decision is made to go ahead with the FORTH method and includes searching for a suitable brainstorming location, choosing the right idea generating techniques and preparing tools for the making and evaluating the product concepts generated. It is also a skill to stimulate the team in advance so that they get into in the right 'mood' for the process. In this I usually ask them to choose a recent innovation which was done about the theme of the brainstorm and to bring it with them. A week before the session I send them a card at home with: 'Creativity is a choice not a gift', designed by Bart Knegt (Figure 6.1). You can also give other stimuli which link with the innovation assignment. For example, before a new product brainstorming session for new snacks I asked the participants to write down what they eat during the day. Do not be afraid that people might find this silly. Everybody reacts positively, from the junior product developer to the member of the board of directors. Of course, you have to use the information during the brainstorming session otherwise the request has no purpose and it will eventually work against you.

The build-up of the creative process in the brainstorming session can be divided into a divergent and convergent phase. In two days you will create attractive new product or service concepts by following nine steps. These nine steps are presented in Figure 6.2. Checklist 9 at the end of this chapter will also help you to determine

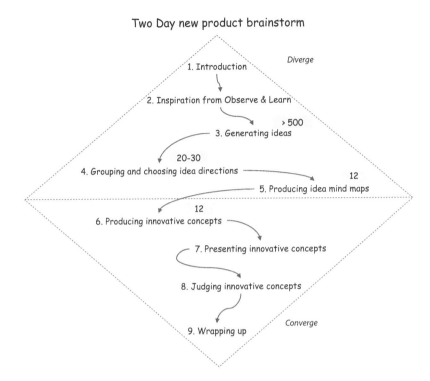

Two Day new product brainstorm

1. Introduction

Diverge

2. Inspiration from Observe & Learn

> 500

3. Generating ideas

20-30

4. Grouping and choosing idea directions

12

5. Producing idea mind maps

12

6. Producing innovative concepts

7. Presenting innovative concepts

8. Judging innovative concepts

Converge

9. Wrapping up

Figure 6.2   The nine steps towards 12 attractive innovative concepts

the purpose for the new product brainstorm. The whole programme is explained step by step, including a global indication of the duration, the techniques to be applied and the points of interest. These nine steps will also be described in more detail later on in this chapter.

Appendix II at the end of the book is another aid for the application of brainstorming techniques. Quite a few of the 30 techniques mentioned regularly form part of the brainstorming programme.

Table 6.1   Thirty brainstorming techniques

Technique	Regular	Optional
A Introductions, energizers and conclusions		
A.1 Photo introduction	X (kick-off)	
A.2 The bunch of keys	X (kick-off)	
A.3 Sequence of play		X (kick-off)
A.4 Getting up you lose your seat	X (kick-off)	
A.5 The dustbin		X (kick-off)
A.6 Energizers	X (all workshops)	
A.7 Finishers		X (all workshops)
B Brainstorming techniques to diverge		
B.1 Spontaneous brain dump	X (brainstorm)	
B.2 Presumptions		X (brainstorm)
B.3 SCAMPER	X (brainstorm)	
B.4 Flower association	X (brainstorm)	
B.5 Biomimicry (nature analogy)		X (brainstorm)
B.6 Comic hero analogy		X (brainstorm)
B.7 Silly things		X (brainstorm)
B.8 Insight game	X (brainstorm)	
B.9 Crawl into the skin of	X (kick-off)	
C Brainstorming techniques to converge		
C.1 Grouping of ideas	X (brainstorm)	
C.2 Selecting idea directions	X (brainstorm)	
C.3 Idea mind mapping	X (brainstorm)	
C.4 With ketchup?	X (brainstorm)	
C.5 Pepper and salt		X (Improvement workshop)
C.6 Improving	X (Improvement workshop)	
C.7 Multi-criteria selection of concept boards	X (brainstorm)	
C.8 I love you	X (brainstorm)	
D Other forms of brainstorming		
D.1 Brainstorm games		X (brainstorm)
D.2 Brainstorm software		X (brainstorm)
D.3 Online brainstorming		X (brainstorm)
E Other techniques		
E.1 TRIZ		X (brainstorm)
E.2 SIT		X (brainstorm)
E.3 Six thinking hats		X (all workshops)

The proposed programme is only a guideline. Should the innovation assignment, the group process or other circumstances ask for something else, deviate from the plan. Each new product brainstorming session is different from the other, especially during the generation phase. For this reason Appendix II also supplies and explains other forms and techniques of brainstorming which is optional and with which the programme can be adapted. For example, brainstorming games or techniques such as TRIZ or SIT can be used for systematic innovation.

The location also determines how the new product brainstorming session will be experienced. This will be discussed in more detail in Section 6.1. There are three other aspects which can help you to create the right atmosphere and thus make the creative process easier.

1. Invite a cartoonist. For years, and with great pleasure, I have been working with the Dutch cartoonist Lex Dirkse, who is also responsible for the cartoons in this book. Cartoons have a very positive effect on the process and result of the brainstorming session. Firstly, with his cartoons he provides the necessary humour regarding the process itself. Furthermore, his cartoons on a user insight or packaging image helps to express the product concept. An image is worth a thousand words. This certainly applies in a new product brainstorming session with an international group where the medium of communication is English and there are possibly only a few native speakers. There might be a few participants who will not be able to clearly express themselves in English (even if they will not admit it) and then the cartoon and brainstorming techniques with images are of great value. Everybody understands a picture. It's that simple.
2. Arrange some music. You can use music to help you to direct the process. It is also an important tool for the facilitator to restrain the energy level. For example, when reading the product ideas on the post-it wall – 'reading music' like *Locatelli* or when evaluating the concept boards – 'evaluating music' like *Vangelis*. You can also allow the group to relax with 'relaxing music' such as *Buena Vista Social Club* or to get them all pepped up with 'pep-up music' such as *I will follow* by U2.
3. Take photographs or films. Capture the whole process, preferably digitally. In this way, during the following FORTH stages, you can allow others to see what the ideation team has done to be able to develop the concepts.

6.4 THE BRAINSTORM LOCATION

You don't brainstorm every day. This certainly applies when brainstorming for a new product with 14 internal and external participants from the company for two days. I would like to warn you not to fall into the trap of brainstorming at the office even if you have the perfect location for it. You then run the risk that your own co-workers will have the tendency of continually going in and out either for a short meeting or for 'urgent business'. A brainstorming location elsewhere reduces this risk considerably. The right location helps with the easing away of fixed thought patterns and it gives extra inspiration. This inspiration can stem from the peace that you find there, the beautiful landscape on which you have a view, the history which is tangible or the great service of the personnel who take care of your every need.

Moreover, you can create an extra dimension by searching for the right location which has a direct link to the innovation assignment. Consider the following:

- A new product brainstorming session about innovative travelling services at Amsterdam Airport, or on board a cruise ship or on board an aeroplane which flies around the world while you are brainstorming.
- A new product brainstorming session about new energy services for large business customers on the Hibernia platform (the largest oil rig in the Atlantic ocean); in one of the largest solar-energy power stations in the world in Parque Fotovoltaico Olmedilla de Alarcón in Spain or in the brightly lit setting of a large horticultural showground in the Westland of the Netherlands.
- A new product brainstorming session about new products for car maintenance in a Kwik Fit branch in England; on the Monza race track in Italy or in the Oshawa Car Assembly Plant, one of the largest car manufacturing companies in Oshawa, Canada.

Of course you can do something less dramatic by finding a lovely and inspiring location close to you.

6.5 THE ROLE OF THE FACILITATOR DURING THE BRAINSTORM

As facilitator you have a contradictory role. On the one hand you are leading the process during the new product brainstorming session and on the other hand you are completely at its service. Even if you are standing in the spotlight, the function of guide is also a serving function. The programme of the new product brainstorm (see Checklist 9) can leave the impression that you have to apply it literally – but be warned. Even though the structured approach has proven its value, it is at the same time only an outline guide in pencil. If there is reason to deviate from this route, because heavy rain showers have made the way impassable and risky, then do it. I have fallen into this trap as well, when I wanted to go through all the intended idea-generating techniques in the original programme while the participants were sitting there like squeezed-out lemons. At the end of the day it is a huge pitfall. As facilitator at that time I was not that fresh either. Always try to remember in this situation that the facilitator must steer the process and that the intended programme must not steer the facilitator. Luckily it will only happen to you once.

The skills necessary to become a facilitator as well as the application of the brainstorming techniques can be developed. Should you want to apply the FORTH method in your organisation you have two options. You can either hire an experienced FORTH facilitator to lead the process or you can train internal facilitators. Both options are possible. At Univé, which have consistently been using the FORTH method, I have trained 15 people with regards to the FORTH method, including managers, project leaders and facilitators. In addition to this I have coached the facilitators, sometimes from the 'back seat' and sometimes from the 'front seat' to apply the FORTH method correctly. Univé VGZ IZA TRIAS is one of the leading insurance companies in the Netherlands and both they and Sanoma Publishers facilitate their own FORTH projects or other innovation processes in a professional way.

Checklist 10 provides other tips for facilitators in practice. The following paragraphs will describe the nine steps of the new product brainstorming session in more detail.

6.6 STEP 1: INTRODUCTION

Throughout the preparation and with the stimuli which they received at home, the core team members, the extended team members and the outsiders come to the brainstorming location with the feeling that it is now or never. It is important to let them 'feel at home' very quickly and to welcome them in a relaxed atmosphere.

Table 6.2   Brainstorm programme (part 1)

Duration	Step	Technique	Points of interest
Day 1: Start 09.00 (entrance from 08.45)			
09.00–09.50	1. Introduction.	• Internal client welcomes all. • Facilitator discusses the programme of the two-day new product brainstorming session. • Go over the rules of the game, the agreements and arrangements. • Participants introduce themselves with objects/photos which relate to the assignment. • They sign a 'mussel pact' (an agreement) regarding confidentiality.	• Create a relaxed atmosphere. • Let the participants, after standing up, sit on another chair.

It is a good idea for the client to formally start the new product brainstorming session after which the facilitator takes over the control and allows the project leader to concentrate on the content. The facilitator then introduces the cartoonist and discusses the brainstorming rules and other arrangements or agreements with the group:

- Privacy outside, openness inside.
- Everybody is equal.
- Postpone your judgement.
- Write or say what you think.
- Listen to others.
- Build on the ideas of others.
- Allow your imagination free reign.
- Be comfortable.
- Mobile phones to be switched off (make arrangements regarding iPhones and other Smartphones).
- Smoking only allowed outside and during the breaks.

For the successful steering of the process it is also useful to have a board, known as the 'parking sign', where important topics which arise during the process but are considered a distraction at that time, can be 'parked'. After the introduction, there is a time to get acquainted as there are two new members in the group, the outsiders. Allow them to get acquainted in an original way, for example with a personal photo or object which they have brought along and which relates to the assignment. Furthermore, it is practical to arrange something regarding confidentiality since there are two people involved from outside the company. I let everybody (even the internal members) sign a simple declaration which I call the 'mussel pact'. You may skip this step if your company already has a specific non-disclosure agreement which the outsider has signed in advance. At this point it is time to roll up your sleeves and get the group working.

6.7 STEP 2: INSPIRE

In the second step of the new product brainstorming session you look back at the results of the previous stage: Observe and Learn. The reason for this is that the outsiders did not go through this stage and they are curious about the experiences of the team members in the market.

It is necessary to allow the internal client to place the innovation assignment at the centre again. In the brainstorming location all results of the Observe and Learn stage are displayed. Each core team member now gets the opportunity to explain the innovation opportunity they have researched. The project leader then points out the trends, technologies and customer frictions they have discovered. The five customer frictions which are the most powerful are individually discussed. It is a good idea to get short positive feedback from the outsiders about the results. It often happens that they are very impressed about the amount of work already done as well as the quality of the sources of inspiration.

Table 6.3   Brainstorm programme (part 2)

Duration	Step	Technique	Points of interest
10.00–11.00	2. Inspire.	• Project leader presents current position of the company, brand or product group (analysis + examples) (15 minutes). • Internal client discusses innovation assignment (5 minutes). • Core team members provide short summary of the results of the six innovation opportunities (20 minutes). • Project leader shortly discusses trends, technology and a few customer frictions (and how they were developed) and the most powerful top five (15 minutes). • Conclude the inspiring round with the most important aspects noticed by the outsiders (5 minutes).	• The innovation assignment. • Sheets of the innovation opportunities on the wall. • Include all customer friction boards. • Feedback of customer visits on the wall. • Pin up the trends and technological overviews.

Figure 6.3   The inspiration from Observe and Learn at the brainstorm

6.8 STEP 3: GENERATING IDEAS

The main purpose of the first day is to generate new ideas for the products, services or business models. The time allocated for this is four hours. This step is interrupted halfway so that the participants can strengthen the body by having lunch and to allow the mind to freshen up.

The techniques for generating ideas, which are applied now, make use of the inspiration gathered during the Observe and Learn stage. By now, the participants are filled with ideas and it is often only a matter of harvesting these ideas.

Table 6.4   Brainstorm programme (part 3)

Duration	Step	Technique	Points of interest
11.10–12.30	3. Generating ideas (I).	• Film about creativity + explanation of how to brainstorm (post-its and so on) + some brainstorming exercises (30 minutes). • Stimulus 1: set the question from the innovation assignment central to create a spontaneous brain dump (50 minutes).	• Inspire the participants regarding creativity. • Refer to the top idea sheet. • Refer to their ideas in their notebook.
12.30–13.30	Lunch		
13.30–16.15	3. Generating ideas (II).	• Stimulus 2: Facilitator: three to five favourite innovation opportunities brainstorming in separate groups (40 minutes). • Stimulus 3: Facilitator: five customer frictions as central point + full brain dump (40 minutes). • Stimulus 4: Facilitator: International solutions for frictions + brain dump (40 minutes). • Stimulus 5: Facilitator: trends and technology as central point in separate groups + brain dump (45 minutes). • Possibility: Silly things technique.	• Make sure that customer insights are presented on nicely designed sheets.

A short explanation of the way in which to brainstorm is given at the beginning, after which it is a good idea for the participants to practise how to brainstorm in order to inspire them to creative thinking and to break through the current patterns of thinking. The aim is to get as many obstacles, inhibitions or restraints out of the way. This can be done through brainstorming exercises or to show a short film about creativity. Personally I find the film very useful.

The generating of product or service ideas starts with the innovation assignment, followed by the task: write down all new product ideas which come to mind. This is called the brain dump. At last, the participants can let go of their ideas, which they have been waiting to do since the kick-off workshop. Remind them of their idea notebooks which they have with them and they are now allowed to get everything off their chests. The new product ideas, which are read out by the participants, lead to new ideas from the others, which lead to more new ideas again and so on. This is the kind of snowball effect you want to achieve. I usually start the brain dump with one of the outsiders as it helps to pull the brainstorming session 'outside the box'. After this first technique from which hundreds of ideas are now on display on the brainstorming wall, lunch is served.

After lunch, the group brainstorms around the most attractive inspirations from the Observe and Learn stage. Three to five innovation opportunities with the most potential are central and the most important customer frictions are placed in the spotlight. International solutions for the customer frictions can serve as a stimulus. Should they have discovered promising trends and technologies use these for inspiration as well to generate new product ideas. Furthermore, you can also choose regular creative techniques and games in order to generate more new product ideas.

Figure 6.4   The harvest of more than 500 ideas for new concepts

Appendix II is a good guide for the application of idea generating techniques in all the steps during the brainstorming process. The order in which you use the different techniques is important as you have to choose a technique which takes you further from home each time. In this way you are taken one step away from the concrete innovation assignment in order to come back to the question, which new product or service idea has this generated? When you draw up the programme, make sure you include different types of activities which you can alternate. You can, for example, brainstorm in small groups and then 'harvest' the ideas with the full team. I always alternate full team brainstorming with brainstorming tasks in groups. In this way there is constant movement and it provides energy.

Recently other kinds of techniques for the creation of new products have come to light. These are techniques for systematic innovation. The origin can be found with TRIZ, a Russian acronym for 'Teoriya Resheniya Izobreatatelskikh Zadatch' which means Theory of Creative Problem-solving. The founder is a Russian engineer Genrich Altshuller who during the 1950s was convinced that systematic patterns form the basis of innovation. Fifty years later TRIZ scientists have analysed more than two million patents. The most important conclusion that can be drawn from this is that innovation can be converted to 40 principles. Furthermore, it seems as if the evolution of technological advances is happening according to predictable patterns. The traditional TRIZ method is a very strong but complex method and not easily accessible to people without a technical or scientific background. Over time other systematic innovation techniques, for example SIT, derived from the TRIZ method, have been developed and are simpler to apply. SIT, Systematic Creative Thinking, functions on the basis of five to seven approaches. My experience is that both these techniques can be very useful during a new product brainstorming session. (For a more detailed explanation see Appendix II.)

If you have completed a few rounds of generating new product ideas, the chance is great that the energy level of the group decreases as brainstorming is both mentally and physically exhausting. Directly after lunch or towards the end of the afternoon the concentration weakens and a 'healthy' reluctance develops. The facilitator must be able to 'feel' when this happens as continuing will become a pitfall. Personally I have fallen into this trap as well. It only generates resistance. At a time like this you need a different activity which can be present at the brainstorm location itself. Go outside, go for a walk, canoeing, rowing, golfing or cycling. However, if time is a problem it could be effective, if the group is up to it, to interrupt the brainstorming programme for a so called energiser. A short physical exercise programme in the brainstorming location through which much energy can be generated (see Appendix II). Before you realise what is happening you are sitting on your knees in a horse race or you are 'in touch' with your toes or you are swinging to the beat of *Sympathy for the Devil* by the Rolling Stones.

After having generated new ideas the participants usually feel like squeezed-out lemons and that is how it should be as the purpose was to get as much out of them as possible. That is then also the sign to end the idea generation phase. During the afternoon and at the beginning of the evening the number of post-its will have steadily grown. It is not unusual to have more than 500 crazy new ideas hanging on the wall – an impressive sight, such an ideas wall.

6.9 STEP 4: GROUPING OF IDEAS INTO DIRECTIONS AND MAKING A CHOICE

After the physical activity, step 4 of the new product brainstorming commences with the convergence phase. The art is, without loss of quality, to nominate all the idea directions which are included in the ideas on the ideas wall.

Table 6.5 Brainstorm programme (part 4)

Duration	Step	Technique	Points of interest
17.00–17.55	4. Make idea directions.	• Each member chooses their two best ideas to elaborate and develop into an idea direction (the best idea near by ... the best idea further away).	
17.55–18.15	5. Choosing 12 idea directions.	• Together we go over the idea directions and choose 12 which have the most opportunity, with the internal client having the last say.	

Ask the participants to walk past the ideas wall and to absorb all the product ideas calmly and then to choose two of their favourite ideas which they believe have much opportunity. Don't be worried as it is not only these two ideas which will be developed further. It is all about using the two best ideas as a starting point for the formulating of an idea direction, on a higher abstract level, for the purpose of combining ideas into one direction. Together with the facilitator the members search for a description of the idea direction. Continue this until all the members are of the opinion that all the relevant ideas have been included. This usually produces 25–30 idea directions. The facilitator then asks the members to choose their favourite seven idea directions. This often produces a clear leading group of directions. Sometimes idea directions can be combined and further developed into one new product concept. The follow-up process leaves room for the development of 12 new product concepts. Together with the internal client, the project leader and the team members determine the ranking and then choose 12. The internal client and the project leader get a 'wild card' during this process as it is, after all, their project.

6.10 STEP 5: MAKING IDEA MIND-MAPS

The final step of this very intensive first day, is the making of mind-maps for the 12 strongest idea directions. These mind-maps will serve as the basis for the new product concepts on day two.

Table 6.6   Brainstorm programme (part 5)

Duration	Step	Technique	Points of interest
18.30–20.00	6. Make 12 idea mind-maps.	• We produce a mind-map for each of the 12 idea directions.	• Let the participants do it themselves.
20.00–20.15	7. Conclusion of Day 1.	• We look back and decide whether we are going to convert the 12 mind-maps into concepts the next day.	

During the first FORTH innovation projects, such as FORTH New Mobility Services, we named idea directions and then we grouped all 500 post-its according to the directions. However, we do it differently now as it took up too much time and did not add much value to the process. After having chosen the idea directions, the group makes a mind map for each idea direction: a large flip-chart board where all the members can individually describe their ideas regarding the 'what?', 'for whom?' and 'how?' of each idea direction.

Finally we look back at the first inspiring, yet tiring day of brainstorming.

6.11 STEP 6: CREATING PRODUCT CONCEPTS

The night between Day 1 (the making of idea mind-maps) and Day 2 (the converting of it into concrete new product concepts) is very useful as the team members have had the chance to allow the idea mind-maps to calmly have an impact on them and they have probably dreamt about it. After breakfast they are fresh and energetic and like an arrow shot from a bow, they are ready to make the product or service concepts, with the slogan: Let's get going, dear friends.

Table 6.7   Brainstorm programme (part 6)

Duration	Step	Technique	Points of interest
09.00–12.30	8. The making of the product or service concepts.	• Discuss the programme for Day 2 of the brainstorming session. • Read the innovation assignment again. • Divide the team into groups of three or four. • Ask each group to choose an idea direction which they will develop into a product concept. • Allocate one hour for this task. • Have three rounds in the same way with the same teams.	• Provide 12 concept boards. • Compose the four teams to include different talents. • Make sure that there are magazines and photos at their disposal to make a mood board.

The facilitator, after consultation with the ideation team leader, divides the team into four groups. Each group has to develop one idea mind-map into a new product concept. Dividing the team into groups is very important. Compose them in such a way that they include various talents as this allows for the product concept to be approached from different directions or angles. For a manufacturing company, the group will consist of a marketer, a salesman, a product developer or product manager and one outsider. It is also important that you put members in a group who get along, as the better they get along the better the cooperation within the group.

It is then up to the groups to create the product or service concept while working at separate tables. I would advise you to not send the groups to different rooms as I have had some bad experiences with this in the past. Rather keep them in the same room but at separate tables. I have noticed that when you 'see work' you 'do work', and it is more practical for the participants, the cartoonist and the facilitator when done in this way. During the process of creating a new product concept the participants must have at their disposal the following:

1. A1-format concept boards. An empty sheet of paper on top of it with relevant aspects from the marketing mix of a new product which they must complete, such as: solved customer friction, product or service characteristics, target group, price, sales channel, positioning, expected turnover, margin and introduction date. Choose specific formulations which relate to the sector or the organisation.
2. A large number of magazines with suitable pictures (of the target group) which can help to visualise the sphere of the product, the users, the user moments, the characteristics of the new product or service and the positioning.
3. The cartoonist, who at the request of the group and after a short briefing, draws a cartoon of the new concept or its packaging.

CREATING NEW CONCEPTS

Furthermore, all contributions of Day 1 are still visible in the brainstorming location: innovation opportunity sheets, reports of customer visits, customer friction boards, as well as all the original post-its and all idea mind-maps. Sometimes the creating of product concepts is taken literally, with the help of parts of different products, new innovative product concepts are created. It is outstanding when it is created in this way.

Each group gets one hour for one new product concept. After it has been completed they collect a second idea mind-map from the wall to create another product concept. They continue in this way until each group has developed three product concepts. The groups are not altered because they usually develop their own method for the creating of the new product concept and by not altering the group it accelerates the creating of the second and third product concept. By the end of the morning there are 12 new product concepts in the form of concept boards covered with photos and cartoons (with manufacturing companies perhaps a prototype).

6.12 STEP 7: PRESENTING THE PRODUCT CONCEPTS

The purpose of this step is to allow the participants to be introduced to all the created product concepts. You yourself are also curious as to what was created. In short 'elevator pitches' one of the participants in each group gets the opportunity to present the product concepts. It is normal that a form of rivalry will develop as they believe that what they have created is better than the other creations. As long as this rivalry develops from a feeling of pride, there is nothing wrong with it.

Table 6.8   Brainstorm programme (part 7)

Duration	Step	Technique	Points of interest
13.30–15.00	9. Presenting the product or service concepts.	• Ask individual participants to present each product or service concept shortly but with much enthusiasm (elevator pitch: max. 5 minutes). • Facilitate 'With ketchup?' for each product concept.	• Ask the group to ask questions without judgement. • Stick green post-its on the concept board for valuable suggestions.

The reason why rivalry usually disappears quickly is because the facilitator asks the participants to withhold their judgement. The most important aspect now is that all the participants understand the essence of each product concept. The listeners may ask questions if something is not clear. After each presentation the technique 'With ketchup?' (see Appendix II, C.4) is applied to give the participants of the other groups the opportunity to make suggestions for improvements. During this phase the possibility for new combinations can still be done. After the 'elevator pitch' they are often applauded enthusiastically.

6.13 STEP 8: EVALUATING THE PRODUCT CONCEPTS

For the first time, a judgement of the new product concept is allowed. The concept boards of the 12 new product concepts are now evaluated individually by the participants.

Table 6.9   Brainstorm programme (part 8)

Duration	Step	Technique	Points of interest
15.00–16.15	10. Evaluation of the 12 new product or service concepts.	• Discuss the evaluation criteria for the new concepts (they have been drawn up during the Full Steam Ahead Stage). • Explain the evaluation boards and the way in which it is to be evaluated. • Ask the participants to evaluate all 12 product concepts on all criteria. • Facilitate the 'I love you' technique and ask the participants to stick their heart sticker simultaneously. • Add the number of points for each concept board. • Present the full range from last to first. • Check where the hearts have been placed with the product concepts which have been ranked. • Ask the participants for their first reaction about the ranking.	• Provide 12 evaluation boards. • Play calm evaluation music. • Should the outsiders find it difficult to evaluate the feasibility, then leave it out (for them). • Allow the participants to do the counting. • Check the scores!

The evaluation takes place on the basis of the five or six criteria which were decided during the Full Steam Ahead stage, in consultation with the management in the innovation focus workshop. To allow for the smooth running of this procedure a product concept evaluation board must be provided for each product concept. Figure 6.5 presents an example of such an evaluation form for a new concept in a business-to-consumer market. With the help of stickers the participants evaluate the 12 product concepts individually according to the five criteria. I am completely aware of the fact that the evaluation in this way happens rationally but there is also the possibility to evaluate with feeling. All participants are asked to place a red sticker (in a heart shape) at the new product concept which has captured their heart even if they cannot give a rational explanation for this.

Concept assessment board	Name idea:.. FORTH Innovation method	
Criteria	Stick 1 to 5 stickers for each criterium	Score
1. Total potential sales volume 3 years after introduction in top 10 markets < 10 million: 1 10 - 30 million: 2 30 - 50 million: 3 50 - 75 million: 4 > 75 million: 5		
2. Perceived value for the consumer versus competitive products 100% me-too: 1 low: 2 reasonable: 3 high: 4 100% unique: 5		
3. Feasibility. Does it fit in present R&D and Production expertise and capabilities Very difficult: 1 Difficult: 2 Fairly easy: 3 Easy: 4 Very easy: 5		
4. Cannibalisation on sales of our present product portfolio Very high: 1 High: 2 Reasonable: 3 Low: 4 Very low: 5		
Total score idea		

Figure 6.5   Example of a concept assessment board in a new product brainstorm

In the meantime the tension is mounting. The scores for each concept are counted by the participants and while they cannot contain there curiosity, the facilitator places the concept boards in the correct order. The most supreme moment of the total new product brainstorming session nears: the presentation of the newly developed concepts according to order of attractiveness, in reverse order. The facilitator then discusses the scores for each concept. In most cases a pattern is discovered; for example, the product concepts which have a high score for attractiveness on the market and for turnover, or with a high score for feasibility. We are looking for a new product concept which scores high on all criteria. Those usually stand out anyway. After the first commotion relating to the result has settled, the facilitator then discusses the hearts. Huge similarities are found between the rational and the emotional and you usually find the hearts of the participants at the top five product concepts. If this is not the case and there is a product concept at the bottom of the range with many hearts, then it is a reason to discuss it extensively and to decide there and then how the attractiveness and feasibility can be strengthened or improved.

6.14 STEP 9: WRAPPING UP

The last step concludes the new product brainstorming session. Tired, but very satisfied, the participants react on that which they have created. With pride they look at the concept boards which are still on display in the middle of the brainstorming location. Do not be surprised when someone in the back of the room, accompanied by loud cheering, opens a bottle of champagne.

Table 6.10   Brainstorm programme (part 9)

Duration	Step	Technique	Points of interest
16.15–17.00	11. Wrapping up.	• Check the (wow) feeling about the product concept with the participants. • Allow the participants some space to react independently on the process of the product brainstorm. • Project leader: mention what comes next on the programme. • Internal client: concluding words.	• Arrange for champagne in the brainstorming location.

At the end of a professional process, it is fitting to reflect back on the course of the two-day new product brainstorming session, under the guidance of the facilitator. But also to look ahead to the next meeting for the core team members, the concept development workshop. As was appropriate in the beginning for the internal client to open the brainstorming session, he/she now has the final word as well.

THE PERSONAL EXPERIENCE OF AN OUTSIDER IN A BRAINSTORMING SESSION (A WILD GOOSE)

When you Google 'wild goose' you will find the most mouth-watering recipes, but also someone who knows nothing about a subject. The funny thing about it is that when you know nothing about a certain subject, but you contribute with your creativity and experience, at the end of the innovation session a feeling arises that you have contributed to a delicious recipe.

It is something to be asked, out of the blue, to participate in a two-day brainstorming session without having the opportunity to prepare yourself properly. I like to be creative, but I also want to be embedded in knowledge of and about the client's market. It is no game because it is serious business wherein the client has invested much time and money and for which he expects good progress in the innovation process. In short, with ambivalent feelings, I agreed to participate at a new product brainstorming session as an outsider.

During a two-day session, a good facilitator knows how to create a relaxed atmosphere whereby his choice of music from the iPod is not insignificant. After getting acquainted and carrying out some general observations, the creativity started bubbling. These sessions were expertly led, in a good mix of business principles, business objectives and surprising stimuli through which different creative approaches were developed into more concrete concepts. Involving outsiders in this process is highly recommended. At one of the brainstorming sessions I had no special affinity with the product group, but due to my detachment, I could contribute ideas without restraint, which served as an important stimulus for the expert group. These combinations led to real new ideas and that is what innovation is all about!

In my experience it is an inspirational process whereby hundreds of product ideas can be generated in a very short time, and then funnelled down to 12 concepts. By evaluating on rational grounds, such as feasibility which scores with many, but also on emotional grounds ('To which concept have you lost your heart?') a commitment is created which forms a good foundation for the successful continuation in the organisation.

Looking back I would like to be invited more frequently. Apart from the good personal interaction, the success of an innovation workshop depends strongly on the quality of the facilitator. A top facilitator knows, like no other professional expert, how to connect atmosphere and emotion: an important condition for a successful new product brainstorm.

John Resink is the Managing Partner of CEMC, the added value partners! And advises and supports concerning strategy, change management, innovation and implementation.

www.cemc.nl/

This is an account of the good experiences of an outsider. Luckily everyone always has a good feeling about the results of a new product brainstorm and I am doing everything so that it stays this way. I have tried, on the basis of my experience with this method in practice, to find the answer to the question, 'What causes a satisfied feeling about the end result?' However, I have discovered that this simple question cannot be answered easily. I do not believe that there is one dominant success factor responsible for this feeling but rather the right combination of many, sometimes minor, aspects. Perhaps the metaphor of a puzzle is the most apt. There are many small pieces necessary to complete the puzzle and if you lose one, the puzzle becomes worthless. My intuition can relate this image to new product brainstorming and that is why it is so important to pay attention to every detail. No puzzle piece should be missing. Anyway, 10 pieces which do contribute to the success of the puzzle are:

1. The momentum has been created: it must happen now.
2. An environment has been created where there is no lack of anything and where everything is directed at the achieving of results (a special venue, music, cartoons and so on).
3. You are busy with it for two days consecutively and without any interruptions.
4. The participants have been immersed into the market for six weeks, as a result of which their subconscious has been busy with it for weeks.
5. An effective combination of brainstorming techniques, which have proven themselves in practice, is used.
6. You are constantly stimulated to find 'the forest trails in your mind'.
7. Outsiders bring a different view or opportunity which can help to break through existing patterns in your organisation.
8. Ideas become more concrete over the two days and are tested by hard criteria.
9. Together with your own colleagues you make the product concept.
10. There is a good coach, sometimes almost unnoticeable, who steers with soft hands.

6.15 CONCEPT DEVELOPMENT WORKSHOP

A good feeling is wonderful, but the real test of the new product concepts only comes in the next stage: Test Ideas. During this stage the new product concepts are tested by those, the intended potential customer, who will determine if they are favourable. This means that all product concepts must be presented in a clear and appealing way. For this reason there is still some work to do between the brainstorming session and the market research and so the FORTH method has included a concept development workshop directly after the brainstorm.

During the new product brainstorming session the participants made concept boards which in a way meant putting the new product concept together. As for design and quality, they will differ greatly if only because the one group has more talent and pleasure. However, for the qualitative concept research it is important that all concepts which are going to be tested are well designed and look professional so that the customer can immediately get a good impression of what it is. Should one concept look better than the others then I know what the result of the research will be, therefore there is still much work to be done.

In a FORTH method for concrete physical products the saying 'the more authentic, the better' applies to the concept research. During a concept development workshop you try to go directly from the concept board to a kind of prototype with the help of external visualisers and product developers. That is if the product type allows for this. Unfortunately this is not possible with most of the new product or service concepts. The only remaining option which I frequently use is the writing up of clear and distinct concept descriptions to present to the customers.

The structure of such a concept description consists of the following parts:

- A description of the situation of the customer
- A description of the needs of the customer
- The customer friction
- A clear description of our solution
- The reasons why we are credible to offer the right solution
- An advertising slogan

This format can be successfully used for both business and consumer services. An example of a concept description for Univé Green Driving you find in Section 6.17 for the FORTH New Mobility Services case study.

The core team members, the outsiders and the market researcher, who will investigate the concepts, will participate in this workshop. In five pairs the participants work for an hour to change the concept board into a concept description. After which the five descriptions are discussed with the whole group. There are two sessions in this workshop: a morning session and an afternoon session. It is hard work as some concepts are more difficult to put into 'normal' words than others. Often one concept perishes at this stage either because it has less added value for the target group or because of the practical feasibility. In practice we usually complete 10 product concept descriptions for the qualitative concept research. It is also advisable to present the worked out concept descriptions to the internal client and extended team members. This brings good feedback and you also keep the support.

6.16 PITFALLS

During the new product brainstorming session a lot of things can go wrong. I have noted down four pitfalls. Furthermore, I provide you with some advice on how to act should you come across these situations in your own practice.

1. The Brainstorming Location Is Not Good

Even if you have checked out the location three weeks before, it does not exclude the fact that when you arrive the evening before the brainstorming session, they have started some renovations or the venue next to yours has been rented out to a pop group for three days.

Reaction: Not good is not good. Don't take any risks as it is an important puzzle piece. If possible make some last minute changes.

2. Participants Don't Turn Up

It happens. It could be due to illness, traffic jams or work related.

Reaction: At the starting time, phone the participants who have not arrived yet. You will not be the first person who phones someone who has made an error in their diary. Arriving at ten o'clock is a pity, but better than one day too late.

3 The Facilitator Does Not Pick Up Signals from the Group Sufficiently

You notice that the facilitator does not sense changes in the group and continues with a specific technique for too long or does not take action when someone oversteps the line.

Reaction: Request a short break to stretch the legs. Talk to the facilitator immediately and privately. They will be very grateful. It could be that they are not yet experienced with the programme or something at home might be bothering them. Always remember when you reprimand the facilitator in front of the group, he/she loses all authority with the group.

4. There Is a Great Amount of Doubt with the Participants on the Evening of Day 1

Do not worry as this is usually the case. Even though there are 500 post-its and 12 idea mind-maps, nothing has been completed yet. It is indeed stressful, but these signs are usually positive as it causes the participants to start the second day with much motivation. This also causes the relaxing time in the bar at night to last only for a short while as everyone realises that they have much to do the next day.

Reaction: Assure the participants that all the puzzle pieces will fall into place the next day.

6.17 CASE STUDY: FORTH NEW MOBILITY SERVICES: RAISE IDEAS

During the getting acquainted evening before the kick-off workshop we realised that it was necessary to enrich the group by inviting someone who was creative by nature. For this reason Cock Meerhof joined the group for the last development workshop. Two other outsiders were also invited for the brainstorming session. Richard Stomp received the invitation because, as a creative idea machine, he could raise the 'outside the box' quality of the group. Jan van der Kleij, director of the Verzekeraars Hulp Diensten (Insurers Help Services), was invited on recommendation of the internal client Jan Dijkstra, because of his expertise regarding new mobility services.

Location

The brainstorm location was carefully selected and visited by Bart Schouten and his assistant Renate Mol. They chose Landgoed 't Laer with overnight stay in the nearby Hotel de Zon in Ommen in the Netherlands. Brainstorming on this real estate added something special as the peace and the rich historical wealth had a calming effect on the usually very busy managers of Univé. The hotel, in walking distance from the brainstorming location, had great rooms and excellent cuisine.

The Two-Day Brainstorming Session

The brainstorming session started at ten o'clock which differs from the usual time. There was, however, a very good reason as the internal client, Jan Dijkstra, had a few questions to discuss with the external accountant regarding the arrangement about the annual accounts. That needed to happen. We decided that Jan would see the accountant before the start of the brainstorming session and that we would then meet at the brainstorming location.

The first day of brainstorming started with the presentation of the innovation opportunities and customer frictions which were collected by the team. After a short film about creativity and the correct mindset in order to brainstorm well, we used seven brainstorming techniques to generate ideas:

Stimulus 1: a spontaneous brain dump (with their idea notebooks on their laps).

Stimulus 2: examples of new services of other insurance companies + brain dump.

Stimulus 3: strategy 2015 + brain dump.

Stimulus 4: brand values of Univé + brain dump.

Stimulus 5: five promising innovation opportunities + brain dump.

Stimulus 6: the top customer frictions + brain dump.

Stimulus 7: international solutions for the frictions + brain dump.

This brainstorm produced 696 post-its with rough ideas and catching phrases – a moment of glory for everybody, even though there were some ideas which were duplicated. The grouping of the post-its, which did not run very smoothly, produced 55 idea directions. During FORTH projects later, this convergence approach was improved considerably. Then the team chose the 12 idea directions which had the most potential and were developed into idea mind-maps on the same evening. The 12 idea mind-maps included the following ideas:

- mobile for life
- car-care plan
- car-repair check
- car-purchasing assistance
- car savings
- the green kit

At approximately 20.30 we strolled, weary but satisfied, back to the hotel where we enjoyed dinner together. During dinner the conversation naturally included what was achieved at the brainstorming session.

After a night of 'incubation' the idea mind-maps were made into concrete product and service concepts in the four groups. A time limit of one hour was given for each product concept. Cartoonist Lex Dirkse provided each concept with a suitable drawing which highlighted the essence of the concepts well. Some of the idea mind-maps also changed during this process. The 12 product concepts included:

- member car market
- car purchasing help
- car purchaser
- car savings
- a fixed price driving plan
- members-for-members
- the green kit
- a bicycle plan

Figure 6.6 shows the concept board for the Green Kit concept.

The presentation of the concepts started after lunch. Everyone got the opportunity by using the 'With ketchup?' technique (see Appendix II Thirty Brainstorming Techniques) to improve the ideas to make them stronger. At the end of the brainstorming session, the concepts were evaluated by the individual participants using the six important criteria from the innovation assignment. In addition to this, the participants could award the concept which stole their heart with a heart sticker. In this way each concept was evaluated. For example, the Univé Green Kit, which shared second position, got a total score of 267:

Figure 6.6   The concept board for Univé Green Kit

- number of customers (41 points)
- direct or indirect profit margin for BU Indemnity Insurance (19 points)
- direct or indirect profit margin for the cooperatives (19 points)
- no cannibalisation (67 points)
- strengthens the Univé brand (66 points)
- introduction possible in 2008 (55 points)

Furthermore, the Univé Green Kit received three hearts.

The two-day brainstorming session ended around five in the afternoon. Everyone was pleased with the results and surprised that they were able to produce so much creativity in two days.

Describing the Concept

The concept boards which are produced during the brainstorming session are beautiful but cannot be presented to the customer in this form for the concept test. For this reason the product concept boards are converted into concrete concept descriptions in the week after the brainstorming session. The core team was helped by Karin Hellema, an external market researcher. This was also an intensive process whereby the concepts become even more concrete. The Univé Green Kit was now accentuated and became the Green Pass of Univé:

> Of course I am concerned about the environment and I would really like to do something about it. But comfort and freedom are also important to me. Even though I know that my car is bad for the environment I don't want to lose it and this makes me feel uncomfortable.
>
> This is why Univé has introduced the Green Pass as supplement to the Univé car insurance.
>
> - For a monthly contribution of €5 you will be able to drive CO_2 neutral. You will receive a Univé registration pass, on which the amount of petrol you put in your tank will be counted. You pay the normal price for petrol.
> - Through the purchasing power of Univé, petrol will become cheaper. The purchasing benefits and your monthly contribution will be invested in environmental projects, such as the planting of trees.
>
> The Green Pass. Naturally from Univé

Not every concept survived this stage. With 11 concept descriptions we moved on to the concept research in the Test Ideas stage.

6.18 PRACTICAL CHECKLISTS

CHECKLIST 9: THE NEW PRODUCT BRAINSTORMING PROGRAMME

Table 6.11 The new product brainstorming programme (Day 1)

Duration	Step	Technique	Points of interest
DAY 1: Start 09.00 (Entrance from 08.45)			
09.00–09.50	1. Introduction	• Client welcomes participants. • Facilitator discusses the programme for the two-day new product brainstorm. • Go over rules of the game, logistics and arrangements. • Participants introduce themselves with objects/photos which relate to the assignment. • Signing of the agreement regarding confidentiality.	• Create a relaxed atmosphere. • Let participants after they get up, go and sit on another chair.

Table 6.11   *Continued*

Duration	Step	Technique	Points of interest
10.00–11.00	2. Inspire	• Project leader presents current position of the company, brand or product group (analysis + examples) (15 minutes). • Internal client discusses innovation assignment (5 minutes). • Core team members provide short summary of the results of the six innovation opportunities (20 minutes). • Project leader shortly discusses trends, technology and a few customer frictions (and how they were developed) and the most powerful top 5 (15 minutes). • Conclude the inspiring round with the most important aspects noticed by the outsiders (5 minutes).	• The innovation assignment. • Sheets of the innovation opportunities on the wall. • Include all customer friction boards. • Feedback of customer visits on the wall. • Pin up the trends and technological overviews.
11.10–12.30	3. Generating ideas (I)	• Film about creativity + explanation of how to brainstorm (post-its and so on) + some brainstorming exercises (30 minutes). • Stimulus 1: set the question from the innovation assignment central to create a spontaneous brain dump (50 minutes).	• Inspire the participants regarding creativity. • Refer to the top idea sheet. • Refer to their ideas in their notebook.
12.30–13.30: LUNCH			
13.30–16.15	3. Generating ideas (II)	• Stimulus 2: Facilitator: three to five favourite innovation opportunities brainstorming in separate groups (40 minutes). • Stimulus 3: Facilitator: five customer frictions as central point + full brain dump (40 minutes). • Stimulus 4: Facilitator: International solutions for frictions + brain dump (40 minutes). • Stimulus 5: Facilitator: trends and technology as central point in separate groups + brain dump (45 minutes). • Possibility: Silly things technique.	

Table 6.11   *Concluded*

Duration	Step	Technique	Points of interest
16.15–17.00	Physical activity	• Going for a stroll	• If necessary, do some exercises when the energy level decreases.
17.00–17.55	4. Make idea directions	• Each member chooses their two best ideas to elaborate and develop into an idea direction (the best idea near by ... the best idea further away).	
17.55–18.15	5. Choosing 12 idea directions	• Together we go over the idea directions and choose 12 which have the most opportunity, with the internal client having the last say.	
18.15–18.30 Snacks			
18.30–20.00	6. Make 12 idea mind-maps.	• We produce a mind map for each of the 12 idea directions.	• Let the participants do it themselves
20.00–20.15	7. Conclusion of Day 1	• We look back and decide whether we are going to convert the 12 mind-maps into concepts the next day.	
Conclusion DAY 1: 20.15 checking in and dinner at 20.30			

Table 6.12   **The new product brainstorming programme (Day 2)**

DAY 2: Start 09.00			
Duration	Step	Technique	Points of interest
09.00–12.30	8. The making of the product or service concepts	• Discuss the programme for Day 2 of the brainstorming session. • Read the innovation assignment again. • Divide the team into groups of three or four. • Ask each group to choose an idea direction which they will develop into a product concept. • Allocate one hour for this task. • Have three rounds in the same way with the same teams.	• Provide 12 concept boards. • Compose the four teams to include different talents. • Make sure that there are magazines and photos at their disposal to make a mood board.
12.30–13.30	Lunch		

Table 6.12   *Concluded*

Duration	Step	Technique	Points of interest
13.30–15.00	9. Presenting the product or service concepts	• Ask individual participants to present each product or service concept shortly but with much enthusiasm (elevator pitch: max. 5 minutes). • Facilitate 'With ketchup?' for each product concept.	• Ask the group to ask questions without judgement. • Stick green post-its on the concept board for valuable suggestions.
15.00–16.15	10. Evaluation of the 12 new product or service concepts	• Discuss the evaluation criteria for the new concepts (they have been drawn up during the Full Steam Ahead Stage). • Explain the evaluation boards and the way in which it is to be evaluated. • Ask the participants to evaluate all 12 product concepts on all criteria. • Facilitate the 'I love you' technique and ask the participants to stick their heart sticker simultaneously. • Add the number of points for each concept board. • Present the full range from last to first. • Check where the hearts have been placed with the product concepts which have been ranked. • Ask the participants for their first reaction about the ranking.	• Provide 12 evaluation boards. • Play calm evaluation music. • If the outsiders find it difficult to evaluate the feasibility, then leave it out (for them). • Allow the participants to do the counting. • Check the scores!
16.15–17.00	11. Wrapping up	• Check the (wow) feeling about the product concept with the participants. • Allow the participants some space to react independently on the process of the product brainstorm. • Project leader: mention what comes next on the programme. • Internal client: concluding words.	• Arrange for champagne in the brainstorming location.

CHECKLIST 10: TIPS FOR FACILITATORS DURING THE BRAINSTORMING SESSION

Tips for the preparation:

- Go to the brainstorming location the night before in order to get everything ready.
- Check that all aids are there (flip-chart, projector and so on).
- Discuss the programme with the catering.
- Ask the ideation team leader to also come the night before.
- Make enough concept and evaluating boards.
- Take enough post-its, stickers, pens and Sellotape with you.
- Take a music system (Apple iPod and Bose Sound dock).

Tips to facilitate:

- The role as host:
  - Welcome everyone at the door with a cup of coffee.
  - Provide a relaxed atmosphere at the start.
  - Arrange for a continual provision of fresh coffee, tea, ice water and so on.
  - If possible play some music.
- The role as facilitator:
  - Present the programme in such a way that it is clear that there can be some deviations.
  - Discuss the rules of the game.
  - Step in immediately (gently) when someone oversteps the mark.
  - Step in and call for a time out if you have the idea that someone seriously oversteps the mark and it has an effect on the atmosphere within the group. Talk to the person separately.
  - Make a parking sign to 'park' some topics until the end of the new product brainstorming session.
  - Control the atmosphere and the energy level with music.
- The role as FORTH guide:
  - Contribute to the discussion with contextual comments or directions if and when necessary. Make it clear that you are doing this in a different capacity.

Everybody is unsure of the results of the process. This type of tension is however necessary to allow the participants to function on a high level. Should the tension turn to doubt, intervene. You can mention that, up to now, every person who has participated in such a new product brainstorming session has gone home satisfied.

CHECKLIST 11: NEW PROPOSITION CHECKER

In my innovation consultancy I have developed a new proposition checker. It consists of 10 criteria whereby you can test a new product or service concept. Five are from a customer perspective and five from a company perspective. They can be applied easily and quickly.

Customer perspective:

1. Is it superior?
2. Does it link to what the customer wants?
3. Can the uniqueness of the products be easily communicated?
4. Can it be easily tested?
5. Is it financially or socially risky?

Company perspective:

1. Does it have turnover potential?
2. Does it cannibalise on any of our other products?
3. Does it link to our positioning?
4. Does it fit in our production processes?
5. Does it ask for huge investments?

CHECKLIST 12: THE IDEAL BRAINSTORMING LOCATION

Demands for the location:

1. Peaceful location.
2. Accommodation, dining and brainstorming all under one roof.
3. Not too simple (managers are used too much) and not too luxurious (especially if you have to consider the expenditure).
4. Distance to the airport not too far when working with an international group.
5. Good catering. With regards to food and drink there should not be a lack of anything.

Try and find an intrinsic 'plus':

Find a location which relates to the assignment:

- Brainstorm for a new travelling service while taking a cruise.
- Brainstorm for a new children's product in Disneyland.
- Brainstorm for new energy services for large business clients on the Hibernia platform in the Atlantic Ocean.

Demands for the room:

1. 8–10 metres wide and 12–15 metres long (100–150 m^2).
2. Not on the ground floor.

3.   Enough daylight.
4.   Situated in a peaceful area (not close to a motorway or terrace accessible to others).
5.   Thirty m² of free wall-space to stick post-its and flip-over sheets.
6.   Ten tables along the walls (where boards and products can be placed).
7.   Fifteen chairs placed in a U-shape (without tables!) plus 4 tables with 4 chairs.
8.   Two flip-chart boards with an endless amount of paper.
9.   A projection screen.

Nice to have:

1.   A location where you are the only group.
2.   Windows and doors which can be opened.
3.   Your own terrace.
4.   An outdoor activity close by to relax body and mind (walking trails, bicycling, climbing, rowing).

Beware of pitfalls:

1.   Always visit the location personally (even if they promise you everything over the phone).
2.   Reserve a specific room with the strict instructions that it may not be changed.
3.   Make sure you can stick things on the wall.
4.   Ask who has rented the other rooms (so that you do not end up next to a jam session or a fierce self-searching course or a competitor busy with training).
5.   Always ask whether renovations have been planned in the hotel or in the area.

CUSTOMER RESEARCH

7   Test Ideas

You have 'desk funny' and 'stage funny'. What I invent in my study, usually does not work on stage.
                                        (Van 't Hek, famous Dutch cabaret artist)

We should do something when people say it's crazy. If people say something is 'good', it means someone else is already doing it.
                                        (F. Mitarai, CEO Canon Corporation)

The biggest risk in innovation lies in sticking too closely to your plans.
                                        (D. Hills, Walt Disney Company)

7.1 INTRODUCTION

The question now is, how attractive and distinctive really are the new product or service concepts? After the brainstorming session and concept development workshop, this is a justifiable question. I would advise you, after the first feeling of euphoria, immediately to reflect on the developed concepts and if necessary improve them or put them in the freezer if the market research shows that you have completely missed the boat, because that can also happen. This stage lasts three weeks: a short period, under great time pressure, to keep the tempo in the FORTH process. At the end of this stage – Test Ideas – the ideation team can plunge themselves into the making of mini new business cases for the best three to five product concepts.

7.2 QUALITATIVE CONCEPT RESEARCH

During the qualitative concept research the customer has the last say. The concept test is done quickly and on a small scale during the second week, if possible in different countries or on different continents at the same time. The qualitative character of the concept research in the ideation phase is without any objections. It is all about acquiring insights into why the customers find the new product concept attractive or not.

When testing the concepts in business-to-business target groups my preference goes to individual in-depth interviews. This is when new concepts are presented to individual customers in the target group. Should you do it as a group discussion with more customers, who are also competitors, then you run the risk that they might feel unable to speak freely. It is better to do it with the business customer at their work or in a research area. If you decide to do the research with the customer at their work, the eagerness is greater as it saves travelling time.

A group discussion with six to eight customers together in a research area is common for new concepts for the consumer market. A strong independent market researcher always makes sure that the opinions of individual extroverts within the group do not overshadow the rest of the group. An important advantage, when the research takes place in a research area, is that the core team members can follow the discussion live behind a one-way mirror or via a TV screen. Through the direct confrontation with the customer reactions they realise that some concepts don't stand a chance and that others should be improved drastically. This is no problem and is also the reason why research has been included in this stage. Moreover, the participants often get inspiration for the improvement of the concept immediately. As a result, during the concept test the chaff is separated from the wheat, as some new product concepts fall short.

An area where groups can be accommodated for testing the product located in a market research consultancy might not have the best atmosphere, but it is a practical solution. Rather consider, before you choose, if perhaps there is a way in which you can present the products or services to the target group in an area where they will be actually used: a concept for a new beer in a bar, a new service concept for car maintenance in a garage or new catering equipment in a modern kitchen for professionals. The only condition is that it must be possible for the team members to watch and listen. If this is not possible, then an interview area in a market research consultancy is the best possible solution.

With regard to the content of the new concept, it is important to get insight into its acceptance by applying the following six aspects:

1. Clarity
2. Relevancy
3. Attractiveness
4. Distinctiveness
5. Does it fit the brand?
6. Trustworthiness

If the innovation assignment includes an international target group, then test the product or service concept in different countries at the same time. There are international networks of market research consultancies that have the same vision, use the same method and are represented in all countries relevant. In most cases, representatives from these countries will also be part of the ideation team. It is then advisable to involve them in steering the direction of the concept research in their country. Checklist 13 at the end of the chapter provides a few practical tips for the qualitative concept research.

TESTING THE CONCEPT WITH CUSTOMERS ONLINE

The testing of the product or service concept is an important step towards its success. A concept test does not only determine the potential of the product but also discovers the best way in which to optimise it, position it, fix the price and how to advertise. This is the reason why Metrixlab has developed an online concept test: CONTEST. In this test the qualitative and quantitative online methods regarding the concepts are combined to give insight into the product through the opinions of the customers and to understand how it performs in relation to other competitive concepts. You get insight into:

- the extent to which it is accepted
- the perceived advantages
- the brand fit
- the position in relation to the competition
- acceptance of the price or price sensitivity
- how the concept can be improved

With CONTEST the online environment is used to the maximum through the creation of 'game-like' questionnaires. Customers first evaluate the concept on their intuition, based on their first impression. The concept is presented by a concept description and is usually accompanied by visual aids. Subsequently, the respondents can then be divided into 'acceptors' and 'rejecters' according to their reactions.

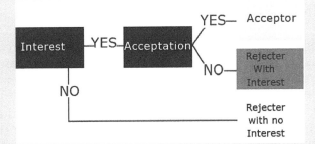

The questions relate to the amount of interest in the concept, the intention of using it and the perception of how much it differs from comparable competition. Some projective questions have also been included, such as: to what extent do you think other people might be interested in the concept, and to what extent will you mention the elements of the concept when talking to friends about this category (an 'advocacy' related question)?

In the concept description, the respondents can indicate with a marker which parts and aspects of the 'formulated benefit' and 'reasons to believe' appeal to them. The acceptors and rejecters are then not only characterised in terms of socio-demographic and physiographic features but also in terms of current brand, product use, brand preference and other variables.

In this way you get an exact indication of which benefits and attributes increase the acceptance, and which are less relevant or less important or even which are not understood. In combination with the price sensitivity metre it can then be established exactly what is the most acceptable price range wherein the largest possible acceptance of the concept can be obtained.

By combining the online information you can accentuate the concept and thus increase the chance for success.

Jaap Vessies
Business Unit Manager NPD and Innovation Research
Metrixlab

Testing new product concepts online is a new development and is currently a brilliant alternative for live concept research. Jaap Vessies, from the leading Metrixlab, describes (above) what is possible online. If your innovation assignment has an international perspective and you need and want to test it in many countries, an online method is worth considering.

7.3 IMPROVING PRODUCT CONCEPTS

The first reaction of potential customers to the new product concepts usually provides a handle to improve even the best concepts. For this reason a development workshop takes place at the beginning of week 3, directly after the qualitative research. In this workshop a brainstorming session is held with all the participants where you want to establish how the negatives can be improved and a choice is made as to which product concepts will be developed in the next stage. The frame below gives an explanation of how to approach this. Checklist 14 provides you with the programme for the development workshop.

APPROACH OF THE DEVELOPMENT WORKSHOP

During the development workshop all core and extended team members are present. The independent market researcher also has an important role to play. Again, I would advise that you arrange this workshop at an external location where you can be more relaxed and have more space available than in the innovation room. Of course all the original idea mind-maps and concept boards from the brainstorming session as well as all drawings and product descriptions from the qualitative research should be present.

It can be very inspiring to start with the recording of the customer confrontations with the new product concepts after which a presentation is given on the market research results. The ideation team leader and the internal client play an important role in the decision-making regarding the following two important questions:

1. Which product or service concepts are we going to improve during this workshop?
2. Which product or service concepts will fall away?

After an enthusiastic defence you, together with the ideation team, must make a decision. The internal client has the final vote but usually it is clear anyway.

Next, the concepts, of which the negative aspects have to be improved, are divided amongst the participants and then the work begins in pairs. Each pair brainstorms regarding the negative aspects from the research about improvements of the concepts and then alters the concept description. The improved concepts are then presented to the whole team who can also add something if necessary. Finally you select which three to five product or service concepts will be developed into a Mini New Business Case (MNBC). I have learned that when developing a mini new business case, it works better in pairs, but you can deviate from this if you wish. The core team members, after conversation with the project leader, are divided into pairs and together it is decided which pair will develop which MNBC in the final stage. In closing, the project leader gives a presentation of the MNBC format in PowerPoint in order to coordinate the expectations of every one involved.

If a new product concept has scored negatively during the test, yet it had a high score from the ideation team, it is recommended that this be discussed. This is especially important when it concerns completely new market innovations. I advise you to think about the statement made by Fujio Mitarai (CEO Canon Corporation): 'We should do something when people say it's crazy. If people say something is "good", it means someone else is already doing it.' Perhaps it will be good to stand firm and to continue to believe in the intuition of the ideation team. Even though the outcome is negative, and it seems contradictory, it might be a good idea to choose to improve the concept and to confidently develop it during the next stage: Homecoming.

7.4 PITFALLS

Even during the Test Ideas stage, situations can develop which raise some questions. Here are six situations with advice on how to deal with them.

1. The Concepts are So Good, We don't Need to do Any Research

During the euphoria of the new product brainstorm, an idea is created to accelerate the process by skipping the concept research. Time-to-market is important, especially for this brilliant new product.

Reaction: It is great that everybody is so enthusiastic but to create the same enthusiasm with others, the voice of the customer is of great value. You might lose three weeks, but you will gain five weeks if you come back with a tested concept.

2. There is Much Pressure to do Large Scale Representative Research

It is stated that the opinion of 18 or 24 people in each country can never be enough to show that the new product concept will really be successful. Why don't we do research on a larger scale?

Reaction: During the ideation phase it is about getting quick feedback in order to understand whether the new product ideas really appeal to the target group or if some important aspects have been overlooked. At a later stage, during the product development phase, you will undoubtedly be able to check the success of the real and sometimes physical product, or service, on a larger scale.

3. We are Only Testing it in One of the Five Countries

Do not make a fuss about it and simply test the new product concept in one country. This saves a lot of work and money as well.

Reaction: However, if your aim is to develop an attractive product concept for five countries which differ in customer behaviour and culture, then do not make any concessions. Discard the work and costs in this situation. If you can mention to the internal parties involved that the concept idea has been checked in their country as well, it gains more support. If you are limited financially, it is great to start with one country to see if it is successful there. Also consider the option to do the research online at a relatively low cost.

4. The Concept Research was not Good

Suppose that the result of the qualitative concept research shows that five concepts have missed the boat, among which were some of the best ideas. Was something then wrong with the research itself?

Reaction: You attended the qualitative concept research yourself, just like the rest of the core team. You have also noticed how the target group reacted to the new product concepts. Now you should be pleased that you have a few concrete handles to bring solid improvements to the new concepts in this ideation phase. Rather focus on that.

5. Your Favourite Concept Gets a Knock

How is it possible that the target group did not appreciate your favourite concept? They don't have any imagination and find it ridiculous.

Reaction: The pitfall is to stop the new concept. Such a big discrepancy always gets my attention especially if it ended in the top three with the ideation team. Perhaps this is a typical concept that should be given a 'wild card' by following your own and the group's intuition.

6. All the Concepts Received an Average to Bad Score

It seems as if 10 concepts have all scored averagely or badly. There are many points to improve. Should we continue?

Reaction: A justifiable question. If the best concepts only score a 6, they are not good enough yet. Then the first step is for improvement after which I would add an extra concept test for the improved concept. If the concepts have scored sufficiently then you have a solid base to draw up a MNBC. However, if not, then it might be a good idea to stop the FORTH method in this direction.

7.5 CASE STUDY: FORTH NEW MOBILITY SERVICES: TEST IDEAS

Concept Research

The 11 product descriptions were presented in a qualitative concept research to four focus groups consisting of six people from the same target groups as during the discovery phase in Assen and Leusden in the Netherlands. The research was conducted by Karin Hellema, an external market researcher in order to guarantee the objectivity.

During the concept research most of the core team members were present and it was for many the first time that they experienced something like this. For them it was the 'moment of truth' and the tension could be cut with a knife. At the moment when someone was very negative about a product concept, you could hear the disapproving groans in the room where they were watching.

The product description was tested on four aspects:

1. Do they recognise the customer situation and need?
2. Do they understand the concept?
3. Is the concept attractive?
4. Does the concept suit the Univé brand?

The result of the concept research was presented to the whole team during the development workshop in Hattemerbroek in the Netherlands on 15 March. It was to be expected that there was some disappointment that not everything was received enthusiastically. Some ideas which, during the brainstorming session, ended at the top, were evaluated differently by the customers and ended further down the list. However, the opposite also happened and with this the concept research was directly of great added value.

During the market research the target group was very enthusiastic about one innovative pioneering concept which the team also valued as number one. Due to the fact that this concept is currently in the idea implementation phase at Univé, I would break the confidentiality if I elaborate more. Immediately after the presentation it was decided to 'park' four of the concepts. With the remaining six concepts we started the development workshop in order to improve the concepts based on the commentary during the research.

At the end of the development workshop, after consultation with Bart Schouten and Jan Dijkstra, it was decided to develop seven concepts into mini new business cases in the next stage.

7.6 PRACTICAL CHECKLISTS

CHECKLIST 13: QUALITATIVE CONCEPT RESEARCH

1. The Qualitative Character

The purpose of the concept research is to test whether the developed new product or service concepts are attractive to the target group. Are you on the right track? It is not only about a yes or a no, but more so about the understanding of the current behaviour and preferences of the target group and to explain their reaction to the new concepts. Why this reaction? Furthermore, you want concrete clues in order to improve the developed products or services.

2. Method and Demands to the Product Concepts

- On a small scale and indicative
- Carry out the research with:
  - prototypes, three dimensional designs or good sketches of the product, or
  - practical concept descriptions for services.
- Conduct it with people in a user-friendly environment:
  - Discuss product concepts for new beer in a bar.
  - Discuss new catering concepts in a restaurant.
  - Discuss new household appliances in the kitchen.
  - For a specific service, this might be a problem, so use the research space.

3. Presenting the Questions

Together with experienced in-depth interviewers from the consultancy, set a structured questionnaire. You might want to consider the following types of questions (apply them specifically to your sector or target group):

- Investigative:
  - What is the current buying and using behaviour? (Why?)
  - What are the most important motives for buying? (Why)
  - What are you using now? (Why?)
  - What do you like about the new offer? (Why?)
  - What don't you like? (Why?)
- Testing:
  - Is the concept clear? (Why?)
  - Is it relevant for you? (Why?)
  - Is it attractive? (Why?)
  - Do you find it distinctive? (Why?)
  - Does it go with the brand? (Why?)
  - Do you find it trustworthy? (Why?)
  - Is it something for you personally? (Why?)
  - Will you buy it? (Why?)
  - What do you think it will cost? (Why?)
  - Would you like to change something about it? (Why?)

4. Target Group

- Choose discussion partners from the target group who were described in the innovation assignment.

Tip: Stick to this.

5. The Participants Who are Involved in the Ideation Team

- Invite all core and extended team members to attend the test.
- Mindset: ask the participants to observe the reactions of those interviewed and to listen carefully to what they say as this might lead to inspiration for possible improvements.
- Make sure that the core team members attend the qualitative research in all countries.

6. Choice of a Research Agency

- There are many good qualitative interviewers and market research agencies. Find people with much experience in the conducting of in-depth interviews, and if possible in the product group or service sector.
- There are also international networks for qualitative market research agencies. Find networks with the same vision who use the same method and are represented in all countries. For the business-to-business concepts, choose agencies that specialise in this.

Tip: Record the interviews, so that feedback from the customers can continue to play a role in the product development process at a later stage. You can use it for example to show the management of the product development team how full of praise or critical the target group was about a specific new product concept.

CHECKLIST 14: PROGRAMME DEVELOPMENT WORKSHOP

Table 7.1   Programme development workshop

Date			
Time	Step	Technique	Leader
Core team and extended team members			
09.00		Arrival and coffee	
09.20	Introduction	Welcome by project leader: introduction over the work done between the brainstorm and now	Project leader
09.20	Results of research	Market research agency presents the results of the concept test	Market researcher
10.20	Break	Short break	
10.40	Conclusion	Which concepts fall away and which have to be improved?	Facilitator
11.00	Improving concepts	Facilitator facilitates the improvement of four concepts in pairs for one hour + its presentation	Each pair one concept
12.00	Lunch		
13.00	Improving concepts	Facilitator facilitates the improvement of the next four concepts in pairs for one hour + its presentation	Each pair one concept
14.00	Break		
14.15	Choose which concepts will continue	Facilitator facilitates the choice of the three to five concepts which will be developed into MNBC. The internal client in consultation with the project leader has the last say	Facilitator
15.00	Mini new business case format	Project leader shows an example of a MNBC and explains what will be done in developing a MNBC	Project leader
16.00	MNBC-final	Make pairs of core team members and assign a pair to each MNBC	Project leader
16.15	Closing		Internal client

RETURNING

8   Homecoming

People are thing-a-ma-jigging too abstract and too much.

(Loesje)

I may not have gone where I intended to go, but I think I have ended up where I intended to be.

(D. Adams)

Everything that a man can imagine, others will be able to bring to life
(J. Verne, French Writer and Pioneer)

8.1 INTRODUCTION

And thus we have sight of the homeport. On the wharf are a group of people not able to contain their curiosity as to what will appear from the ship's hold. In the seventeenth century it was spices from the East. The VOC ships of then are the ideation teams of now. In the twenty-first century mini new business cases will come from the hold of FORTH: well-founded business cases which will confirm the potential of the new product concepts. The highlight is presenting it to the management, who will make the decision for it to be taken up into the regular development process. Presentations will also be given to the line managers, after which the knowledge and experience will be transferred to the teams who will develop the product. An ideation logbook will be made to record the experiences in the current process, handy tips and developed formats for the next voyage of discovery. The activities of this final stage last for four weeks.

8.2 MINI NEW BUSINESS CASES

The product concepts are not only attractive for the customers but more so for the organisation. During the Full Steam Ahead stage you have already decided which criteria they have to meet and therefore it is important during this stage to show, in a recognisable and convincing way, that the new concepts do meet the criteria. Although the concept boards and well-developed designs and concept descriptions are a good beginning, it is still too vague, especially for the managers responsible for the turnover and profit. Everyone can make nice pictures, but they often think in the form of business cases: a clear, strategic, commercial, professional and financial business case for a new initiative or a new investment.

In your company during the innovation phase it might have been possible that a business case was drawn up but during a later phase and just before the new product is introduced in the market: Gate 5: decision to launch (see Chapter

3, Figure 3.1). In order to prevent confusion, I call the business case for a new product concept in the ideation phase of FORTH, a Mini New Business Case. This also helps when it comes to controlling the expectation of the management. It is a kind of 'preview' of the possible business case for later: not so detailed yet and with more uncertainties than its 'big brother' in Gate 5. However, you strengthen the persuasiveness by highlighting the attractiveness of the strategic, commercial, and professional aspects of the innovative product or service. The five aspects of the mini new business case can be seen in Figure 8.1.

By drafting a mini new business case the ideation team can also learn much. In this way, the core team members realise that not only do creative or technological aspects play a role in the decision-making, but also strategic, commercial, professional and financial aspects are important. In the previous stage it was decided to draft a mini new business case for three to five product concepts. In this stage it is highly likely that some might be dropped as the ideation team, during the development of the concept, are not totally convinced of its attractiveness or feasibility. Checklist 15 will help when drafting a mini new business case.

On the basis of these mini new business cases the ideation team will choose which new product concepts to present to the management to actually be developed.

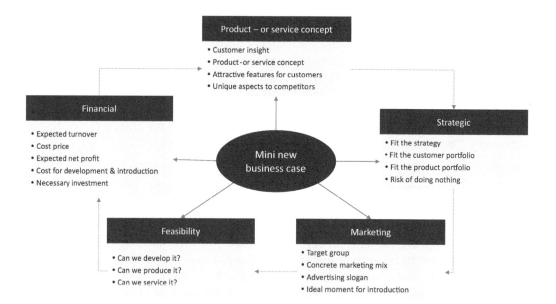

Figure 8.1   Five relevant aspects of the mini new business case

8.3 PRESENTATION TO THE MANAGEMENT

It is important to present the chosen three to five mini new business cases as soon as possible to the board of directors and managers who have to make the final decision (Gate 3: decision to develop). Therefore, during this stage you arrange a meeting which will be attended by the whole ideation team and where you take the management on a creative FORTH journey. A journey from the beginning to the end and which includes the innovation assignment, the sources of inspiration, the customer frictions, the new product brainstorm, the concept descriptions and the qualitative concept research of the three to five mini new business cases. At the end of the meeting there is usually an instant decision as to which new product concepts will be further developed.

However, after this formal decision, you are still not finished yet. Managers and co-workers who have not been closely involved in the FORTH journey, but for who the product development is relevant, are also important, especially if their business units, countries or departments are going to be involved with the product development or the introduction into the market. After the final decision has been made you can arrange, with much pleasure and enthusiasm, a presentation for them. For those who stayed at home, it is nice not only to see the mini new business cases but also to get insight into the preceding creative process. An 'outside the box' presentation of the creative process by giving a 'tour' around the innovation room is also a suitable way of getting them involved. If you have applied FORTH internationally, then do not hesitate to take the same creative presentation to the countries involved. What it costs now will later be paid back double. Co-workers will now feel privileged that they are allowed to be informed in such an original way at the beginning of the innovation process.

8.4 THE TRANSFER TO THE DEVELOPMENT TEAMS

The ideation phase ends with the admission of the new product concepts to the innovation process. There are three activities which are now meaningful in rounding off.

Firstly, it is significant to transfer the knowledge and experience gained to the development team. In this way you try to capture 'the soul' of the product or service concept. In the frame below you can find various starting points in how to do this.

TRANSFERRING KNOWLEDGE AND EXPERIENCE

In the mini new business cases for the product concept the attractiveness of the concept was shown in a very business-like manner – call it the 'hard side'. However, it is important to also transfer the 'soft side'.

TINY NEW BUSINESS CASE

A few starting points which are necessary when describing the concept are:

- This is what we have learned about the target group.
- Customers with these characteristics are attracted to this concept.
- The original idea was the solution to this customer friction.
- The product concept developed itself during the process.
- These are the strongest qualities of the product concept.
- The product concept is specifically meant for ...
- This is the weakness of the product concept.
- The product concept is not meant for ...
- This is what makes the product concept so unique.
- If I had to characterise the product as an animal, it would be a ...

During the product development phase a new team is set up as different skills and abilities are now required. At the start of the development team it is advisable to arrange a transfer workshop where the ideation team can transfer the product or service concept to the development team. This is a typical moment to go over the mini new business case as well as the 'soft sides' of the product concept. Furthermore, the original idea mind-map, the original concept boards, the first concept description and all the sketches and designs can now be transferred creatively and thoughtfully.

In addition to this, for the sake of continuity I fervently advise that one or some of the ideation team members be included in the development team who now have to realise the new product concept. After all, the participants from the ideation team know, as no other, the origin and background of the concept and are also aware of why certain conscious decisions were made in choosing specific product or service characteristics. Their function in the development team can be to 'guard the concept'.

The final activity which must be rounded off is something for the project leader who now has to draw up the ideation log book. In this log book you record the positive and negative experiences during the FORTH journey and evaluate it with the ideation team. Moreover you can lay out all the developed business formats ready for the next ideation team which will start the FORTH journey.

And so you have reached the end of stage five, the end of the journey. The ideation team has achieved its goal: three to five attractive, new and splendid product or service concepts are in the innovation pipeline to be further developed. Congratulations Columbus!

IDEA-DEVELOPMENT-TEAM

8.5 PITFALLS

Even in this last stage things can go wrong, and to quote the Americans: 'It ain't over 'til the fat lady sings.' Below are the final seven pitfalls.

1. The Calculations are for the Financial Man

Everybody has their own qualities but it is better that the controller in the ideation team does all the calculations.

Reaction: Of course you have to make use of each other's expertise. However, the controller can make a uniform calculation module wherein he records the procedure for the financial estimations, to be made by every pair. When it specifically concerns estimating the market range and calculating the turnover for the next three years, that is your job.

2. You Cannot Estimate the Market for a Product or Service Which is not There Yet

Reaction: Yes, it is more difficult for revolutionary new market innovations than for top-of-the-market innovations or bottom-of-the-market revolutions. For the top and bottom market innovations you still have the existing market on which you can base your estimations. For the new market innovations it is advised that you draw up an investigative mini new business case where you try to estimate the potential number of customers and how much turnover and profit it involves. If there is anybody who can do it, it is a member of the ideation team, therefore you!

3. I Am Not Successful in Drawing up an Attractive Mini New Business Case for the Most Favourite New Product Concept

Reaction: The pitfall here is, just as in the previous stage, to stop the new concept especially if it is in the top three. Continue to follow your own and the group's intuition. Present the product concept to the management anyway and inform them about the contradictions. Should they have the same feeling, you will probably get a 'wild card' to develop the product in the next step.

4. If Only Three to Five New Product Concepts are Allowed to Go Through to the Next Round, not One Might Reach the Finish Line

In Chapter 1 it was mentioned that in order to have one successful product entering the market you need seven new product ideas, and now there is every likelihood that you might end up with nothing at the end of the development process.

Reaction: The ratio of 7:1 is for companies who start with product ideas which have not been tested or structured at all. The chance to introduce a successful product will therefore increase by using the FORTH method. With the product concepts we have now already reached Gate 3 of the development process instead of still being at the beginning of Gate 1 (see Figure 3.1, Chapter 3).

5. The Management Has Decided to Choose Only One Product Concept from the Suggested Three to be Developed Further

Reaction: One new concept in the pipeline is a good start. Check why the other two were not chosen as they might only be 'on hold' to accelerate the development of the one chosen and will be ready to be developed as soon as the capacity to develop is available again.

6. Must I Present the Confidential Product Concepts? New Products are Promising but also Very Confidential

Reaction: This may never be an excuse to withhold information from, or not to involve, the co-workers in your company who will play a role in the development process or in the introduction of the product into the market. Enthuse them!

7. The Product Development Team is not Interested in a Transfer Workshop

Reaction: It is important to find out the reason behind this immediately. If it is due to a lack of time, explain that the transfer workshop will save time at a later stage. If you have the feeling that they do not want to commit themselves to the new product or service concept fully, try to talk to them. Anyway, arrange your own 'farewell party' with much enthusiasm.

8.6 CASE STUDY: FORTH NEW MOBILITY SERVICES: HOMECOMING

MNBC Format

The Univé format for the mini new business cases was previously produced in the form of a PowerPoint presentation with eight sheets. The most important aspects from the innovation assignment were included in the presentation. The aims of the MNBC were presented to the core and extended team members at the improvement workshop in order to manage the expectations.

Teams and Method of Working

In this FORTH project and in this phase seven mini new business cases were developed. Each core team member adopted a product concept over which they were very enthusiastic and were given the role of 'puller'. Then everybody adopted a second idea in the role as 'pusher'. In this way each member had a 'sparring-partner'. During the interim progress meetings with the core team members the

MNBCs were presented to one another and problems with the drawing up were shared and solved. Project leader, Bart Schouten, kept in contact with each core team member individually and tried to help as much as possible during the drawing up of the MNBCs.

Presentation and Decision-Making

The final presentation of the MNBCs by the core team members to the whole group, including the internal client Jan Dijkstra, was planned for 5 April. The outline of each concept was developed and included the basis for the financial potential and the estimated feasibility. Every core team member experienced, yet again, the feeling that this is the moment of truth. Their involvement with their concept was great and with much passion they held their presentations. The internal client was overwhelmed with not only the quality but also the quantity of information he received. He could not make a decision overnight and asked for some time out to decide with which MNBCs he wanted to continue. After a few days consideration he made the following choices:

- The innovative pioneering concept: start directly with more elaboration (long-term project).
- Two short-term innovations: start a follow-up directly and develop it into a full business case, including the Green Driving concept.
- Two idea directions which are of strategic value which transcend the BU Indemnity Insurance of Univé: to be presented to the group level innovation board.
- A good idea which did not fit within the innovation assignment, but has great value will be passed on to the line organisation to start with immediately.
- An idea with a disappointing mini business case stops immediately.

The FORTH process, the best mini new business cases and the decision about what to do was presented to the management team of BU Indemnity Insurance, within two weeks after the last presentation in the FORTH process. Subsequently the results were presented by Bart Schouten and Jan Dijkstra to the Innovation Board on group level and included Edwin Velzel, the chairman of the board of directors. The innovative pioneering concept was immediately accepted by the top management. It was then decided to start an innovation project, on group level, to estimate the concrete feasibility of the pioneering idea with the main purpose to draw up a clear and full business case. There was also much support for the decision to develop the two short-term innovations on a business level.

Evaluation

Immediately after FORTH New Mobility Services the FORTH project was evaluated by each member individually. FORTH New Mobility Services received an eight on a scale of ten, a score with which the project leader Bart Schouten and I are still very proud. However, more significant than a number are the quotes about the experiences of some of the participants.

- 'A unique accomplishment within Univé to come up with concrete results' (Jan van Raalte).
- 'A positive atmosphere, good involvement, really innovative and more than enough mini new business cases' (Cock Meerhof).
- 'It has exceeded all my expectations' (Aletta Dokter).
- 'An inspiring and thorough process. Good supervision. The session with the customers were educational and interesting' (Jan Dijkstra).

For me, it was a good and educational process too.

8.7 PRACTICAL CHECKLIST

CHECKLIST 15: DRAFTING MINI NEW BUSINESS CASES

The product or service concept is central in the mini new business cases. The purpose of these cases is to be commercially convincing and to supply a good foundation, as to what extent and why the product concept has met all the criteria set in the innovation assignment.

A. The format of the mini new business case

- Choose a PowerPoint presentation, according to the scheme below. Limit yourself to a maximum of seven slides for each product concept.
- Draw up a calculating module. In it you record the method of working for the financial calculations so that the financial foundation for each product or service concept can be calculated in the same way. If you and the group controller agree to these principles then you already have 'one partner in crime'.

B. The drafting of the mini new business cases

- Divide the core team into groups of two. For each group choose participants who complement each other with regards to expertise and skills. Allow each group to choose which product concept they want to develop. The size of the group will depend on the number of participants and the number of product concepts. Stimulate the groups to make use of each other's expertise.
- The drafting of the mini new business cases takes four weeks, and during this time you organise three MNBC meetings lasting one day each. After a week and a half allow the groups to present the first version (mini new business case 0.3) to each other. The purpose is to help each other with the problems they have encountered up to now.

- Halfway through the third week the groups present the mini new business case 0.8 to each other again. The purpose is to continue to help with improvements.
- On the MNBC day in the fourth week, allow the groups to have the last say on the selected mini new business cases. Give sharp feedback. After some changes and improvements the 1.0 version for all the product concepts is available. This will then be presented to the management on the final presentation in the FORTH project including the extended team members.

C. The six sub-divisions of the mini new business case:

1. The product or service concept (2 slides):
   - This is how the idea was created.
   - Product concept:
     - This is it.
     - This is what it looks like.
     - This is what it does.
   - This is what makes the product or service attractive!
     - It solves the following customer frictions.
     - It provides the following needs.
     - This is the target group for this product.
   - This is what makes the product concept unique!
     - Current behaviour of customer.
     - Current solutions and competitors.
     - Distinctiveness of our concept.

2. Strategy (1 slide):
   - This is how it fits into the strategy of the company.
   - This is how it fits into the strategy of the branch.
   - This is how it fits into our strategy for the target group.
   - This is how it fits into the product portfolio.

3. Commercial (1 slide):
   - Target group.
   - Concrete marketing mix:
     - Product or service
     - Positioning
     - Price
     - Distribution channel
   - This is the advertising slogan for the product.
   - This is the ideal moment to introduce the product into the market.

4. Organisation (1 slide):
   - We can develop it.
   - We can produce it.
   - We will probably have to invest.
   - We have the knowledge (or we know where to find it).
   - These are possible internal obstacles.
   - This is the development process.

5. Financial (1 slide):
    - This is what it will contribute (one to three years after introduction into the market):
        - Number of customers
        - Estimated turnover
        - Estimated profit
    - It is going to cost:
        - Estimate R&D costs
        - Estimated investment
        - Estimated costs for market introduction

6. Recommendations (1 slide):
    - These are the reasons why we should develop it.
    - These are the risks if we do not develop it.
    - These are the most important doubts.
    - We suggest that we must or must not do it.

Tip 1: Do not calculate the turnover, cost price or profit up until the last decimal, because the only sure thing is that you will miscalculate anyway. At this stage it is all about managing the expectations of the board of directors. Will the innovative product or service generate an annual turnover of €100,000, €5 million, €25 million or €100 million? Be sure to make the right choice and to provide concrete reasons for your choice.

Tip 2: Use the expertise of the participants of the innovation team as well as others in the organisation as much as possible. Make time available for the ideation team to help you and each other.

BACK HOME...

Conclusion

He who is on his way to a star, does not turn back.
                                         (L. Da Vinci, Italian artist and scientist)

It is not how many ideas you have, it's how many you make happen.
                                         (Text for advertising consultancy Accenture)

The best ideas lose their owners and take on lives of their own.
                                         (N. Bushnell, Founder Atari)

At the end of a journey, after everyone has welcomed you home and you have handed out souvenirs, you unpack your suitcase. This also applies to FORTH. While unpacking your suitcase you find many things which you have collected during the innovation journey. Looking back, you realise that they have great value too.

9.1 PARTICIPANTS WITH A DIFFERENT VIEW AND GREATER SKILLS

Twelve participants from your organisation have, for six weeks, immersed themselves in what is happening in the market. They have talked to customers and have searched for customer frictions. Many of them now look back with a different view on the market. Furthermore, they have worked with colleagues and learned from each other how to interview customers, how to position an innovative product or service in the market or how to draw up a mini new business case. All the participants have gained new experiences and have increased their skills. This is something that not only the participants personally but also the company will benefit from in the future. Johan Buigholt, one of the core team members in FORTH New Mobility Services, talks about his experiences below.

THE EXPERIENCES OF A 'SENSIBLE FORTH PARTICIPANT'

The Observe and Learn stage was the most inspiring for me. I visited customers at home to ask them what they think. I also did extensive desk research and had appointments with marketers from other branches. All these activities gave a whole new perspective on the market within which we operate and led to new insights and surprising and feasible forms of cooperation with other companies.

All the information which was collected created an explosion of ideas during the two-day brainstorming session. More than 600 ideas! Then I had a moment of doubt as to whether we could bring it back to a few usable ideas without throwing away some good ones.

The testing of the final concept descriptions by customers in the market research during the stage Test Ideas was a unique experience. Those concepts which we pushed forward did not make it and concepts over which we weren't very enthusiastic were given a high score. The highlight was Jenny, a participant during the focus group in the Observe and Learn stage. Based on one of the frictions discovered by her, a specific concept was created as solution. By coincidence, Jenny was also part of the panel that was evaluating the concepts. You can imagine that the expectation and tension were high. But you have probably guessed it: Jenny did not think much of it at all. Research has shown that interaction with your customers is fundamental. Your own belief that something is either good or not, is not necessarily the opinion of your customer.

The most important aspect of the FORTH innovation method is that the approach works. The journey is educational and inspiring. However, it is all about the end result and we are extremely pleased with the mini new business cases which it has produced.

Johan Buigholt
Manager Strategy and Innovation
BU Indemnity Insurance Univé VGZ IZA Trias

9.2 MINI NEW BUSINESS CASES WHICH DID NOT MAKE IT

It is possible that you find in your suitcase a Mini New Business Case which did not make it in the end either because it was not technically feasible or not yet attractive enough for your organisation as the others were better. Do not throw away the MNBC. Find a safe place where you can store it. It might even be possible that the MNBC can be brought back later when a new product concept, while developing in the innovation pipeline, unexpectedly drops out.

9.3 DROPPED-OUT CONCEPT DESCRIPTIONS

You will also discover new product or service concepts which have dropped out after the qualitative research. They did not endure the criticism of the target group. It will not be a good idea to throw them away either. Imagine that you suddenly find a solution for the weakness of the concept. It is not something that you will start working on immediately, as the priority lies with the product concepts which are adopted in the product development phase. But just imagine …

9.4 TEN IDEA DIRECTIONS NOT WORKED OUT

At the bottom of your suitcase you find 10 flip-over sheets with undeveloped idea directions, together with, in total, about 400 or more post-its with product ideas.

You did not get around to these during the brainstorming session as 12 other idea directions had priority. However, should you take a look at them about eight weeks down the line you might still find some 'nice looking pieces of granulated sugar' which you can still polish to make them shine just like the new concepts which are currently in the pipeline. It will be a good idea to look at these idea directions with other participants again. Who knows, you might even find something useful.

9.5 CUSTOMER FRICTIONS AND MARKET EXPERIENCES

The market experiences and customer frictions were used to gather inspiration for the 'business of tomorrow'. It might even be possible that they are useful for the 'business of today'! Visit division or sales managers in your organisation who concentrate on these issues and discuss your experience of the journey with them. There is nothing nicer for them (or for you) than to share the experiences in a creative way with the sales and marketing people who will also get inspiration in this way.

And so your journey has finally ended. I trust that FORTH has helped you with this. Well, *'partir c'est mourir un peu'* as the French say, or are you already secretly thinking about your next voyage of discovery?

If you are going FORTH more often, like Univé, there is one other spin-off. The different FORTH stages and integrated method can become part of the regular innovation practice of marketers and innovation specialists. This is the experience of Bart Schouten, Business Innovation Director, Univé VGZ IZA Trias.

THE SIDE EFFECTS OF THE FORTH INNOVATION METHOD

As innovation manager I am deeply impressed with the FORTH method. It is par excellence the method to involve people and get great results, especially in a less creative organisation. The expectations which I had before were all realised. After the first FORTH innovation project, another followed; one was more successful than the other. Besides the direct results there are other spin-offs as well.

Firstly the word 'awareness' comes to mind. More attention has been paid to customers. This might sound strange as we have been working for them, after all. Everybody was busy indeed with customers, but it often happens that we look at the situation from our own perspective as we, with the best intention, think for the customer. The FORTH innovation method forced us to make contact with the target group and not to be satisfied with a written report from a research consultancy but with 'live' customers. FORTH also made us aware of the fact that our own opinion might be good and nice, but that each one of us suffers from 'company blindness'. Visions and strategies allow for dreams but customers bring you back to reality and give you a large portion of perspective and a rich insight.

The way in which you are busy with the environment in FORTH takes you away from internal company discussions. We value our customers but it often happens that internal discussions decide how we solve customer problems. By literally going outside you are separated from the company. The world outside comes at you absolute and direct and teaches you what the discussions should be about. After FORTH you also notice that some people keep on looking around them and by doing so get positive stimuli and ideas which serve the interest of the customer.

Furthermore, FORTH forces you to structured thinking and to not take your own personal and preferred way. When you take the time to look further and to investigate the successes or failures of others, you prevent disappointing results. You have to be patient and not just take the road on the spur of the moment. Make sure that you go further to get better answers.

FORTH lets you blossom. When you mobilise people with good supervision, they are more creative than they ever thought they could be. This gives positive energy with which you can achieve much. In this way everybody can get much better answers than the first one which you might have had in mind already.

In the following stages of the innovation process or in other projects you notice that the above mentioned insights have been given a place. FORTH components can be traced back in various places and in various projects within our organisation. The FORTH method is a wonderful instrument but not always the best solution for a problem. Through knowledge and experience we find that, apart from FORTH, we can now choose which components are a good mix for which problem.

In short: with FORTH a world has opened up for our company and we now have many innovative resources with which to develop answers.

Bart Schouten
Director Business Innovation
Univé VGZ IZA Trias

Appendix I

CERTIFIED FORTH INNOVATION FACILITATORS

The practical FORTH innovation method was introduced in 2006 by Gijs van Wulfen.

The use of this inspiring and effective method has grown and with it the need for experienced facilitators to guide and supervise the ideation process professionally. During the past few years a network of FORTH innovation facilitators has been developed. They are trained and certified in the application of FORTH. They also share 'best practices' with each other on a regular basis. The certification is extended annually based on good results.

The following FORTH innovation facilitators will gladly facilitate a professional FORTH process in your company or organisation wherever you are. Feel free to contact them for a personal appointment.

Founder of the FORTH innovation method:

Gijs van Wulfen
Company: FORTH Innovation Group
Telephone: +31–651483575
Email: gijs@forth-innovation.com
Internet: www.forth-innovation.com

Certified Facilitators

Benjo van den Boogaard
Company: Boester
Telephone: +31–645640770
Email: benjo@boester.nl
Internet: www.boester.nl

Rogier Braak
Company: Pezy Product Innovation
Telephone: +31–651578545
Email: r.braak@pezy.com
Internet: www.pezy.com

Enno Meines
Company: Ennovatief
Telephone: +31–655104501
Email: info@ennovatief.nl
Internet: www.ennovatief.nl

Ina Mohrmann (Germany)
Company: IdeaKitchen
Telephone: +49 (0) 176 32399428
Email: info@ideakitchen.de
Internet: www.ideakitchen.de

Mathijs Niehaus
Company: WEL klantgericht innoveren
Telephone: +31–505497345
Email: mathijsniehaus@daaromwel.nl
Internet: www.daaromwel.nl

René Salemink
Company: GOWIN
Telephone: +31–655716177
Email: rene.salemink@gowin.nl
Internet: www.gowin.nl

The following FORTH innovation facilitators work as internal innovation facilitators in companies and organisations which have used this method for a flying start to innovation:

Isabel Verhoeven
Company: Sanoma Publishers
Position: Business Development Manager

Arjan Evers
Company: Univé VGZ IZA Trias
Position: Senior Consultant Innovation

Marien Gramser
Company: Univé VGZ IZA Trias
Position: Senior Consultant Innovation

Pieter van Haren
Company: Univé VGZ IZA Trias
Position: Programme Manager Care Innovation

Ewoud Liberg
Company: Univé VGZ IZA Trias
Position: Innovation Consultant

Alexandra Luyk
Company: Univé VGZ IZA Trias
Position: Business Innovation Programme Manager

Cock Meerhof
Company: Univé VGZ IZA Trias
Position: Innovation Manager

Carolien Nauta
Company: Univé VGZ IZA Trias
Position: Manager Customer and Care Market

Actual information regarding certified FORTH innovation facilitators can be found at www.forth-innovation.com. If you are interested in becoming a certified FORTH innovation facilitator, contact Gijs van Wulfen – Telephone: +31–651483575. Email: gijs@forth-innovation.com

Appendix II

THIRTY BRAINSTORMING TECHNIQUES

This appendix provides, as help for determining the most effective FORTH programme, a description of 30 techniques. Some of these techniques are regularly part of the kick-off workshop, the brainstorming session and the development workshop. Should the assignment, the group process or other circumstances cause you to change, then it would be wise to deviate from your programme. This is just a guideline and therefore also other techniques will be explained which, if and when required, can be included in the FORTH method.

Table A2.1   Thirty brainstorming techniques

Brainstorming techniques	Regular	Optional
A Introductions, energisers and conclusions		
A.1 Photo introduction	X (kick-off)	
A.2 The bunch of keys	X (kick-off)	
A.3 Sequence of play		X (kick-off)
A.4 Getting up you lose your seat	X (kick-off)	
A.5 The dustbin		X (kick-off)
A.6 Energisers	X (all workshops)	
A.7 Finishers		X (all workshops)
B Brainstorming techniques to diverge		
B.1 Spontaneous brain dump	X (brainstorm)	
B.2 Presumptions		X (brainstorm)
B.3 SCAMPER	X (brainstorm)	
B.4 Flower association	X (brainstorm)	
B.5 Biomimicry (nature analogy)		X (brainstorm)
B.6 Comic hero analogy		X (brainstorm)
B.7 Silly things		X (brainstorm)
B.8 Insight game	X (brainstorm)	
B.9 Climb into the skin of	X (kick-off)	

Table A2.1   *Concluded*

Brainstorming techniques	Regular	Optional
C Brainstorming techniques to converge		
C.1 Grouping of ideas	X (brainstorm)	
C.2 Selecting idea directions	X (brainstorm)	
C.3 Idea mind-mapping	X (brainstorm)	
C.4 With ketchup?	X (brainstorm)	
C.5 Salt and pepper		X (Improvement workshop)
C.6 Improving	X (Improvement workshop)	
C.7 Multi-criteria selection of concept boards	X (brainstorm)	
C.8 I love you	X (brainstorm)	
D Other forms of brainstorming		
D.1 Brainstorm games		X (brainstorm)
D.2 Brainstorm software		X (brainstorm)
D.3 Online brainstorming		X (brainstorm)
E Other techniques		
E.1 TRIZ		X (brainstorm)
E.2 SIT		X (brainstorm)
E.3 Six thinking hats		X (all workshops)

The two-day brainstorming session in the stage Raise Ideas are built up around the principles of the original brainstorm. This approach is divided into a divergence and convergence phase. The techniques have been placed into the stage in which they can be used. Section A gives an explanation of three help techniques: ways in which to facilitate getting acquainted, physical exercises to get more energy in the group and to conclude a brainstorming session. Section B describes ten techniques for the divergence phase and Section C seven techniques for the convergence phase. In Section D three different other types of brainstorming techniques are explained. Finally, Section E presents three extra techniques.

The brainstorming techniques are explained according to the following five questions:

1. What: what type of brainstorming technique is it?
2. Why: why do I use this technique?
3. When: in which situations are these techniques useful?
4. Where: where during the brainstorming process, are these techniques effective?
5. How: how do I enforce this technique?
    a) Timing: how long does the technique take?

b) Participants: with how many participants can I enforce this technique?
c) Process: which steps do you, as facilitator, complete?

Three other ways to brainstorm are: brainstorming games, brainstorming software and online brainstorming. Depending on the innovation assignment and situation, these brainstorm variants can also be applied in the FORTH method. They are also shortly explained. Two other techniques are TRIZ and SIT. Originally they are not brainstorming techniques as they apply to systematic innovation. However, experience has taught us that components of both techniques can be very useful in a new product brainstorm and that is why they have been included in this list. They are described based on how they will be applied in a new product brainstorm. Of course, these techniques are also useful in brainstorming about other subjects or for other purposes, and in practice there is not much difference.

At the end of each category for brainstorming techniques you will find a reference to informative websites which can help you for a more in-depth study of the techniques.

SECTION A: TECHNIQUES FOR GETTING ACQUAINTED AND SOME ENERGISERS

For the effectiveness of every workshop or brainstorm it is important the participants feel at ease. Many factors contribute to this such as feeling safe in the group, which is an important condition in order to be willing to say what you think.

The number of participants in a new product brainstorm varies between 12 and 14 people. There are always two outsiders (external participants) present. There is also the question whether the participants from the same organisation know each other. This might not be the case especially if the company is big and the participants come from different branches or from different countries. Furthermore, the participants, the brainstorm facilitator and the cartoonist see each other for the first time. It is very important that they all get well acquainted. This contributes to the creating of a safe atmosphere within the group from the start.

Everybody has their own experience with a spontaneous 'getting to know one another' where each person introduces themselves. As people don't really know each other they also don't really know what to say. At that moment they are still inhibited and don't get much further than saying their name and their position in the company, and afterwards they nervously look at their neighbour as if to say that it is their turn now. Luckily there are techniques which can help the getting acquainted phase go a bit smoother. Below you will find four techniques explained. There is a fifth technique but with a different character which can also be useful for a good start, and to minimise negative experiences with product development in the past. After these techniques have been explained it is followed by the energisers.

A.1 Photo Introduction

Timing:

- 20–30 minutes

Participants:

- 12–14 participants

Process:

- Place a collection of 100–200 photos on one of the tables.
- The facilitator asks each person to choose a photo which says something about them personally.
- The participants choose one photo and take their seats again.
- The facilitator then asks an extrovert person, who has already shown that they are at ease, to start the introduction with the help of the photo. The rest follows.

An effective alternative:

You can ask the participants to take their own photo and to bring it with them. It is also a nice idea for them to link it with the innovation assignment. In a new product brainstorm about travelling products you can ask the participants, when invited, to bring a photo of their favourite holiday. Or at a brainstorm about new services in car-crash testing you could ask them to bring a photo of their own car. Websites with photos:

- www.flickr.com
- www.faganfinder.com/img

A.2 The Bunch of Keys

All participants have keys with them. This is a nice way to get an insight into someone's life: the key of their second home, the neighbour's key, the key from the children's (who have left home) house, the office key, the car key. This technique always creates a funny and relaxed atmosphere especially when everybody can relate to the person who has no idea what a specific key is for.

Timing:

- 20–30 minutes

Participants:

- 12–14 participants

Process:

- The facilitator asks each participant to introduce themselves and show each key from their own bunch of keys. What kind of key is it and why do they have it?
- The facilitator chooses an extrovert, who is already at ease, to say something about themselves with the help of their bunch of keys. The others then follow.

An effective alternative:

Instead of using a bunch of keys, the participants are asked to introduce themselves with the help of the content of their wallet or purse. These usually contain photos of partners or children and a wide variety of credit cards, business cards and social cards. If you are brainstorming in the sector for car leasing, retail, banks or insurance companies you immediately create a link to the innovation assignment.

A.3 Sequence of Play

Immediately after the introductions with photos, keys or wallets, you can get the participants going by playing the sequence game. In this way you get them motivated as they have to cooperate with each other immediately and so learn something more about each other.

Timing:

- 10 minutes

Participants:

- 12–14 participants

Process:

- The facilitator asks the participants to make room and to get together and see how quickly they can work together.
- The facilitator gives instructions which they have to perform as a group.
- The instructions could be: Stand in order of:
  - height
  - age
  - number of children

- distance from brainstorm location
- number of kilometres driven with current car

Tip: When the participants stand in order, let them say the numbers out loud. In this way you learn something about each other and you can also check if they have done it correctly.

A.4 When You Get Up You Lose Your Seat

It often happens that at meetings like this, the participants will go and sit next to somebody they know and, if you don't do something about it, they will consider that chair as 'their' place. It is good to break through these patterns immediately. In this way, the external participants will also become part of the group quicker. A simple rule to follow: when you get up you lose your seat. The facilitator explains that every one who gets up to get some coffee or put ideas on the ideas wall, has to sit somewhere else. Only apply this rule on the first morning of the first day of the brainstorming session. The group forming after that will make this rule unnecessary.

A.5 The Dustbin

Participants of a new product brainstorm might have some negative experiences in the past at their organisation. Perhaps their company was recently re-organised. When you, as the facilitator, get the feeling that this plays a role and that it will influence the brainstorming process negatively, then it is good to do something about it. It will not be possible to discuss all these negative experiences at that moment but you can give it a place – a physical place – in the dustbin.

Timing:

- 10 minutes

Participants:

- 12–14 participants

Process:

- The facilitator asks the participants if they had any recent negative experiences within their organisation. They are then asked to write these experiences (one by one) on a post-it and are given the assurance that it will not be discussed with the group.

- The facilitator then takes a big black bag and asks the participants to throw their post-it in it. And in this way they can leave all negative experiences behind them.
- The facilitator closes the bag and asks someone to place it outside the room. Usually you will notice a more relaxed atmosphere as if the tension has been released.

A.6 Energisers

It often happens that the energy level of the group decreases at some point during the brainstorming workshop as brainstorming is mentally very tiring. The time after lunch or at the end of the afternoon, are moments when the concentration can weaken and these moments ask for an activity. If you can use the facilities available at the brainstorming location, then that will be great. Go outside for walking, canoeing, rowing or cycling. However, if you do not have the time or the opportunity to do this, then if the group is up to it, interrupt the brainstorming programme for an energiser. These are short physical exercises in the brainstorming room which provide energy. The following three energisers can be used.

A.6.1 The horse race

Timing:

- 10 minutes

Participants:

- 12–14 participants

Process:

- During the horse race the participants pretend to participate in a real horse race on a track. The facilitator plays the role of the commentator of the race. The participants are then asked to sit on their knees in a circle close to each other. As soon as the race starts, they start tapping on the floor with open hands thus imitating the sound of the horse's hooves. While they are continuously tapping on the floor, they have to react to the commands given by the facilitator, in five movements:
  - the horses are on their way – tap on the floor;
  - the horses are going through a trough of water – tap on the thigh;
  - turn to the left – everyone leans to the left;
  - turn to the right – everyone leans to the right;
  - passing the stands – everyone does the wave!

It is an art to keep it fun and to increase the tempo so that the actions are done faster. It is also a challenge on the energy levels, especially that of the facilitator.

A.6.2 Swinging to music

Timing:

- 10 minutes

Participants:

- 12–14 participants

Process:

- Place the chairs to the side. The facilitator then asks everybody to stand in the middle and announces that all the participants are going to move and swing to different kinds of music. Choose the music carefully and build it up from relaxed to quick. The following order is suggested: new age music, classical music, ballads, rock-and-roll and techno house. It is important that the facilitator also participates and sets an example. Some might be hesitant at first but make sure they know that anything goes, whether you move fast and furious or move slow and relaxed. Ensure that the tempo and volume of the music ends with a grand finale.

  Source: Marcel Karreman (2002). *Warming-ups and energizers*. Zaltbommel: Thema.

A.6.3 In touch

Apart from creating energy, this kind of exercise also allows the participants to get into contact with one another.

Timing:

- 15 minutes

Participants:

- 12–14 participants

Process:

- Place the chairs to the side. The facilitator asks everyone to stand in the middle. He then announces that they are going to do an exercise to get them moving.

Ask everyone to walk through the room, not in a circle following each other, but randomly. At the command of the facilitator they must walk slower or faster. As soon as the facilitator mentions a body part the participants should make contact via that body part with everyone they encounter. Start with the hands – that is easy. After that you can mention the back of the head. Toes are also nice and you can continue with hips, noses and cheeks. Allow the participants to set their own boundaries and stop on time.

Source: Marcel Karreman (2002). *Warming-ups and energizers.* Zaltbommel: Thema.

A.7 Finishers: The Compliment Game

At the end of a workshop or brainstorming session everybody is obviously tired but pleased with the good results and an atmosphere of excellence fills the room. Of course you end with champagne or prosecco. If you, as the facilitator, still have the energy it is always nice and meaningful to end the session with the compliment game, especially at the last meeting. What makes this game so perfect is that everyone receives a 'gift' about themselves which they can take home: a handful of compliments.

Timing:

* 20 minutes

Participants:

* 12–14 participants

Process:

* Each participant is asked to write a compliment about the other participants. One compliment on one post-it.
* Then they have to stick one compliment on the back of each person. The compliment should be a word which describes their strengths, such as 'open', 'practical' or 'creative'.
* When this is completed, you ask them to stand in a semi-circle. You, as the facilitator, collect the post-its from the first participant and ask them to read the 'gift' aloud. Then they collect the compliments from the back of their neighbour and give it to them to read it out.
* Continue until each participant has had a chance.

Source: Mieke van de Pol. www.decreatievetrainer.blogspot.com, 8 September 2007.

You can find more information about ice breakers, energisers and finishers at:

* www.wilderdom.com/games/Icebreakers.html
* www.zhaba.cz/index.php?id=95

SECTION B: BRAINSTORMING TECHNIQUES TO DIVERGE

B.1 Brain Dump

1. What?

The brain dump is the start technique for every new product brainstorm in the divergence phase to 'catch' the first spontaneous ideas. The participants dump their first ideas and the facilitator harvests them.

2. Why?

During the Full Steam Ahead and the Observe and Learn stages everything has been done to get the creative process going. Many participants have already created ideas even before the brainstorm in the Raise Ideas stage. They now want to get rid of them as soon as possible.

3. When?

A brain dump is organised at all brainstorming sessions.

4. Where in the process?

The best moment is at the start of the divergence phase. During the FORTH method the participants have been working towards this moment and now they are allowed to let go and write all their ideas on a separate post-it. The additional effect is that it creates room in the mind to get new ideas and insights during the brainstorming session.

5. How?

Timing:

* For as long as it lasts …
* Usually with 12–14 participants for about 45 minutes

Participants:

- The facilitator
- Usually with 12–14 participants

Process:

- The facilitator reads the innovation assignment and asks the participants to write down their first ideas (in a few key words) on a post-it. One idea per post-it.
- The facilitator harvests the ideas.
  - The participants read their ideas, one by one, and give them to the facilitator who then asks them to stick them on the post-it wall.
  - The facilitator asks the rest of the participants to listen well and write any new ideas on a post-it.
  - This continues until there are no more ideas left.

Tip 1: During the new product brainstorming session participants from both inside and outside the company take part. The outsiders have only been involved since this stage whereas most of the other participants have gone through stages 1 and 2 already. It is very useful at this stage to 'harvest' the post-its of those who have just joined. You will notice that they bring in a new perspective from those who have been involved for longer. When the participants react to each other positively, an 'idea explosion' develops through the pollination of the ideas from the outsiders and the rest of the team.

B.2 Presumptions

1. What?

A creative technique whereby the presumptions implied by the assignment or challenge are made clear, discussed and eliminated.

2. Why?

In existing markets, products and services start looking alike more and more as competitors watch each other carefully and then copy the successful ones. In this way, without realising it, fixed patterns based on the reality of today are formed. By mentioning these patterns and implied presumptions and eliminating them, new angles are created which can lead to 'outside the box' product or service ideas.

3. When?

The presumption technique can be applied in many new product brainstorming sessions. This usually happens at the beginning of the divergence phase in order to reverse the habitual conventions in the product market or within the company. The TRIZ and SIT techniques, described later, work in the same way and are very useful as a booster when generating new product ideas.

4. Where in the process?

The best moment is at the beginning of the divergence phase in the new product brainstorming session, directly after the assignment and the first brain dump.

5. How?

Timing:

- For as long as it lasts
- Usually with 12–14 participants for about 30 minutes

Participants:

- The facilitator
- Usually 12–14 participants

Process:

- The facilitator asks:
  - What are the key concepts of the assignment?
  - Allow the participants to write down the key concepts for themselves.
  - Allow the participants to mention these key concepts.
  - Choose the most important three to five key concepts.
- Generate ideas by eliminating the presumptions from each key concept:
  - The facilitator makes a list of the presumptions for each key concept.
  - The facilitator asks the participants to eliminate the presumptions.
  - The facilitator then asks the participants to invent new product ideas without the presumptions and write them on post-its.
  - The facilitator continues until there are no more new ideas.
- Continue with the next key concept until the harvest has been exhausted.

B.3 SCAMPER

1. What?

SCAMPER is an acronym which consists of the first letters of the seven approaches which one can use to change a product or service. This technique was developed by Bob Eberle, an American author who has written many books about creativity. SCAMPER is very useful when brainstorming for new products. It can be compared to the presumptions technique, but is easier to apply for new products. All implied characteristics come to the forefront.

2. Why?

SCAMPER asks seven questions about the product. Brainstorming about each of the seven approaches leads to new 'outside the box' product ideas.

3. When?

SCAMPER can be used in many new product brainstorming sessions. It usually happens at the start of the divergence phase to discard product characteristics which have been the same for years. The TRIZ and SIT methods work in the same way and are useful as boosters when generating product ideas.

4. Where in the process?

The best moment is at the start of the divergence phase during the new product brainstorming session, directly after the assignment and the first spontaneous brain dump.

5. How?

Timing:

- For as long as it lasts
- Usually with 12–14 participants for 1 hour

Participants:

- The facilitator
- Usually 12–14 participants

Process:

- SCAMPER places seven approaches central:

- S = Substitute. What can I replace in the composition, the material, the appearance and the size, and so on, of the product?
- C = Combine. What can I combine with the product to improve it?
- A = Adapt. Can I adapt the product to something else or can I copy something from other sectors?
- M = Magnify/Minimise/Modify? What can I magnify, minimise or modify about the product?
- P = Put to other uses. Can I use the product for something else?
- E = Eliminate. What can I eliminate?
- R = Reverse/Rearrange. Is there anything I can reverse, turn inside out or do in a different order?

• Generate ideas by dealing with the questions about the seven approaches of SCAMPER one by one.
  - The facilitator mentions all the questions for each approach.
  - The facilitator asks the participants to create new product ideas and write them down on a post-it.
  - The facilitator continues with the next approach and harvests the post-it.

B.4 Flower Association

1. What?

The basic principle of an association is that it brings forth another thought. A flower association is the first investigation of the context about a specific core concept in the assignment.

2. Why?

It helps the participants to set the first step to become detached from the most logical directions by naming elements people associate with the core concept.

3. When?

A flower association is a useful basic technique which can form part of many brainstorming sessions in order to investigate the territory and get an image of the context. This technique is useful during the new product brainstorm to identify the enclosed thought patterns about the product offer, the distribution channel, the target group, the buying and user behaviour.

4. Where in the process?

A flower association usually happens as one of the first creative techniques in the divergence phase after the presumption and brain dump. However, it can also be used in between.

5. How?

Timing:

- Usually with 12–14 participants and different 'flowers' for 30–45 minutes

Participants:

- The facilitator
- Usually 12–14 participants

Process:

- Determine the core concepts
- What are the core concepts in the assignment or in the market?
  - Allow the participants to write down the core concepts.
  - Allow the participants to name the core concepts.
  - Choose the most important three to five core concepts.
- Do the flower association.
  - Questions:
    * What do you associate this concept with?
    * What type of aspects does the concept have?
    * What does the concept remind you of?
  - Write down all the words (like flower leaves) around the concept which take central place (hence flower association).
- The facilitator asks which new product ideas the participants have created. After a while the facilitator harvests the ideas.
  - The participants read their own ideas. The facilitator collects the post-its and asks the participants to write new ideas on new post-its again.
  - The facilitator continues until there are no more new ideas.
- The facilitator continues with the next concepts and the next flower association.

B.5 Biomimicry (Nature Analogy)

Biomimicry is derived from bios (life) and mimesis (imitate, copy). Life on earth is millions of years old and nature, through evolution, has found many solutions. Biomimicry is a relatively young science which studies nature and uses it as a source of inspiration for the challenges with which people are confronted. Janine Benyus, the promoter of Biomimicry, wrote about it in 1997 *Biomimicry: Innovation Inspired by Nature*. Biomimicry is commonly used to solve technical (design) problems. This is a fairly simple brainstorming technique which uses nature as a source of inspiration.

1. What?

Two things are analogous when they have something in common. Through nature analogy you search for 'something in your surrounding area' that resembles a core concept in the assignment. This can be an animal, tree or natural phenomenon. When you relate back to the innovation assignment based on the characteristics of the analogue subject, it forms a source of inspiration for new product ideas.

2. Why?

We try to investigate surprisingly new possibilities which will lead to 'outside the box' product ideas by taking a step to things which surround us in order to relate back to the assignment.

3. When?

This method can be easily applied in many new product brainstorming sessions, to find out what the 'things in our biotope' bring to mind.

4. Where in the process?

Not at the beginning of the divergence phase, but somewhere in the middle or at the end.

5. How?

Timing:

- For as long as it lasts
- Usually with 12–14 participants for 30 minutes

Participants:

- The facilitator
- Usually 12–14 participants

Process:

- The facilitator asks:
  - When you consider the assignment (or the product, or the customer) as starting point, of which animal or object does it make you think?
  - The facilitator writes down the names of these animals or objects.
- The facilitator then chooses one animal or object. Choose one which is known by all and which can give inspiration.

- Relate back to new product ideas based on some of the characteristics.
  - What are the characteristics of the animal or object?
  - Use these characteristics as a source of inspiration for new product ideas and ask the participants to write it on a post-it.
  - The facilitator continues until there are no more new ideas.
  - Continue with the next characteristic until all have been completed.

You will find more information about Biomimicry at:

- www.biomimicryinstitute.org
- www.designboom.com/contemporary/biomimicry.html

B.6 Comic Hero Analogy

1. What?

In comic strips everything is possible. The heroes are not bothered by the fixed patterns in reality. Furthermore, in comic strips the fixed patterns are broken through and the boundaries are moved. And this is exactly what we are looking for during the brainstorm. We stimulate our own fantasies by 'climbing into the skin' of our favourite comic hero of our youth. Then we ask ourselves which new product ideas will they come up with.

2. Why?

We try to find surprisingly new possibilities to investigate which will lead to 'outside the box' product ideas by taking a step into the world of fantasy and then relate to the assignment.

3. When?

The comic hero analogy is easy to apply in many new product brainstorming sessions in order to come up with different thoughts generated by our comic strip heroes from our youth.

4. Where in the process?

Not at the beginning of the divergence phase, but somewhere in the middle or at the end. This technique can be used with success after the nature analogy.

5. How?

Timing:

- For as long as it lasts
- Usually with 12–14 participants for 30 minutes

Participants:

- The facilitator
- Usually 12–14 participants

Process:

- The facilitator asks:
  - What was your favourite comic strip hero when you were young?
- Relate back to the innovation assignment via the imaginary hero.
  - Put yourself in place of the comic strip hero. Which new product ideas would Asterix or Donald Duck create? Ask the participants to write these ideas on post-its.
  - The facilitator continues until there are no more new ideas.

Tip: Should the participants not have any specific comic strip hero, then you can ask them about a fairy tale figure or a film star they liked when they were young.

B.7 Silly Things

1. What?

With this creative technique you confront the participants with an object which lies completely outside the context or theme of the new product brainstorm, such as a garden gnome, rattle or binoculars. The 'feedback' based on the characteristics of the object can lead to inspiration for new product ideas.

2. Why?

We are trying to get surprising connections which will lead to real 'outside the box' product ideas by confronting the participants with something which is completely outside the context and to relate it back to the assignment.

3. When?

The silly things technique is easily applied in many new product brainstorming sessions, to find out what this strange object can bring to mind.

4. Where in the process?

If you do it too early during the divergence phase you run the risk of losing the rational thinkers: 'I have better things to do than to write down ideas with a garden gnome in my hand.' Therefore, don't do it at the beginning of the divergence phase, but somewhere in the middle or the end. After two or three other divergence techniques you can easily lead the group to associations which are further removed from reality.

5. How?

Timing:

• Usually with 12–14 participants for 30 minutes

Participants:

• The facilitator
• Usually 12–14 participants

Process:

• The facilitator hands out a completely random object which has nothing to do with the product or the market.
• The participants study the object and are then asked to think about the specific characteristics of it.
• Relate back to the assignment based on these characteristics.
  – What are the characteristics of this object?
  – Use the characteristics as a source of inspiration for new product ideas and ask the participants to write them on post-its.
  – The facilitator continues until there are no more new ideas.

Tip: A box full of strange objects can be made up as follows: Go to a huge warehouse and pick the third object you see on every shelf. Within 10 minutes you will have a box with 25 'silly things'.

B.8 The Insight Game

1. What?

The Insight Game is a divergence technique whereby new product ideas are generated around the most important customer frictions (which were discovered during the focus groups in the Observe and Learn stage) in combination with the strengths of the organisation. For this technique you can make a board game that might need some adjustment on the spot. The participants work in groups of three or four.

2. Why?

The combination of the discovered customer frictions during the Observe and Learn stage together with the strengths of the company creates a beautiful source of inspiration for innovation. By making a special board game and by working in groups it brings a welcome change from the usual way of brainstorming.

3. When?

The Insight Game, included in the FORTH method, is only useful during the new product brainstorming session when, during the Observe and Learn stage, the focus groups and the conversations with the customers have been done and customer frictions have been discovered. (Or when the customer frictions have been discovered via online research.)

4. Where in the process?

The best time for the Insight Game is during the divergence phase of the new product brainstorming session. At this moment there are probably new participants who have not done any customer visits during the Observe and Learn stage. The game is an effective way in which to involve them with the new insights.

5. How?

Timing:

- Flexible: 1–2 hours

Participants:

- The facilitator
- The participants who have observed the focus groups and customers in the Observe and Learn stage
- The outsiders
- A maximum of 14 participants, a minimum of 12

Process:

- Choose the most relevant customer frictions.

All the customer friction boards from the Observe and Learn stage are on display in the brainstorming room. Each participant receives four stickers which they have to stick on those customer frictions they think are most favourable in the light of the assignment. During the FORTH method this takes place in the last Observe and Learn workshop in the Observe and Learn stage.

- Choose the strengths of the organisations.

  Each participant receives green post-its on which they write a maximum of four strengths of the company which can serve as a competitive advantage in the light of the assignment. The facilitator then sticks the post-its on the wall. Each participant receives four stickers and sticks them on the strengths they find most favourable in the light of the assignment.

- Play the game.

  Each group (four in other words) is given a four-by-four matrix with the client frictions in the rows and the strengths of the company in the columns. Number it 1 to 16. Write the customer frictions and strengths on it.

- Play the board game.
  - The facilitator divides the participants in groups of three or four. Each group receives a board game, a dice and a pawn.
  - Player one throws the dice and moves the number of squares indicated on the dice. He then lands on a square which is a combination of an insight and a strength. The players brainstorm together over the combination and note their ideas on a post-it.
  - Should the brainstorming end, player two throws the dice and the game is repeated.
  - The combinations which have already been used, are crossed out and you continue until all 16 squares have been used.
  - At the end of the game the players choose the three squares which have generated product ideas with the most potential.
  - At the completion of the game the participants read all their post-its from the chosen combinations and they are then stuck on the idea wall.

Tip: Use extra brainstorming techniques. The facilitator chooses one or more of the most favourable squares and uses another divergence technique to brainstorm around this combination of insight and strength. Consider: Flower association, Nature analogy or Super hero. Maybe even the Presumptions.

B.9 Climb into the Skin of …

1. What?

With this brainstorming technique ideas are generated by climbing into the skin of another human being from the target group. When the participants imagine themselves as 'this person' then ideas are created in their new role.

2. Why?

By climbing into the skin of another human being from the target group you create different angles from which new ideas can come. This technique helps when brainstorming for the business-to-consumer markets as suddenly abstract customers now become 'real people'. However, it can also be applied when brainstorming for a business-to-business market. In this case the rational and respected manager becomes 'an unsure person in a difficult decision-making process' right in front of their eyes.

3. When?

This technique is useful when a concrete target group has been established which is not too far removed from those who are going to brainstorm.

4. Where in the process?

This technique can be used during the kick-off workshop to be able to imagine you as part of the target group and so identify innovation opportunities. Another moment where it is also useful to apply the Climb into the Skin technique is during the divergence phase of the brainstorming session. The participants have by then done customer visits and they can draw from their own experience.

5. How?

Timing:

- Flexible: ½–1 hour

Participants:

- The facilitator
- 12–14 participants

Process:

- Ask the participants, maybe with the Flower association technique, to distinguish the 'types' or 'characters' from the target group.
- For the consumer market:
  - the seemingly uninterested adolescent
  - the energetic 70 year old who is travelling the world
  - the 24/7 X-Box gamer
  - the beer-drinking motor biker in the neighbourhood (with all due respect)
- For the business-to-business market, for example the energy market:
  - the desperate buyer who is taking great risks with the rising energy prices
  - the manufacturing manager for who continuity is the most important aspect
  - the controller who does not want to deviate when it comes to cost-price calculations
  - the director who does not want to spend one cent more on energy than is necessary
- Ask either the individual participants or the groups of three to four, to climb into the skin of a real person fully, including a name, address, daily activity, work, hobby and so on. Stimulate them in such a way that they will imitate their chosen 'type'. By using caricatures it eases the imagining process, causes great pleasure and through exaggeration it generates effective angles of approach for new ideas.
- Ask the individual participants (after they have finished laughing) to create new product or service ideas through this 'new person' and to write them down on a post-it.
- Harvest the post-its.

More information about brainstorming techniques during the divergence phase can be found at:

- www.mycoted.com/Category:Creativity_Techniques
- www.d-sciencelab.be/newpic/glossary/index.html
- www.creatingminds.org/tools/tools.htm
- www.brainstorming.co.uk/tutorials/creativethinkingcontents.html
- www.mindtools.com/brainstm.html
- www.innovationtools.com/resources/brainstorming.asp

SECTION C BRAINSTORMING TECHNIQUES TO CONVERGE

C.1 Grouping of Ideas

1. What?

With this technique the convergence phase starts. The idea wall is full of post-its, hundreds of them, some useful and others useless. Do not be surprised when after Day 1 of the new product brainstorming session there are more than 500 post-its on the wall. This technique helps you to group those post-its which are linked to one direction.

2. Why?

With the grouping of the post-its you create order in the 'chaos'. Product ideas which are identical or are closely related are now brought together. The purpose is to uncover the different directions of all the ideas. This technique does not allow you to make a choice, but to only group the ideas.

3. When?

The grouping is done to give a first insight into the different directions of the ideas.

4. When in the process?

The convergence phase usually starts with this technique.

5. How?

Timing:

- Usually with 12–14 participants for 45 minutes, depending on the number of post-its

Participants:

- The facilitator
- Usually with 12–14 participants

Process:

- The facilitator asks the participants to study the 'wall of post-its' well. Explain that all the ideas will still be part of the brainstorming session at the end of this stage. For now, they have to choose the two post-its which they believe are the strongest. Allow 5–10 minutes so that they can study the impressive wall well. Ask them to choose a post-it which is 'close to home' and another which 'lies further away'. In this way you do not only get feasible solutions but also outside the box ideas.

- The facilitator asks the participants to read out the post-it. Subsequently the group chooses a name which represents the idea direction. Each idea direction gets a title. In this way the facilitator deals with each selected post-it. Should two post-its indicate the same direction they are stuck next to each other. The facilitator continues until the group has the impression that all possible idea directions have been completed. At a new product brainstorming session 20 to 30 idea directions are not unusual.
- During earlier FORTH brainstorms the rest of the post-its were also grouped under the named idea directions. As there are often more than 500 post-its, it is very intensive and takes too much time. These days, I do not do this anymore and in practice it has shown that it does not have detrimental consequences for the quality of the final concepts. I continue directly with the selection of the strongest idea directions.

C.2 Selecting Idea Directions

1. What?

This technique often follows the grouping and naming of the 20 to 30 idea directions. With this technique you make sure that the strongest directions are chosen and developed further into idea mind-maps in the next stage.

2. Why?

During Day 2 of the new product brainstorming session there is not enough time available to develop the 20 to 30 idea directions into concept boards. On the morning of Day 2 you can however, with 12–14 participants, develop 12 new product or service ideas into concept boards. In groups of three or four participants each concept is worked out in an hour. This is repeated three times. In practice you will notice that after the development of three new product ideas the participants are 'done'. Having done the selection on Day 1 you now focus the attention on the 12 strongest idea directions as decided by the participants.

3. When?

You select the best idea directions in any way. The idea directions which fall off, you save. They will not be developed further in the brainstorming session, yet they can still be very useful later on. For this reason the flip-charts, with the idea directions not selected, stay in sight. They might possibly serve as inspiration when it comes to the development of the concept boards on Day 2 or they might even still be useful in the development process which follows the brainstorm.

4. Where in the process?

The selection of the idea directions happens after the grouping of the ideas during the convergence phase.

5. How?

Timing:

*   Usually 12–14 participants for 30 minutes, depending on the number of directions

Participants:

*   The facilitator
*   Usually 12–14 participants

Process:

*   The facilitator hands out stickers and asks the participants to stick them on the idea direction they believe to be the strongest. In other words, they must choose the idea directions which they would like to develop into a concrete product or service idea on Day 2. Each participant is only allowed to stick one sticker on an idea direction.
*   After this has been done, the facilitator determines, in collaboration with the internal client and the project leader, which directions are the strongest. The principle of the one with the most stickers is the strongest, work best. I often give the internal client a 'wild card' so that he/she might also make a choice and maybe give a 'hidden pearl' a second chance.
*   The chosen 12 idea directions are then developed into idea mind-maps by using the next technique.

Tip: The number of stickers depends on the number of directions. Experience has taught that with 20 to 30 idea directions, seven stickers per participant give a good division between stronger and weaker idea directions.

C.3 Idea Mind-Mapping

Mind-mapping is a well-known brainstorming technique. Tony Buzan, an English psychologist, has made this technique popular. When mind-mapping you place the main theme in the centre and around it you write keywords associated with the theme. You usually use different colours and you can also add drawings. It is a simple technique which is also very visual as everybody immediately sees what it is all about.

1. What?

With this technique an idea direction is developed into an idea mind-map. The idea is central and the participants brainstorm to individually add various ideas about the 'what?' 'for whom?' and 'how?'. In this way a mind-map is developed for each idea direction where each participant has added their own associations.

2. Why?

Individually each participant adds their 'own taste' to the development of the idea directions by adding key words. In this way the idea directions becomes more concrete without having to make a specific choice for the development yet. In practice you will notice that many of the original post-its now return in a different combination. With this technique you also end Day 1 of the two-day brainstorming session in a good way.

3. When?

Mind-mapping is a universal technique and can be useful when wanting to make an abstract idea more concrete. However, it can also be used to unravel a problem or to summarise something.

4. Where in the process?

During the brainstorming session you use the mind-mapping of idea directions in the convergence phase. The purpose is to diverge a bit and then to develop possible differences with which the idea becomes more visible. During the next stage the idea will actually be developed more concretely into a specific direction on a concept board.

5. How?

Timing:

- Usually with 12–14 participants and 12 idea directions for 45 minutes

Participants:

- The facilitator
- Usually 12–14 participants

Process:

- The facilitator explains how mind-mapping works and discusses a mind-map sheet. On a flip-chart page the idea direction, written on a post-it, is placed in the centre. It already has three sub-divisions: 'what?' 'for whom?' and 'how?'. In total there are 12 empty mind-map sheets, one for each idea direction.
- The facilitator gives the participants a marker and asks them to add what they associate with the idea on the sheet, either in the form of words or drawings. Of course judgement should be left for later.
- The participants are allowed 20–30 minutes in order to enrich the 12 idea mind-maps with their ideas about its development.
- As soon as everyone is done, the facilitator asks the participants to each read out an idea mind-map. In this way everybody gets a good image of the possible developments for each idea. This activity then concludes the first day of the two-day brainstorming session.
- More information about mind-mapping can be found at:
  - www.buzanworld.com
  - www.12manage.com/methods_mind_mapping_nl.html
  - http://www.mindtools.com/pages/article/newISS_01.htm

C.4 With Ketchup?

1. What?

The product concepts are explained in a sales pitch, a short verbal explanation of 5 minutes. With this technique an attempt is made to improve the concepts, presented one by one.

2. Why?

To give the participants in the brainstorming session, who have not been directly involved in the development of the concepts, the opportunity to, with their good ideas, help to improve the concepts.

3. When?

It can be used when you have the feeling that the participants who were not directly involved with the concept idea, have valuable suggestions.

4. Where in the process?

At the end of the convergence phase in order to improve the concept ideas.

5. How?

Timing:

- Usually with 12–14 participants for 5 minutes per product idea

Participants:

- The facilitator
- Usually 12–14 participants

Process:

- The facilitator asks one of the participants to present the concept board to the whole group in a few minutes.
- The facilitator asks the rest of the participants if they have any ideas which will make the concept stronger and then to write it on a post-it.
- The facilitator discusses the additional ideas, and sticks the extra post-it with the idea on the concept board.
- The facilitator continues with the next concept board and the process is repeated until all the concepts have been presented.

The original deviser of the 'With ketchup?' technique is Richard Stomp, who was my client for the design of the ideation approach at the ANWB (the Dutch AAA).

C.5 Salt and Pepper

1. What?

The purpose of this technique is to attempt to improve a good basic idea which was not selected during the brainstorming session on Day 1 but with possible interesting additions, by making the main ingredient more tasty with salt and pepper (ideas). This happens during the convergence phase.

2. Why?

An idea is never complete, not even at the end of a new product brainstorming session. By combining the developed product idea in the convergence phase with other ideas it may just become a more attractive product idea.

3. When?

You may add this technique to the programme when you have the feeling that, besides having selected the best ideas and developed the concept boards, there are still some qualities hanging on the wall of ideas on the rest of the post-its. By spicing up the developed concept boards with the rest, a tasty meal is created. Salmon with curry, perhaps?

4. Where in the process?

At the end of the convergence phase, to make a good idea even better.

5. How?

Timing:

- Usually 12–14 participants with approximately 20 minutes for each product idea. As it takes a lot of time, use this technique selectively

Participants:

- The facilitator
- Usually 12–14 participants

Process:

- The facilitator, in consultation with the group, chooses one of the developed concepts where, according to all the participants, there is still a lot of room for improvement. One of the participants is asked to explain the idea.
- The facilitator then asks the participants to walk past the original idea wall and choose one idea which can function as 'salt and pepper' for the original concept. In other words: 'Choose the idea which can make this concept better.'
- Each participant then explains their 'salt and pepper idea'. The group discuss this and choose which elements are added and which are not.
- The process is repeated with the next idea.

Tip: Give the group who has developed the concept board the right to choose which ideas will be added and which ideas will not. In this way the group continues to be 'the owner' of the idea.

C.6 Improving (Improving the Negative Aspects)

1. What?

With the help of this technique an attempt is made to improve a developed product idea by quickly adding up the plus and minus aspects and developing the negative aspects. This technique is similar to the 'salt and pepper', but in this case the positive and negative aspects are mentioned explicitly. These positive and negative aspects will also appear as a result of the qualitative concept research with customers during the Test Ideas stage.

2. Why?

To make a developed product concept (in the next stage) even better.

3. When?

- When, during the presentation of the concept boards, you notice that the group still finds too many negative aspects about the developed product idea and you quickly want to improve it.
- When you notice from the qualitative market research that the developed new product concept can (drastically) be improved.

4. Where in the process?

- During the convergence phase, to make the first selected ideas even better.
- After the qualitative concept research of the new product concept with the target group in the Improvement workshop.

5. How?

Timing:

- Usually with 12–14 participants for about 60 minutes per product concept

Participants:

- The facilitator
- Usually 12–14 participants

Process:

- The facilitator, in consultation with the group, chooses which developed product ideas are eligible for further development. Usually the qualitative research in the Test Ideas stage will provide the answer immediately.
- The facilitator divides the participants into groups of two or three and then, in consultation with the project leader, divides the product concepts amongst the group. In this way four to seven concepts can be improved simultaneously by the group. The improvements are adapted on the original concept description immediately.
- The participants present the improved concepts to each other. More additions from the group might be added.
- You continue until all eligible concepts have been discussed.

C.7 Multi-criteria Selection of Concept Boards

1. What?

With this technique the final rank order of the 12 developed product ideas on the concept boards are determined.

2. Why?

It is all about choosing the product ideas with the most potential and which according to the participants have met the criteria mentioned in the assignment. This takes place at the end of the brainstorming session.

3. When?

You involve all 12 developed concept boards in the selection. It is about determining the rank order. All the developed product or service ideas on the concept boards go through to the next phase of the FORTH method: the concept description workshop. It is possible that the decision of the participants regarding the attractiveness of the developed ideas will change in the follow-up processes after the reflection on the concepts by customers.

4. Where in the process?

This technique is applied at the end of the convergence phase to determine the rank order and attractiveness.

5. How?

Timing:

- Usually with 12–14 participants with 12 concept boards for approximately 60 minutes

Participants:

- The facilitator
- Usually 12–14 participants

Process:

You have already made evaluation boards. All concept boards with the product ideas are displayed on the tables along the wall. For each concept board there is one evaluation board. The facilitator shows the evaluation boards and discusses the way in which evaluation should take place. This is an important moment, so make sure to allow enough time. It is also good to show the participants that much thought has gone into the way in which evaluation takes place and that the criteria have been chosen in close consultation with the project leader and internal client.

- The facilitator explains that each developed product idea is evaluated on five criteria. For each criterion the participants have the possibility to give the idea 0 to 5 points (stickers). 0 = low; 5 = high. The categories for each criterion are explained with the help of the evaluation board.
- The facilitator hands out the sticker sheets with the task to evaluate each product idea according to the five criteria.
- After all the participants have evaluated all the concept boards, the facilitator gives the sign that all the stickers for each board are counted. The facilitator is the first to know the rank order of attractiveness of the developed product ideas. He keeps the result a secret.

Tip: With 14 participants and 12 concept boards, each concept board is occupied. The participants walk around randomly until the next board is free. Suggest that each one place their initials on the concept boards onto which they have already placed their stickers. In this way they know which concepts they have evaluated. It is also a useful way of controlling whether all the participants have evaluated each product idea.

C.8 I Love You

1. What?

This nice technique gives 'extra magic' to the previous technique, where the final evaluation is determined. With an 'I love you' sticker in the shape of a red heart the participants can now give their favourite idea extra support with this final evaluation.

2. Why?

It can happen that you fall in love with a product idea and it 'doesn't want to let go of you'. You have actually given it your heart. However, it can happen that through the rational character of the previous multi-criteria selection the idea ends in the middle or at the end of the group. Why then should we not allow, apart from the rational, also the gut feeling to play a role in the evaluation?

3. When?

When you, as facilitator, want to add playfulness at the end of the rational process.

4. Where in the process?

At the end of the convergence phase, together with the multi-criteria selection.

5. How?

Timing:

- At the same time as the previous technique. Experience has shown that it does not take much extra time.

Participants:

- The facilitator
- Usually 12–14 participants

Process:

- The facilitator hands out only one 'I love you' sticker to each participant with the request to openly declare their love to the developed product or service idea which has stolen their heart.

- The participants then stick their heart, together with the evaluation stickers, on the selection board of their choice.
- At the presentation of the final rank order the facilitator not only pays attention to the number of stickers of the previous technique but also to the concepts which have received the most hearts.

Tip: In most cases the hearts go to the concepts which end high. If that is not the case, then it should be pointed out to the group in order to find the reason for this. How is it possible that the concept boards which received the most hearts have scored so low? The participants have the right to alter the rank order on the basis of a contextual discussion, certainly if there are solid grounds for it.

The original deviser of the 'I love you' technique is Richard Stomp, who was my client for the design of the ideation approach at the ANWB (Dutch AAA).

More information about brainstorming to converge can be found at:

- www.mycoted.com/Category:Idea_Selection
- www.creatingminds.org/tools/tools_selection.htm
- http://www.innovationtools.com/Articles/EnterpriseDetails.asp?a=351

SECTION D: OTHER FORMS OF BRAINSTORMING

Apart from the regular brainstorming with a divergent and convergent phase in a group there are also other forms of brainstorming. Many new brainstorming games (D.1) are entering the market. Some are suitable for brainstorming in groups, other for brainstorming on your own. Digitalising also creates practical alternatives for brainstorming. For this reason this appendix also pays attention to brainstorm software (D.2) and online brainstorming (D.3).

D.1 Brainstorm Games

Brainstorming brings to mind something playful and nice to do. It is therefore not surprising that many games have been created to either brainstorm in a group or individually. The games are usually very simple and often take over the role of the facilitator. Below you will find four popular games which can help you to brainstorm individually or in a group.

D.1.1 Brainstorming games to brainstorm individually

- Free the Genie Cards (www.ideachampions.com/free_the_genie.shtml):
  Free the Genie is a set of 55 creative thinking cards for open-minded people.

- The KnowBrainer (www.solutionpeople.com/kbtool):
  A useful tool with 180 cards which include questions, quotes, words and images to provide you with inspiration for new ideas.

- Thinkpak (www.creativethinking.net):
  A set of brainstorming cards by Michael Michalko to stimulate creativity and get new ideas.

- Innovative Whack Pack (www.creativewhack.com):
  A set of cards made by Roger von Oech with 60 creative ways and inspired by the old Greek philosopher Heraclitus.

D.1.2 Brainstorming games for groups

- IDEO method cards (www.ideo.com/work/item/method-cards):
  A set of 51 cards by the world famous designing agency IDEO, which contain various ways in which the designer teams can understand the target group better.

- Metaforio (www.mytholius.com):
  An instrument for visual and creative development based on the technique of visual thought. The game consists of a set of 53 inspiring training cards based on the garden metaphor.

D.2 Brainstorm Software

Brainstorm software is available in large numbers. The focus lies in two areas: software for mind-mapping and software to support the whole brainstorming process. Below are some examples of both types:

- CREAX Innovation Suite (www.creaxinnovationsuite.com):
  An extensive and user-friendly package regarding systematic innovation, based on TRIZ (see E.1) from Creax in Belgium. It offers a step-by-step approach to the whole innovation process.

- Flashbrainer (www.solutionpeople.com/flashbrainer):
  A brainstorming programme which consists of four steps (Investigate, Create, Evaluate and Activate) and it leads you through the innovation process.

- Mindmanager (www.mindjet.com):
  The most well-known and extensive mind-map package. It has various editions and all sorts of 'add-ons'.

- Visual Mind (www.visual-mind.com):
  A software program for mind-mapping. An 'add-on' has recently been made (The Realizer) which helps you to generate and evaluate ideas in a practical way.

D.3 Online Brainstorming

There are many idea generating tools available on the internet. They are free of charge and are usually practical and simple instruments to bring you to new ideas, such as the 'Ideagenerator' described below. Websites where you can mind-map online without any software, such as 'Mindmeister', are also very popular. Other sites allow you to generate and evaluate online ideas immediately within a group, such as 'Brainreactions' and 'Brainstormnet'.

- Mindmeister (www.mindmeister.com):
  A mind-mapping tool with which you can create mind-maps online and in a group.

- Ideagenerator (www.tdbspecialprojects.com):
  When you click on the free online idea generator you unexpectedly receive original word combinations which can create new ideas within the group.

- Brainreactions (www.brainreactions.net):
  Online brainstorming rooms, where together with others, you can generate and evaluate around a self chosen challenge.

SECTION E: OTHER TECHNIQUES

E.1 TRIZ

TRIZ is a Russian acronym for Teoriya Resheniya Izobreatatelskikh Zadatch, which means Theory of Inventive Problem-solving. The founder of TRIZ is the Russian engineer Genrich Altshuller. He began the development of his theory in 1946 while working at a patent office of the Russian navy. There he was fascinated with the question as to how an invention is created. Are inventions unique and brilliant occurrences? Are they coincidental treasures? Or are there systematic patterns which lie at the base of it? Altshuller did not believe in the trial-and-error method for which Thomas Edison is known (innovation is 1 per cent inspiration and 99 per cent perspiration) and started looking for a more effective and systematic method. He became convinced that the basis of the inventions lies in systematic patterns. To prove this he studied hundreds of thousands of patents regarding mutuality and repeated patterns. In the meantime TRIZ scientists have collectively analysed more than a million patents.

At the end of the 1980s TRIZ scientist developed, under the guidance of Altshuller, a series of very strong but also very complex instruments. The skill to be able to use these, which are now known as the Traditional TRIZ, requires prolonged training and practice. After the Iron Curtain came down the investigation and the developed TRIZ theory received more attention. At the beginning of the 1990s TRIZ moved from Russia to the United States and Western Europe. The most important results of the investigation are that all innovations can be relayed to a number of principles and that the evolution of the technological advancement passes through a number of predictable patterns. TRIZ authorities, Boris Zlotin and Alla Zusman of Ideation Inc. have produced hundreds of these evolution patterns.

Traditional TRIZ is powerful but complex and not easily accessible to people without any technical background. TRIZ experts Darrel Mann in Europe, CREAX in Belgium and the sympathetic Russian Valeri Souchkov in the Netherlands have made it more accessible. In the United States Zlotin and Zusman, after many years of research, have successfully joined the instruments of the Traditional TRIZ in one integrated system, known as I-TRIZ. This system is even more powerful but at the same time much more accessible and user friendly because of the new software. Over the years other, more simple, systematic innovation techniques derived from TRIZ have been created. They are easier to apply, such as SIT (see the explanation E.2). The table below gives a description of the 40 TRIZ-principles from the Traditional TRIZ, with a short explanation and a practical example wherein you will recognise its application.

Table A2.2   Forty TRIZ-principles as a source of inspiration for new product ideas

N	Principle	Description	Product Example
1.	Segmentation, fragmentation or division	Divide the product into independent parts in order to isolate or integrate useful or harmful characteristics.	Shop-in-the-shop concept
2.	Taking out, omission, separation or isolation	Separate one or more of the interfering or harmful parts or properties and/or use the only necessary property.	Caffeine-free coffee.
3.	Local quality	Change the structure from uniform to non-uniform (locally) of one of the products to get the desired function.	Easy opening of a carton of juice
4.	Asymmetry, symmetry change	Change the shape of an object from symmetrical to asymmetrical.	A special vase for tulips
5.	Merging, combining, consolidating, integrating	Bring functions, characteristics or parts of a product together in time and space so that a new, desired or unique result is produced.	Mobile telephone with navigation system
6.	Universality, multi-functionality	Make a product more uniform, universal, extensive and multi-functional.	A drill with which you can also screw

Table A2.2 *Continued*

N	Principle	Description	Product Example
7.	Nested doll	Products which fit against, next to or in each other.	Patio chairs which when stacked up, use less space
8.	Anti-weight	Compensate for a negative aspect of the product with an opposite power from the environment (and so create a uniform division).	Hovercraft
9.	Preliminary anti-action	Analyse in advance what can go wrong and then take actions to eliminate, decrease or prevent it.	Sun-tan oil
10.	Preliminary action	Perform an action before another action or event. Do something in advance.	Local anaesthetic
11.	Beforehand cushioning	Realise that nothing is perfectly trustworthy so compensate in advance.	Car wax to protect the paintwork
12.	Equipotentiality	Make sure that there is no tension in or around a system or make them all equal.	Anti-wrinkle cream
13.	The other way around	Apply an opposite or reverse action. Turn it upside down or inside out.	Heinz squeeze bottles
14.	Curved or spherical shape	Replace linear aspects (for example, shape, movement, power) with a curved or spherical shape.	Black & Decker 'Mouse'-grinding machine
15.	Dynamics	Make a product, condition or aspect short lived, temporary, moveable, adaptable, flexible or changeable.	Discount for early bookers
16.	A bit more or less, partial or excessive actions	Use 'a bit more' of one action or substance than necessary and deal with the results. Use a 'little less' of an action or substance than necessary and deal with the results.	Extra-thick soup
17.	Another dimension	Change the orientation of a linear (straight) product from vertical to horizontal, from horizontal to diagonal, from horizontal to vertical and so on. Work in another dimension or in several layers.	Cookies with different layers
18.	Mechanical vibration	Use shaking, vibrations or oscillations to get a positive effect of a desired function.	Power plate
19.	Periodic actions	Replace continuous actions with periodic or pulsating actions. Change the way in which an action is performed.	Philips Sonic electric toothbrush
20.	Continuity of useful action	Create a continuous stream (circulation) and/or remove all useless, interim and unproductive movements to increase the efficiency.	Internet booking without tickets
21.	Hasten, skipping, running ahead	If something goes wrong at a specific tempo, then do it more quickly.	Broadband internet

Table A2.2 *Continued*

N	Principle	Description	Product Example
22.	Blessing in disguise	Find ways in which disadvantages can be used to add value. Turn a disadvantage into an advantage.	Slow-food restaurant
23.	Feedback	Feed the output of one system back into the system as an input to improve the control of the output.	Telephone number for complaints on the packaging of products
24.	Intermediary	Mediate a temporary connection between incompatible parties, functions, events or conditions. Use a temporary carrier, barrier or a temporary process which can be removed easily again.	Packaging of a microwave meal
25.	Self-service	Allow an object or system to carry out certain functions on its own or to organise it independently.	Online investment
26.	Copying	Use a copy, replica or model instead of using something too valuable, vulnerable or unavailable.	Crash simulators for cars via computer models
27.	Cheap short-living products	Use cheaper, more simple or disposable objects to decrease the cost, and to increase the user friendliness and so on.	Disposable crockery
28.	Mechanics substitution	Replace mechanical inter actions with physical fields or with other forms, actions or conditions. This principle is about the changing or replacing of the operational principle of a system.	Bicycle with an engine.
29.	Pneumatics and hydraulics	Replace the components or functions of one system with pneumatic (air) or hydraulic (water) components or functions.	Bicycle with springy fork.
30.	Flexible shells and thin films	Replace traditional constructions with constructions of thin films or flexible/pliable membranes.	Hansaplast liquid plasters
31.	Porous materials	Change the characteristics or functions of an object, system or material (solid, liquid or gas) by making it more porous. Create cavities and add a useful substance or function.	Porous plaster with iodine which allows air to pass through.
32.	Colour changes	Change the colour or other optical aspects of an object or system to increase the value of the system or to discover problems.	Tefal pan with red mark
33.	Homogeneity, uniformity	When two or more objects or substances influence each other, then it is better to consist of the same material, energy or information.	School uniforms
34.	Discarding and recovering	Throwing away of parts of a system and recycling is basically the same. Throwing away removes something from the system. Recycling brings something back to the system in order to use it again.	Recycling of packaging

Table A2.2 *Concluded*

N	Principle	Description	Product Example
35.	Parameter changes	Change the characteristics of a system to gain a useful advantage.	Hosepipe with sprinkler holes
36.	Phase transition	Use the phase transition (for example, from a solid to a liquid or from a liquid to a gas and so on) of one material or situation to implement an effective change or to create a change in the system.	Singing kettle
37.	Thermal expansion	Change heat energy into mechanical energy or action.	Bimetallic strip in a thermometer
38.	Strong oxidants	Strengthen oxidative processes to improve an action or function.	Extra oxygen in a cutting torch
39.	Inert atmosphere	Create a neutral (inertia) atmosphere or environment to support a desired function.	Vacuum electric cooker
40.	Composite materials	Change a homogenous structure of a material to a compound structure.	Insulating material

Sources: D. Mann, S. Dewulf, B. Zlotin, A. Zusman (2003). *Matrix 2003: Updating the TRIZ Contradiction Matrix*. Ieper (Belgium): Creax Press (principles and sub-principles) and G. Altshuller (2005). *40 Principles: TRIZ Keys to Technical Innovation. Extended Edition*. Worcester, MA: Technical Innovation Centre Inc (descriptions).

My gratitude to Karel Bolckmans who helped to generate many examples.

These TRIZ principles can be applied in a new product brainstorming session as a source of inspiration for the generating of new product ideas. It is advisable to start TRIZ at the beginning of the divergence phase.

How?

Timing:

- Approximately 1½–2 hours for the explanation and application of the TRIZ principles as triggers for new product ideas

Participants:

- The facilitator
- Usually 12–14 participants

Process:

There are 40 TRIZ principles. It is too many to apply in a group with 16 participants. It is therefore advisable to concentrate on the principles which you suspect have added value in the divergence phase. A work form is chosen where the TRIZ principles are applied in four sub-groups of four participants each. In this way you can use 16 TRIZ principles as a source of inspiration for new product ideas. Choose those which apply to the innovation assignment and the type of product. Sixteen TRIZ principles which have much potential are for example:

1. Segmentation
2. Omission
3. Asymmetry
4. Merging
5. Universality
6. Anti-weight
7. Preliminary anti-action
8. The other way around
9. Dynamics
10. A bit more or less
11. Another dimension
12. Continuity of useful action
13. Every disadvantage has an advantage
14. Self-service
15. Porous materials
16. Colour changes

Make sure that the above-mentioned principles are written on a separate card, with a short explanation and an example.

Choose the subject: the product category and target group from the innovation assignment.

- Explain the origin and background of the TRIZ method with everybody.
- Discuss all 16 principles which will be used for the TRIZ brainstorming and give all the participants a card with one principle.
- Divide the participants into four groups. Try to make the diversity of the participants and the TRIZ principles as big as possible.
- Ask the participants at each table to take 5 minutes for one principle and based on that write down as many product ideas as possible. After 5 minutes give a sign so that the participants can start with the next principle. Ask the participants, after four slots of 5 minutes, to sit in the U-shape again and then ask each participant to read their ideas for each TRIZ principle.
- Harvest the post-its and stimulate the participants to listen to each other and in this way generate more ideas.

More about the TRIZ can be found at:

- www.ideationtriz.com

- www.innovation-triz.com
- www.realinnovation.com/methods/triz_theory_of_inventive_problem_solving. html
- www.xtriz.com

E.2 SIT

SIT stands for Systematic Inventive Thinking. This technique which comes from Israel is closely related to the TRIZ method described above. It is a simple and easily applied version. Just like TRIZ this technique is not a brainstorming method, as in the traditional brainstorming method an attempt is made to invent new and breakthrough product ideas by moving away from the current product situation. SIT and TRIZ do it in an opposite manner as it stays with the current product as much as possible. In the meantime many versions of SIT have been developed. Depending on the version, SIT works on the basis of five to seven creativity templates. Scientific research has shown that the SIT creativity templates form the foundation of about 70 per cent of all innovations.

SIT concentrates on the existing building stones of the current product and its environment. The application of the creativity templates leads to change in the building stones of the product. SIT first focuses on the change in the product itself and then asks if the effect that it created is good or bad.

SIT works according to seven creativity templates.

1. Displacement: an essential part of the product is removed, and the task is not taken over by another part; for example, omitting the water from a tin of soup and you have Cup-a-soup.
2. Replacement: an essential part of the product is removed, as the task is taken over by another part; for example, you remove the key board of a computer and let the screen take over this role and you have a touch screen.
3. Multiplication: copy an existing part of the product and change something about it; for example, you copy the holes which control the amount of content from the package of a product and change it so that it becomes many garnishing holes.
4. Breaking symmetry: to break through an existing symmetry to solve a problem; for example, you make the spare tyre of a car smaller to solve the problem of space. It creates the 'getting home' wheel: a small, thin spare wheel for short distances.
5. Attribute dependency: create a new dependability between two parts or remove an existing dependability; for example, make the colour of the bottom of the pan dependable on the temperature of the pan and you have the Tefal thermo-spot pan (with red spot).
6. Division: divide the product or parts into something else; for example, divide a group of customers into cardholders and the rest and organise a special late night shopping for the first group.

7. Unification/Component control: find a new connection between a part of a product and the environment so that the product gets a new extra task which used to be the task of another product; for example, Becel (Benecol) Pro-Activ which lowers cholesterol.

The seven creativity templates implicitly set the presumptions of the product combination, the use of the product and the groups of customers at the forefront. The SIT creativity templates also have, in the divergence phase of the new product brainstorm, an added value as a trigger for new ideas. It is best to apply the SIT creativity templates at the beginning of the divergence phase.

Source: Annina van Logtestijn, Youri Mandour (March 2004). Zeven stappen naar succesvollere innovaties. *Magazine for Marketing.*

How?

Timing:

• Approximately 1½–2 hours for the explanation and application of the SIT creativity templates as triggers for new product ideas

Participants:

• The facilitator
• Usually 12–14 participants

Process:

Here I have chosen a way of applying the SIT with the whole group.

• Choose the topic, product category and target group from the innovation assignment.
• The facilitator initiates a brain dump on all possible product parts and attributes of the product category.
• The facilitator applies the seven creativity templates:
    1. Displacement: an essential part of the product is removed and the function is not taken over by another part.
    2. Replacement: an essential part of the product is removed and the function of this part is taken over by another part.
    3. Multiplication: copy an existing part of the product and change something about it.
    4. Breaking symmetry: breakthrough an existing symmetry to solve a problem.
    5. Attribute dependency: create a new dependability between parts or remove an existing dependability.

6. Division: divide the product or parts thereof into parts which do not become something else (in time and space).
7. Unification: form a new connection between parts of the product and the environment so that the product gets a new extra function which up to now was done by another product.
- For each creativity template the participants write their product ideas on a post-it. The facilitator harvests the post-its.

A variation: You can also apply the SIT method in groups. More information about SIT can be found at:

- www.sitsite.com/blog
- www.start2think.com
- www.sit-netherlands.com

E.3 Six Thinking Hats

1. What?

The six thinking hats is a technique by Edward de Bono. The added value of this technique during the creation of new products or services is that a product idea can be improved by putting on different thinking hats. In this way possible improvement suggestions can be devised.

2. Why?

Even after the new product brainstorming session the product idea is not completed yet. By looking at it from different perspectives in the test or development process later, you can get a better insight into the weaknesses of the idea. By putting on different hats, you can generate possible improvements.

3. When?

To strengthen the idea or developed concept. The six thinking hats can therefore be used as a type of test when it comes to the creation or development process of the new products after the new product brainstorming session.

4. Where in the process?

In the FORTH method the six thinking hats technique can best be used during the Test Ideas and Homecoming stages. However, it is also useful during the product development process in order to identify the weaknesses.

5. How?

Timing:

- Approximately 3 to 4 hours for each concrete new product in development

Participants:

- The facilitator
- Usually 10–14 participants

Process:

- The facilitator explains the principles of the six thinking hats which is actually very simple. Together, the different angles of approach produce a more complete image than each individual angle. The essence of the different thinking hats are as follows:
  - The white thinking hat: virginal white thinking in the form of facts, figures and information.
  - The red thinking hat: a red haze in front of the eyes in the form of emotions and sentimental evaluation as well as suspicions and intuition.
  - The yellow thinking hat: sunshine, clarity and optimism, positive evaluation, constructive contribution, searching for chances (opportunistic).
  - The green thinking hat: fertility, creativity, seeds which germinate and grow, movement, provocation. Alternative and new ideas are welcome.
  - The black thinking hat: the devil's advocate, negative evaluation, why something will not function.
  - The blue thinking hat (the hat of the facilitator): distant and controlled, the conductor of the thinking, thinking about the thinking.
- The facilitator finds four places in the available working space and puts down a white, red, black and yellow hat and a flip-over sheet. The blue hat is for the facilitator and the green hat will be used collectively at the end.
- The participants are divided into four groups (minimum of two persons). Each group starts with a specific colour thinking hat and they must also wear it! The facilitator asks the participants to write down their impressions of the new product idea from the specific angle of approach. After 10 minutes the participants must change places. The hat and the flip-over sheet are left behind and are used by the next group. This continues until each group has done each angle of approach.
- After 40 minutes the facilitator hangs the white, red, yellow and black sheets on the wall and discusses the results with the participants. The sheet for the black hat must be done at the end.

- Subsequently the facilitator asks the participants to put on the green thinking hat collectively and to find solutions for each negative aspect or disadvantage of the product idea. These solutions are then written on green post-its and the facilitator harvests the post-its. The best solution for the weakness is chosen.
- The group then continues with the next weakness. The original product or service ideas are now enriched by a few new product aspects and changes which can improve them totally.

More information about the six thinking hats can be found at:

- www.mindtools.com/pages/article/newTED_07.htm
- www.debonothinkingsystems.com/tools/6hats.htm
- www.edwarddebono.com

Bibliography

ABOUT CREATIVITY

Chris Barez-Brown (2006). *How to Have Kick-ass Ideas*. London: HarperCollins.
Igor Byttebier and Ramon Vullings (2007). *Creativity Today*. BIS.
Michael Dahlen (2008). *Creativity Unlimited*. John Wiley.
Ap Dijksterhuis (2009). *Het slimme onbewuste*. Bert Bakker.
Michael Gelb (1999). *Denken als Leonardo da Vinci*. Baarn: de Kern.
Dan Heath and Chip Heath (2007). *De Plakfactor*. Amsterdam: Pearson Education.
Peter ten Hoopen and Marleen Janssen Groesbeek (2008). *Oh, wat zijn we creatief!* Amsterdam: Het
    Financieele Dagblad.
Joost Kadijk and Cyriel Kortleven (2007). *En. Actie!* Zaltbommel: Thema.
Marcel Karreman (2002). *Warming-ups and energizers*. Zaltbommel: Thema.
Max van Leeuwen and Hans Terhurne (1999). *Innovatie door creativiteit: Vijftig tools om problemen
    creatief op te lossen*. Deventer: Kluwer.
Fons Trompenaars and John Cleese (2007). *Creativiteit en innovatie*. Nieuw Amsterdam.
Koen de Vos (2006). *Brainstormen*. Amsterdam: Pearson Education.
Shira White (2002). *New Ideas About New Ideas*. London: FT Prentice Hall.

ABOUT INNOVATION

Rob Adams (2008). *Branchmarking – Over inspiratie, ideeën en innovatie*. Six Fingers.
Jonathan Cagan and Craig M. Vogel (2002). *Creating Breakthrough Products – Innovation from product
    Planning to Program Approval*. Upper Saddle River: Prentice Hall.
Henry Chesbrough, Wim Vanhaverbeke and Joel West (2008). *Open Innovation*. Oxford University
    Press.
Clayton M. Christensen (1997). *The Innovator's Dilemma*. Boston: Harvard Business School Press.
Clayton M. Christensen and Michael E. Raynor (2003). *The Innovator's Solution: Creating and
    Sustaining Successful Growth*. Boston: Harvard Business School Press.
Robert Cooper (2005). *Product Leadership*. New York: Basic Books.
Patrick van der Duin, Rob de Graaf and Ton Langeler (2009). *Innovatie uit de polder*. Business
    Contact.
Elaine Dundon (2002). *The Seeds of Innovation*. New York: American Management Association.
Wichert van Engelen, e.a. (2007). *Ideeën genoeg*. Amsterdam: Pearson Education.
Ernest Gundling (2000). *The 3M Way to Innovation, Balancing People and Profit*. Tokyo: Kodansha
    International.

Harvard Business Review (1997). *On Innovation*. Boston: Harvard Business School Press.
Denis J. Hauptly (2008). *Something Really New*. American Management Association.
Paul Heere, Dorien van der Heijden and Yousri Mandour, e.a. (2005). *Doelgericht Vernieuwen*. Academic Service.
Tim Hurson (2008). *Think Better*. London: McGraw-Hill.
David E. Hussey (1997). *The Innovation Challenge*. New York: John Wiley and Sons.
Robert Jones (2001). *The Big Idea*. London: HarperCollins.
Annina van Logtestijn and Yousri Mandour (March 2004). *Zeven stappen naar succesvollere innovaties*. Magazine for Marketing.
David Nichols (2007). *Return on Ideas – A practical guide to make innovation pay*. John Wiley and Sons.
Bettina von Stamm and Anna Trifilova (2009). *The Future of Innovation*. Farnham: Gower.
Anthony Ulwick (2005). *What Customers Want*. McGraw-Hill.

ABOUT MANAGEMENT

R. Meredith Belbin (2005). *Management Teams: Over succes- en faalfactoren voor teams*. Den Haag: Academic Service.
Ruud Boer (2007). *Brand Design: Het vormen en vormgeven van merken*. Amsterdam: Pearson Education.
Andy Boynton and Bill Fischer (2005). *Virtuoso Teams – lessons from teams that changed their worlds*. Pearson Education.
Linda Gorchels (1996). *The Product Manager's Handbook*. Lincolnwood: NTC Business Books.
Spencer Johnson and Kenneth Blanchard (2007). *Wie heeft mijn kaas gepikt?* Business Contact.
Al and Laura Ries (2004). *The Origin of Brands: How Product Evolution Creates Endless Possibilities For New Brands*. New York: HarperCollins.

ABOUT TRENDS

Adjiedj Bakas (2005). *Megatrends Nederland*. Schiedam: Scriptum.
Adjiedj Bakas and Rob Creemers (2007). *Leven zonder olie, Megatrends energie, natuur, vervoer*. Schiedam: Scriptum.
Patrick Dixon (1998). *Futurewise: Six Faces of Global Change*. London: HarperCollins.
Hilde Roothart (2005). *Zien, Trends van vandaag, markten van morgen*. Business Contact.
Hilde Roothart and Wim van der Pol (2001). *Van trends naar brands*. Deventer: Kluwer.

ABOUT TRIZ

G. Altshuller (2005). *40 Principles: TRIZ Keys to Technical Innovation. Extended Edition*. Worcester, MA: Technical Innovation Center Inc.

D. Mann, S. Dewulf, B. Zlotin and A. Zusman (2003). *Matrix 2003: Updating the TRIZ Contradiction Matrix*. Ieper (Belgium): Creax Press.

INSPIRING BOOKS ABOUT TRAVEL

Tania Aebi (1989). *Solo: Een achttienjarig meisje zeilt alleen de wereld rond*. Baarn: Hollandia.
Shona Grimbly (2002). *Atlas van de Ontdekkingsreizen*. Utrecht: Veltman.
Heinrich Harrer (1999). *De Witte Spin: De beklimming van de Eiger*. Berlijn: Ulstein Buchverlag.
Tristan Jones (1990). *De ongelooflijke tocht*. Baarn: Hollandia.
Jolanda Linschooten (2007). *Keerput Alaska*. Haarlem: Hollandia.
Aron Ralston (2004). *KLEM: Zes dagen die mijn leven veranderden*. Utrecht: Kosmos-ZandK.
Paul Theroux (1991). *Het drijvende koninkrijk*. Amsterdam: De Arbeiderspers.

Glossary

Brainstorming A way of thinking whereby groups can create new ideas for a problem or a challenge according to certain guidelines. The founder of the brainstorming technique, who also introduced the term in 1941, was Alex Osborn. Osborn's guidelines on how to generate new ideas are, for example – try to think of as many ideas as possible, postpone your judgement, pay extra attention to 'silly' ideas and allow for cross-pollination of ideas.

Brain Dump A technique with which the divergence phase of each new product brainstorm starts to 'catch' the first spontaneous ideas. The participants 'dump' their first ideas and the facilitator harvests them.

Business Model The way in which you can obtain turnover and profit with a product or service. A few examples: pay when you buy (supermarket such as Carrefour), pay in advance (magazine subscription such as National Geographic), rent (car renting such as Enterprise Rent-A-Car), pay in instalments when leasing (aeroplanes such as Boeing), free of charge paid by advertisers (search engines such as Google) and so on.

Concept Board A board used during the new product brainstorming sessions on which a concept outline is described both in words and images. (Stage: Raise Ideas.)

Concept Description A practical description of a new product or service which includes: a description of the situation and need of the customer, the customer friction, the solution brought about by the new concept, arguments as to why it provides the right solution and an advertising slogan. (Stage: Raise Ideas.)

Concept Development Workshop A workshop whereby the core team members develop 12 concepts from the new product brainstorming session into concrete descriptions on paper or into other forms such as a design or prototype. (Stage: Raise Ideas.)

Convergence Phase A phase during the new product brainstorming session when the best ideas are selected according to certain criteria based on the innovation assignment. These ideas are then improved and presented by the participants. It is a skill to be able to, without loss of quality, develop the best idea directions which are included in all the ideas. (Stage: Raise Ideas.)

Core Team Member An internal participant to the FORTH team who goes through all the stages. Core team members are chosen based on specific contextual expertise and personal skills. A FORTH team includes six to eight core team members.

Creativity A way of observing and thinking using different angles and combinations which cause a breakthrough in the existing patterns of thinking. It is stimulated by postponing your judgement.

Customer Friction A (re-)discovered relevant need, impulse or wish from a specific target group in a recognisable situation, which is not sufficiently satisfied and which we use as the basis for a new distinctive product or service concept. (Stage: Observe and Learn.)

Customer Insight A new and unique insight into the motives, wishes and behaviour of the customer which forms the basis for an appealing and relevant new concept. (Stage: Observe and Learn.)

Development Workshop A workshop where all the participants brainstorm about how the negative aspects of the concepts from the customer research can be improved. Furthermore, during this workshop the choice is made regarding which three to five product concepts will be developed into mini new business cases during the last stage of the FORTH innovation project. (Stage: Homecoming.)

Divergence Phase A phase during the new product brainstorming session where, with the help of brainstorming techniques, as many new appealing ideas as possible are generated for new concepts. (Stage: Raise Ideas.)

Source of Inspiration A source of inspiration with which you can learn much about a specific innovation opportunity. Think of experts, organisations which excel in a certain area, interesting existing concepts in other countries or on other continents, websites which give much information and inspiring places to visit and so on. (Stage: Observe and Learn.)

Extended Team Member An internal participant in the FORTH team who only goes through the highlights, such as the internal client or other members of the board.

Facilitator The guide of the FORTH innovation process in all stages. He/she also functions as partner and confidante of the project leader of the ideation team. A good facilitator is very important and their role as a success factor is often underestimated.

Focus Group A conversation with six to eight people from the target group under direction of the facilitator to investigate their motives, behaviour and needs. The purpose is to highlight relevant customer frictions while the core team watches from a different room. (Stage: Observe and Learn.)

Front End The front end of the innovation process. This term is usually associated with the starting phase where ideas are created. As this usually happens with great difficulty and is unclear, it is also known as 'fuzzy front end'.

Full Steam Ahead The first stage in the FORTH innovation method where the innovation focus is chosen and recorded in the innovation assignment. The internal team is set up and invited to participate.

Homecoming The fifth stage in the FORTH innovation method wherein the three to five most attractive and tested product or service concepts are developed into mini new business cases including the market expectations, turnover and profit.

Ideation Phase The first phase of the innovation process, where attractive new concepts for products or service ideas are created. The FORTH innovation method is one way in which to approach the ideation phase where the new concepts are developed into mini new business cases.

Ideation Team An internal team who go through the first phase of the innovation process, where attractive new concepts for products or services ideas are created.

Idea Direction An idea direction is the red thread behind a group of concrete ideas, a higher abstract level where you can combine ideas under one denominator. The best idea directions are developed into an idea mind-map during the new product brainstorming session. (Stage: Raise Ideas.)

Idea Mind-Map An idea mind-map of an idea direction (what?, for whom?, how?) with which the participants of the new product brainstorming session can add their own suggestions in the convergence phase. The idea mind-map serves as basis for the development of the concept boards. (Stage: Raise Ideas.)

Innovation The ability to create something new in the form of concrete new ideas, concepts, products, services, business models or processes which break through existing patterns and in practice have long-lasting added value.

Innovation Assignment A concrete description of the assignment for the FORTH team. It gives direction about the market and the target group and indicates for whom the ideas for new products or services are developed and specifies which criteria the new concepts must meet. (Stage: Full Steam Ahead.)

Innovation Focus Workshop A workshop preceding the kick-off workshop with the top managers concerned as well as those who will lead the FORTH method. At this workshop the purpose, innovation assignment, the participants and the planning are realised. (Stage: Full Steam Ahead.)

Innovation Opportunities A subject, theme, technology, trend, area or target group which provides great opportunity to realise the innovation assignment.

Innovation Process The process whereby concrete new ideas, concepts, products, services, business models or processes are created, developed and introduced in the market. This process is usually divided into various steps. One of the most used processes for innovation is the Stage-Gate process by Robert G. Cooper. FORTH is an innovation method for the start of the innovation process.

Inspiration Compass An aid to find the correct sources of inspiration. The compass consists of four, closely linked directions: the customer, trends, technology and the promising innovation opportunities for innovation from the kick-off workshop. (Stage: Observe and Learn.)

In the Box To think within existing patterns and conventions.

Mini New Business Case A small business plan for a new developed concept consisting of seven to 10 sheets where a strategic, commercial, professional and financial foundation is presented. (Stage: Homecoming.)

New Product Brainstorm A two-day brainstorming session with the core team members, the extended team members and the outsiders where new product or service ideas are practically generated and developed into product concepts. (Stage: Raise Ideas.)

New Product A new offer which is attractive for customers, distinctive on the market and which has the potential for extra turnover and profit for the organisation. A new product or service can be new to the company, new to the market or even new to the world.

Observe and Learn The second stage in the FORTH innovation method where you gain insight into what the potential target group really finds relevant and what they struggle with and you investigate innovation opportunities, trends and technologies.

Observe and Learn workshop A workshop which included the whole FORTH team during the Observe and Learn Stage where the insights concerning trends, technology, customer frictions and the progress of each innovation opportunity is discussed. (Stage: Observe and Learn.)

Online Research Research amongst customers which take place via the internet to gain insight into customer motives and frictions (Stage: Observe and Learn) or to test the attractiveness of the newly developed concepts. (Stage: Test Ideas.)

Outside the Box To be able to think outside existing patterns and conventions.

Outsider An external participant who is included in the FORTH team on a temporary basis during the two-day brainstorming session and the concept development workshop because of their expertise and/or creative skills. (Stage: Raise Ideas.)

Product Idea A concrete idea about a new offer that is attractive for the customer, distinctive in the market and which has sufficient extra turnover and profit potential for the organisation.

Raise Ideas The third stage in the FORTH innovation method where new concepts are created and developed into product concepts during a two-day brainstorming session and a concept development workshop.

Stage Gate Process A blueprint for the product development process which was developed by Robert G. Cooper. In the original Full Stage-Gate model it is divided into five stages. Each stage ends with a gateway which serves as a quality control and as a go/no go moment of decision for the management. This model has been used by many large international companies during the last decade. The suitability as well as the effectiveness regarding additional insights (fuzzy gates), the number of stages in the project result (newness, complexity) and dependability has been enlarged. Nevertheless, the use of it is still open for discussion.

Test Ideas The fourth stage in the FORTH innovation method where the newly developed concepts are tested by the potential target group. In the Improvement workshop which follows, the negative aspects of the new concepts which were mentioned by the customers are improved.

TRIZ A technique for systematic innovation. TRIZ is a Russian acronym for 'Teoriya Resheniya Izobreatatelskikh Zadatch' which in English is: the Theory of Inventive Problem-solving. The founder of the TRIZ technique is the Russian engineer Genrich Altshuller. According to the TRIZ theory all innovations can be converted to 40 principles. Furthermore, it seems as if the evolution of technological progress follows predictable patterns.

The FORTH Innovation Method An inspiring practical innovation method in five stages with which you can create and develop new products and services with the help of a internal team. FORTH® is an acronym for: Full Steam Ahead, Observe and Learn, Raise Ideas, Test Ideas and Homecoming. This method effectively links the daily 'in the box' management practice with 'outside the box' creativity.

Index

For Product Safety Concerns and Information please contact our
EU representative GPSR@taylorandfrancis.com Taylor & Francis
Verlag GmbH, Kaufingerstraße 24, 80331 München, Germany